GEORGE OPPEN

GEORGE OPPEN
A Critical Study

Lyn Graham Barzilai

McFarland & Company, Inc., Publishers
Jefferson, North Carolina, and London

Frontispiece: George Oppen (Mary Oppen Papers, Mandeville Special Collections Library, University of California, San Diego)

Poems of George Oppen copyright ©1962, 1965, 1968, 1972, 1975 by George Oppen. Used by permission of New Directions Publishing Corporation.

LIBRARY OF CONGRESS CATALOGUING-IN-PUBLICATION DATA

Barzilai, Lyn Graham, 1950–
    George Oppen : a critical study / Lyn Graham Barzilai.
       p.   cm.
    Includes bibliographical references and index.

    ISBN-13: 978-0-7864-2549-5
    softcover : 50# alkaline paper ∞

    1. Oppen, George — Criticism and interpretation.
    2. Oppen, George — Literary style. I. Title.
    PS3529.P54Z55   2006
    811'.54 — dc22   2006013602

British Library cataloguing data are available

©2006 Lyn Graham Barzilai. All rights reserved

No part of this book may be reproduced or transmitted in any form or by any means, electronic or mechanical, including photocopying or recording, or by any information storage and retrieval system, without permission in writing from the publisher.

On the cover: Portrait of George Oppen by Mary Oppen. Mixed media. Photograph by Scott McCue courtesy Linda Oppen. Mary Oppen Papers, Mandeville Special Collections Library, University of California, San Diego

Manufactured in the United States of America

McFarland & Company, Inc., Publishers
  Box 611, Jefferson, North Carolina 28640
  www.mcfarlandpub.com

To the
memory of my father, John Graham,
and my sister, Fiona Ferguson

Acknowledgments

I would like to thank the University of Haifa for their financial support at various stages of the process of my work, thus facilitating the publication of this book.

And my grateful thanks go to Oppen's daughter Linda, whose assistance throughout this writing project has been much appreciated. Thank you, Linda.

Contents

Acknowledgments vi
Preface 1
Introduction 3

ONE • Oppen's Primitive Modes 9
TWO • Oppen and Language 20
THREE • Oppen's Materials 32
FOUR • What Is There 56
FIVE • Cityscapes 79
SIX • Light and Water 114
SEVEN • Into the Eyes of the Tiger 132
EIGHT • Primitive 151
NINE • Recurring Threads 179

Conclusion 198
Appendix: Additional Reading 207
Notes 209
Bibliography 217
Index 221

Preface

I first became acquainted with George Oppen's poetry when a friend lent me his "bible"—a collection of Oppen's poems—to read. I found the poems, with their fractured syntax and idiosyncratic phrasing, obscure and sometimes impenetrable; at the same time, their impact was powerful and moving. They were full of sharp, clear images which carried their own light and which acknowledged themselves in my mind over and over—long after I had, reluctantly, returned the book to its owner. During the next few years I pursued my study of Oppen's work in my doctoral dissertation, and discovered that although there exist quite a number of articles (and several dissertations) on Oppen's poetry, providing insight into his poetic approach and concerns, no single book has been written which evidences a systematic analysis of the individual poems. For a poet whose 1969 collection of poems, *Of Being Numerous*, won the Pulitzer prize, this seems a sad critical omission. Whether the reason for the omission is related to the obscure nature of Oppen's writing, or whether he is simply viewed as belonging to the Objectivist movement and therefore treated within the framework of a larger body of poets does not matter; Oppen deserves closer critical attention than he has received up until now. This book aims, at least in part, to fill that gap. Although the book focuses primarily on primitive modes as they appear in Oppen's poetry and therefore, by its nature, chooses to explore only those poems which manifest some aspect of the primitive, it takes a close critical look at a large number of individual poems from all of Oppen's work, ranging from the earliest collection to his last published volume, *Primitive*.

Preface

Since there is relatively little critical material on Oppen's work compared to that of many prominent poets of the twentieth century, any intensive research on Oppen's poetry must lean on the few collections of articles available in books and journals. These include a volume of extremely informative and enlightening essays on Oppen, titled *George Oppen: Man and Poet*, edited by Burton Hatlen, as well as special editions of journals such as *Ironwood* and *Paideuma* which are devoted to Oppen's writing. The autobiographical work *Meaning a Life*, by Oppen's wife Mary, also provides an interesting glimpse into Oppen's background and personality, and Rachel Blau DuPlessis's *The Selected Letters of George Oppen* offers the reader of Oppen's work a further understanding of the poet's views on many topics.

This critical study of Oppen's poetry takes a primarily poststructuralist and postmodern approach to the texts discussed. Although Oppen's work spans a long period beginning after World War I and continuing into the 1970s, the poet's handling of language and poetic devices lends itself to a poststructuralist analysis. For this reason, the book is organized in such a way as to supply the reader with both an understanding of the concept of primitive modes as I see them in the poems, and background information on critical theories and ideas pertinent to a poststructuralist interpretation. Chapter one investigates different kinds of primitive modes appearing in the poetry, while chapter two looks at the work of poststructuralist thinkers such as Jacques Derrida, Roland Barthes, Jacques Lacan and Julia Kristeva, whose ideas illuminate and put into perspective Oppen's often unique way of writing. Each subsequent chapter is devoted to an analysis of specific poems from one particular volume of poetry, following a chronological sequence, while the last chapter provides an overview of Oppen's recurring themes and ideas. Informing this study as a whole is the notion that much of what Oppen has to say is conveyed not *in* language but *through* it.

In offering such an individual and particular study of Oppen's body of poetry, I hope to encourage the reader of this book to investigate, grapple with and ultimately savor the work of a poet whose obscurity — paradoxically — veils a poetic integrity and clarity of vision more deserving of discovery and attention than has been granted them till now.

Introduction

George Oppen, a Jewish American poet born in 1908 in New Rochelle, New York, has received relatively little attention from critics, in spite of having won the Pulitzer Prize in 1969 for his collection of poems *Of Being Numerous*. Although the way Oppen employed language in his poetry has been scrutinized by some critics, many critical reviews of his life and work have focused mainly on his inclusion in the group of poets who founded and wrote out of the Objectivist movement at the beginning of the 1930s, following the example of William Carlos Williams and led by two other Jewish American poets, Louis Zukofsky and Charles Reznikoff. Williams offered a definition of Objectivism in a review of *An "Objectivists" Anthology*:

> They are successfully displayed to hold an objective view of poetry which ... show[s] it not to be a seductive arrangement of scenes, sounds and colors so much as a construction of each part of which has a direct bearing on its meaning as a whole, an objectification of significant particulars.[1]

The Objectivist poets wrote an austere and emotionally neutral form of poetry, using words sparingly and preferring small, concrete nouns. They believed that words are their own substantiality existing independently of the things they represent, while those "things" are set in the poems as distinct, discrete units of representation. Hugh Kenner compares the Objectivists to a camera: "Like the Western camera, the Objectivist poet is the geometer of minima."[2] Oppen's first book of poetry, *Discrete Series*, was written in the Objectivist tradition, following, as its title implies, the principles of the Objectivist movement. Oppen's frequent use of "small words" in this collection, and in his subsequent poetry, is explained in the following two references he made during an interview with L.S. Dembo: "All the little nouns are the ones I like the most, the deer, the sun and so on" and "The little words that I like so much, like 'tree,' 'hill' and so on are, I suppose, just as much a taxonomy as the more elaborate words" (p. 162).[3] In fact, the frequent appearance of the "small words" has become a hallmark of Oppen's poetry, and it appears that this is not incidental to the themes he evolved in the poems.

In 1935 Oppen and his wife Mary, perhaps influenced by the left-wing politics of the Objectivist poets, put aside their lives as artists in favor of a politically active life in the Communist party, working with the unemployed. In the previously mentioned interview with L.S. Dembo in 1968, Oppen explains this move:

> If you do something politically, you do something that has political efficacy. And if you decide to write poetry, then you write poetry, not something that you hope, or deceive yourself into believing, can save people who are suffering.... In a way I gave up poetry because of the pressure of what ... I'll call conscience [p. 164].

Oppen did not return to poetry until 1958. In the interim he worked as a die cutter in a factory, was drafted into the army in 1942 and was wounded, then worked as a carpenter after the war. As a result of his affiliation with the Communist party, Oppen was forced to leave the country in 1950; he lived in Mexico City for the next few years, running a furniture factory, until he returned to New York and began writing poetry again in the late 1950s. The kind of manual work that Oppen did during those years — factory operator, carpenter — and the fact that he worked with basic materials (metal and wood) find a parallel in the poetry he wrote: Oppen's poems are carved out of the simple stuff of life: they are composed of basic nouns, concrete objects, elemental images, things rather than ideas. Even the titles of some of his collections of poems — *Discrete Series, The Materials,* and his last publication, *Primitive*— point to his preoccupation with the tangible, the concrete, the elemental. This preoccupation becomes particularly evident in the last collection, *Primitive*, although it also pervades the previous volumes of poetry.

Introduction

This in Which, written in 1965, is introduced by an epigraph from Heidegger (whose philosophical views were well-known to Oppen at the time): "...The arduous path of appearance." Oppen's poetry often chronicles his struggle to bring to light in language certain fundamental elements which constitute a kind of "primary aura" in the poetry; this aura can be evoked but not entirely articulated in the words on the page. Heidegger's phrase summarizes what appears to be the underlying motif in much of Oppen's work, particularly in *Primitive*. Many of the poems in this collection are self-referential: they deal with the crafting of poetry itself, charting how the poem is shaped, like a piece of furniture, from basic materials (elemental images of stone and water, simple discrete nouns) until it emerges, complete, in the last few lines. This is a recurring theme in Oppen's work. His poetry functions in two diametrically opposed directions: a movement from primary to secondary process in the construction of the poem itself, and a movement from the sophisticated to the elemental as language is broken down, dismantled, to get at the elemental energies which are the foundation of the poem. Oppen's work is often obscure as a result of this dismantling of language; the syntax is fragmented, often a series of noun phrases juxtaposed without conjunctions, a set of images linked only by dashes and an apparent mismatch of disjointed items.

One of the most striking aspects of Oppen's poetry is this obscurity. It is extremely difficult, even after many readings, to pierce the core of meaning in some of the poems. This difficulty evolves from Oppen's fragmentation of normative units of meaning. The aforementioned use of simple nouns, often without conjunctions, the disruption of a logical sequence of events and the breakdown of the flow of the lines all make for a poetry which is not only obscure, but also surreal in its strange juxtaposition of phrases and ideas, conjuring up a pictorial and conceptual jigsaw of experience. Most of the critical readings of Oppen's poetry have focused on this somewhat unorthodox approach to language, understanding it to be intrinsically bound up with the themes in the poems. In a conversation with George and Mary Oppen, Burton Hatlen asks the poet about this dislocation of language:

> BH [Hatlen]: Are these disruptions of syntax the result of a consciously thought-out set of poetic principles?

> GO [Oppen]: Yes, definitely. All along I've had a sense that the structure of the sentence closes off the little words. "The" and "and" are the greatest mysteries of all [p. 36].⁴

Oppen's poetry, from the beginning, attempts to reveal or at least approach those "greatest mysteries of all"—not only the little words, but the mysteries of experience itself—by foregrounding the seemingly insignificant and abstract "the" and "and" words in his poems, giving them visual prominence and presence, so that they do not become swallowed up in long complex strings of verbs, adverbs and adjectives, but rather force the reader to reappraise their significance. Thus they retain a presence and mystery which echoes the mystery of experience itself, also something often beyond concrete representation. These mysteries lie at the deepest level of our consciousness, and they are ultimately impenetrable. Like the philosopher Martin Heidegger (whose Theory of Being appealed to Oppen and was reflected in his work), Oppen believes in the independent existence of basic entities—they are "just there." Heidegger's approach is described by David Halliburton:

> In our everyday experience, for example, we encounter things that are just there, before us, such as trees or hills or birds or rivers or rocks. Because such things are indubitably present, are really "right there," and because they are so without necessary orientation toward human interest, Heidegger calls their mode of Being "presence-at-hand" (*Vorhandenheit*).⁵

Oppen frequently makes use of "things that are just there"—the "small nouns" like stones, trees and the sun—and his comment in the interview with L.S. Dembo (reprinted in *Contemporary Literature*) that "the absolutely unitary is somehow absolute, that, at any rate, it really exists ... the atom, for example" reveals an elemental quality in his poetry. In the previously mentioned interview with Burton Hatlen, the interviewer comments on the frequent appearance of "stone" and "sea" in Oppen's *The Materials*, and Randolph Chilton attempts to explain Oppen's motives for including so many simple, basic nouns: "In using such words he intends partly to return us to his own perception of the elemental."⁶

Oppen generally deals in a direct representation of the elemental through the elements themselves, rather than through intermediary sit-

Introduction

uations. This sometimes makes for a static quality in Oppen's representation of the primitive; in Oppen's poetry, elemental entities simply exist, independent of any human influence. Randolph Chilton, discussing Oppen's poem "Party on Shipboard," affirms this point: "Beyond individual apartments, beyond any assertive 'Me!,' beyond consciousness itself lie the rocks, emblems of pure existence, which in the absence of all else ties us together."[7] Oppen sets elements like rocks, water and fire in his poems as the genesis from which everything else evolves; he is, as Diane Wakoski notes, a poet of beginnings, tapping into the well-spring of existence at its source. Wakoski calls him

> a 20th century philosopher who has rejected the artifice of 20th century philosophy — its language. He speaks of unities, of being, of beginnings, ends, life death and I suppose the metaphor we all use today — that poetry is life and the poet's vision is what lifts him from the limitations of death.[8]

Oppen's poems do, indeed, as Wakoski says, deal in "being" and "beginnings"— not least the being and beginning of the poem itself. There is a certain self-referentiality about much of Oppen's poetry, the poem chronicling its own appearance on the page, speaking of itself in the lines, as the poet reaches back, through his primary images of stone, water and fire, to the sources of the poem itself. Oppen is concerned not only with human existence, but also with the sources of poetic creativity rooted in an elemental state beyond words. His poems simultaneously synthesize and fragment: the poem takes shape from within itself, building on those primary images which are its beginning, until it emerges as a complete entity in the final lines, while the language of the poem is broken down into its simplest units (the "small nouns") and a fragmented syntax through which the meaning of the poem accumulates. His poems speak of themselves as they unfold; phrases such as "the voice of the poem a wandering foreigner" and "the poem discovered in the crystal center of the rock" appear in Oppen's last volume, *Primitive*. This consciously expressed unfolding of the poem is often achieved through a fragmentation of the actual language that is creating the poem. In a letter to Rachel DuPlessis, Oppen comes close to defining this complementary process of synthesis and interdependence:

Introduction

> One's awareness of the world, one's concerns with existence — they were not already in words — And the poem is NOT built out of words, one cannot make a poem by sticking words into it, it is the poem which makes the words and contains the meaning.⁹

Oppen's poetry, then, is at once simple — concrete nouns, the basics of existence, pre-verbal primary levels of existence — and at the same time complex, in its accumulation of ideas through a form of language which is disjointed and fragmented. Oppen arrives at the elemental and the primitive both through the simplification of language into its smallest and most concrete units of meaning, and by his primary images of stone, water and fire.

ONE

Oppen's Primitive Modes

The nature of the primitive modes under discussion in Oppen's poetry implies a more psychological and social orientation, rather than an anthropological one, synchronic rather than diachronic. Nevertheless, an examination of several mythic sources will clarify and add dimension to the primitive modes being discussed, since these mythic sources embody symbolic elements which transcend time and are therefore not tied down to any particular anthropological development. Rather, they articulate a set of images which belong to what Carl Jung termed "the collective unconscious," a well-spring of primary symbols which express a universal significance underlying all human experience. These mythic symbols can be seen to embody *pre-verbal* elements, since they already existed in societies which had not yet developed linguistic definitions of the concepts they stood for, as well as functioning to reinforce sub-verbal, symbolic dimensions of all poetic discourse.

In order to invoke a primal state there must be a reaching-back or a reaching-down into a deeper, more basic level of existence that lies beyond civilized consciousness and social discourse. In an exploration and study of myth, Mircea Eliade calls this primal state the *illud tempus*—"that time" or the "time of origins." For Eliade, this is the time of "primordial revelation" where sacred myths are re-enacted through ritual repetition in order that man may regenerate himself by reliving that event.[1] Although Eliade regards the re-enactment of myth as a sacred and religious event, he makes it clear that the primordial revelation, the projection into *illud tempus* is not the exclusive experience of the religious human being: "every individual is fundamentally a 'spiritual' being. His most secret self is a part of the secret world he is periodically trying to recontact."[2] The realization of the "secret self" by re-entering primal consciousness is the underlying concept of T.S. Eliot's "still point," where the temporal, or historical, and the atemporal or ahistorical merge in a moment of illumination. Eliot's "still point" lifts those who experience it into a sphere of existence beyond the temporal—a realm defined by the mystical, revelatory and spiritual. This sphere of existence is independent of, but always accompanies, the temporal, fallible world, and can be accessed through poetic and mythic thinking; it reveals a condition both ulterior and primary which enriches the inner self. The revelation of the primal condition and the enrichment of the inner self also occupy the attention of Oppen, in his tracing back to the creative origins of poetry.

According to Eliade, myths were originally perpetrated by primitive societies in an effort to return to sacred origins — to thrust themselves out of "profane" time and into eternity. These myths were expressed in symbols: "it is too often forgotten that the workings of primitive thought were not expressed only in concepts or conceptual elements, but also, and primarily, in symbols."[3] In his chapter on symbolism and psychoanalysis, Eliade makes it clear that, for him, symbolic thinking is an added dimension of perception that takes place outside the boundaries of language: "Symbolic thinking is not the exclusive privilege of the child, of the poet, or of the unbalanced mind: it is consubstantial with human existence, it comes before language and discursive reason."[4] Eliade elaborates on this concept of symbolic thinking in a book which traces the links between the symbol, ancient pre-verbal rites and their representation in the arts, saying:

> the symbol itself may be considered as a language which, although conceptual, is nevertheless capable of expressing a coherent thought on existence and on the World. The symbol reveals a pre-systematic ontology to us, which is to say an expression of thought from a period when conceptual vocabularies had not yet been constituted.[5]

As an example he points out that the concept of "becoming" is not given linguistic designation until long after its symbolism is in evidence through

One: Oppen's Primitive Modes

myths from archaic cultures. He mentions images of light emerging from shadow, phases of the moon and waves as expressions of the idea of movement and passage from one mode to another in order to illustrate this point. Eliade goes on to draw our attention to the fact that symbols "succeed in distilling structures of the real, which much later and in certain cultures had been signified by concepts" and claims that they "maintain contact with the deep sources of life," contrasting symbols with conceptual language which "does not succeed in communicating the existential significance which accompanies the disclosures of the deep structures of reality."[6] An examination of Oppen's work reveals many primary, mythic symbols such as light and dark, the moon and waves. These symbols will be elaborated on in later chapters.

In order to understand Eliade's approach fully, it is essential to examine how he links the concept of "primordial time" with psychoanalysis. Eliade draws to our attention the significance acquired by a return to "primordial time" within the framework of Freudian psychoanalysis, which places this "primordial time" in earliest childhood, at the pre-language state. He explains:

> One of Freud's discoveries above all has had portentous consequences, namely, that for man there is a "primordial" epoch in which all is decided — the very earliest childhood — and that the course of this infancy is exemplary for the rest of life. Relating this in terms of archaic thinking, one might say that there was once a "paradise" (which for psychoanalysis is the prenatal period, or that time before weaning) ... and that whatever the adult's attitude may be towards these primordial circumstances, they are none the less constitutive of his being.[7]

Eliade goes on to call the vestiges of this primordial epoch "archaic modes of psychic life, 'living fossils' in the darkness of the unconscious." He believes, like Julia Kristeva, that the unconscious is far more poetic and mythic than the conscious. The "living fossils" of primordial time embedded in the unconscious, which belong to the paradisal time of infancy, can be retrieved through psychoanalysis, but they also emerge through "symbolic thinking" — in dreams, slips of the tongue, and also in poetry.

For Oppen, the primitive elements in his work reflect the attempt to re-enter a sub-verbal state where images and symbols embody some sort of genesis, a primal condition he wishes to explore. This, of course, is where the poetic paradox comes into play, since the translation of these symbols into a concrete terminology annuls their power to convey essential experiences which are felt but cannot be easily articulated. Symbolic thinking reflects a sense of rhythm and pattern which often eludes concrete expression. Oppen, therefore, must bring into force the other elements of poetry which can convey this mode of symbolic thinking (in addition to the symbolic images themselves), such as rhythm, spaces and breaks in syntax through which the symbolic meaning can "leak through."

Sub-verbal elements, which may be conveyed through mythic and symbolic modes of thinking, can also be expressed in other ways, such as through the "Deep Image." The work of Deep Image poets is examined by such critics as Jonathan Holden and Karl Malkoff. The latter labels these poets "Deep Imagists"; his definition of Deep Imagist poets would, I think, be applicable to Oppen as well, since Oppen is concerned with primitive modes which reflect a deeper and more basic level of experience. Although Malkoff defines the Deep Image as a subjective one, a definition which would apparently contradict Oppen's Objectivist approach, there is no real contradiction. Subjectivity plays as integral a part in Objectivist poetry as objects do. In his essay "George Oppen, *Discrete Series*, 1929–1934," Tom Sharp defines how Objectivist poetry functions: "Objectivist ... poems ... rely on inspiration." Inspiration, according to Sharp, can be defined in Objectivist poetry as "an inward movement of an objective thing such as myriad lights or faces in a crowd."[8] Subjectivity therefore plays an important part in Objectivist poetry in spite of the apparent linguistic contradiction: objects in the Objectivist poems function as a trigger for the poet's own subjective response to them. Malkoff's description of how Deep Images function in poetry undoubtedly applies to Oppen no less than to other Deep Imagist poets. He emphasizes the image as the central component of the poem in Deep Imagist poetry, an image which rises up from the substrata of the poem and is not connected to any single word or phrase: "emphasis should be shifted from the syllable ... to the image as the poem's crucial component." He elaborates on the function of the image, giving as an example an image from a Robert Bly poem ("Waking from Sleep") depicting whole fleets of ships accompanied by seagulls on a sea which is, in fact, the blood in one's veins. This is an image drawn from the inner world of the unconscious, not directly couched in a single concrete term, as are the images and symbols used by Romantic and Symbolist poets, but rather is sensed as a turbulence in the blood, a primal "eddy" which permeates the whole poem, as opposed to being pinpointed in a single image.[9] The Romantic Image reverberates outwards; the Deep Image percolates up through layers of consciousness, acting as a kind of "primal blueprint." The difference lies not in the qualities the image possesses, but in its representation. Frank Kermode describes the Romantic Image as. "Analagous not to a machine but to an organism; coexistent in matter and form; resistant to explication; largely independent of intention, and any form of ethical utility; and itself emblematized in certain recurrent images, of which ... the Dancer is the most perfect."[10]

Both the Romantic Image and the Deep Image are organic, "rationally accessible with difficulty" (a phrase used by Eliade on page 6 of *Symbolism, the Sacred and the Arts*) and non-didactic. But whereas the Romantic Image is "emblematized" in concrete form (the urn, the dancer, the tree), the Deep Image is one which surfaces as an *overall* permeating image, not tied to any one word or line but construed in the poem as a whole. According to the view of how images function in Deep Imagist poetry, Malkoff describes Deep Imagist poets as those who "question the legitimacy of the ego as providing the perspective from which reality is viewed."[11] Since the ego functions at the conscious, social level, and Oppen is delving into more primary levels of experience, the ego becomes impotent, to a certain extent, to deal with those deeper levels. This is also true for modes of symbolic thinking, although the symbols and images which appear as a manifestation of mythic or symbolic thinking do tend to be more concrete: the circle, the moon, the shadow. Deep Images and mythic symbols express the primitive mode in different ways; nevertheless, there may be overlap. The shadow, for example, may be an emblem of mythic or symbolic thinking, reflecting primitive notions of dark and light, substance and lack of substance; but it may also surface in a Deep Image poem as a manifestation of dark primordial forces which pervade the poem as a whole, subtly undercutting, or reinforcing, other elements which appear in more concrete form.

Deep Imagist poets, then, employ images and symbols drawn from the well-spring of the unconscious, a deep vein of energy which is sub-verbal and not easily translated into rational terms. An examination of the poetic use of images by W.S. Merwin serves to illustrate how Deep Image poetry draws on sub-verbal material, grappling with the paradox of how to express this material through the medium of language in the same way that Oppen attempts to present primitive sub-verbal modes within the framework of language. In an article reflecting on Merwin's career, *The Atlantic*'s poetry editor Peter Davidson discusses the movement and activity of Merwin's poetry "which seem to flow up from an underground river that lies beneath mere speech, as though written in some pre-verbal language of which all later language have proved to be a mere translation."[12]

Many of Merwin's images (a figure swimming blindly, the silence of a seashell, gathering mushrooms at dawn) approximate Oppen's use of elemental images and states to represent the generic sources of poetic energy, the blind beginnings of a poem. For Merwin, this is a silent space of absence on which he draws to produce the "presence" of a poem; for Oppen, the concrete images constitute the bedrock upon which the poem is founded. Merwin's starting-point is not a bedrock or foundation, as Oppen's is; he begins with lack (in this case, lack of sound) and defines it, using a vacuum as a state to make something of. Merwin takes up the concepts of silence and absence and imbues them with "an informing presence" as Charles Altieri describes it: "Language, for example, need not be only a process of supplementation: in the silence within the overlapping words trying to define and judge experience, an informing presence might be taking shape."[13] He quotes from Merwin's book *The Lice* (p. 38) to explain his point. Several of Merwin's poems look beyond language to a more "fundamental beyond," a pure, primitive state of beginnings. This idea parallels several of Oppen's poems which deal with generic states where the creative process begins; these generic states are defined by concrete images such as crystal and rock, and by fragmented syntax which allows Oppen to break open language and reach a fundamental, silent space underneath. Merwin explores the generic state in several other poems included in *The Lice*; for example, in a poem titled "Looking for Mushrooms at Sunrise" he imagines a natural, pre-conscious world of simple existence, personified by mushrooms growing up through a dark space which he seems to recognize, and which calls to him. This dark space where the mushrooms grow retains a sense of the fundamental, a "beginning place" which Merwin seems to recognize as belonging to "another life." It carries reverberations not only of a personal memory but also of a larger human experience, something akin to Jung's collective unconscious, a state of origins. This state is, according to Jung, a relic from another time: it is "something strange that derives its experience from the hinterland of man's mind, as if it had emerged from the abyss of prehuman ages, or from a superhuman world of contrasting light and darkness."[14] Jung goes on to call this a "primordial experience" which he suggests may be a "vision of other worlds ... or of the primal beginnings of the human psyche[.]" Twentieth century poets, particularly T.S. Eliot, writing during the period when Jung was developing his theory of the collective unconscious, tapped into this storehouse of primal images, reviving in their poetry some of the deep symbols and rhythms inherent in natural cycles of light and darkness, growth and decay, from which the collective unconscious derives. This aspect of the primitive, in addition to the overt use of myth, is treated in the poetry of Oppen, and his contemporaries (such as Robert Bly and W.S. Merwin), as they draw on these deep primal currents, evoking myth and symbolic imagery to reinforce their themes. These primitive modes employ images which cannot always be defined within the framework of language. They often refer to states which evade or precede linguistic definition. Jung cites the example of an abstract symbol which appears in Stone-Age rock drawings and which existed before it was "named":

> There appears ... an abstract pattern — a double cross contained in a circle.... It is the so-called sunwheel, and since it dates from a time when the wheel had not yet been invented, it cannot have had its origin in any experience of the external world. It is rather a symbol for some inner experience.[15]

Not only does this symbol belong to an unconscious, internal reservoir of images, it also defies linguistic naming. It is a *pictorial* symbol, defined by a sensory, rather than a verbal, image. It resides in the realm of primordial experience which precedes language, although it can be evoked and shaped by words.

These primitive modes, which draw on deep-seated images reaching back through human experience to man's psychic beginnings, are of a psychological or symbolic nature. Other primitive modes display a more concrete or physical quality, such as those which deal with animals and instincts. It seems significant that those poets who investigate the psychological and symbolic aspects of primitive modes also write poetry about animals, exploring the realm of sub-verbal communication through instincts, gestures and emotional response. In addition, animals — like the archetypal images which reach back through the collective unconscious to our deepest primary experiences — embody an unfettered, primordial energy. In fact, as creatures of instinct who communicate by gestures, sounds and scent, animals are deeply connected to the basic rhythm of life. This contrasts with our own human environment of overloaded and overdeveloped communication where social discourse has evolved to the point where our natural drives have been misdirected or repressed. The animals who appear in Oppen's poems — serpents, buzzards, wolves and of course deer in the celebratory "Psalm"— strip away the clutter of civilized discourse to show us a simpler and more basic mode of existence, sometimes frightening in its stark energy, but always in tune with natural urges, rather than the distortion of those natural drives manifested by our own human culture: animal behavior is dictated by instincts and the responses they trigger. Donald Abel discusses and quotes Freud's concept of instincts: "Freud posits the id as the most basic element of the mind; the ego and superego develop from the id. The id, in turn, is 'the repository of the instinctual impulses.'" Freud's theory of human nature derived from his assertion that "'the deepest essence of human nature consists of instinctual impulses which are of an elementary nature, which are similar in all men and which aim at the satisfaction of certain primal needs.'" Therefore, "'the core of our being ... is formed by the obscure *id* ... Within this id the organic *instincts* operate.'"[16] Freud saw the id as the unconscious aspect of the psyche, an instinctual self springing from basic drives. The superego, or conscious "social" self, is in charge of repressing many of the actions and thoughts that derive from this basic aspect of the self, a conscious being which channels our primary urges. It therefore curbs and sublimates what might otherwise become destructive behavior; but it also disguises and distorts our innermost thoughts and emotions, causing human responses and communication through language to become devious, misleading and unreliable, a falsification of our true, organic selves. Of course the superego acts as a necessary restraining force on instinctual urges which would otherwise cause havoc in our civilized patterns of behavior; but it also catapults us from an inner organic reality into the empty world of language where words are slippery and their meaning elusive.

Animals do not misinterpret instinctual and emotional responses in other animals. Displays of emotion in animals, based on natural urges, are an authentic means of communicating information and provoking certain responses in other animals. These displays function to communicate courtship and mating rituals, warnings, dominance or submission hierarchies and distress signals. Interaction in the animal kingdom, then, functions according to the same impulses from which the id derives. Furthermore, the instinctive behavior displays exemplified by animals are based on elementary, primary emotions such as fear, anger and satisfaction. These emotions are purer and less complicated than secondary or more complex emotions (such as shame, envy and remorse) which characterize much of human discourse and behavior. Many of these complex emotions are interpreted as negative in our human culture, and are therefore repressed, modified or disguised, making it difficult to assess a person's true feelings or responses to certain situations. We censor our own thoughts and feelings, making real communication about our essential nature difficult to achieve. Verbal reports about our emotional states may deflect away from our true emotional responses; they can be deceptive in describing how we really feel. Robert Plutchik calls our attention to "the inherent ambiguity of language," which he examines in a chapter on the language of emotions:

> Words are not precise symbols that have a single, unequivocal meaning. They are inherently ambiguous and depend on context to help establish meanings.... Thus, the statements one makes about one's own

> inner emotional states are partially dependent upon the kinds of words available to the individual and the kind of linguistic community he or she is in. The point is simply that many factors influence verbal reports of inner, private, emotional states and therefore, the nature of the inner states will always remain an inference that requires confirmation by independent sources of evidence.[17]

Plutchik here is concerned here about the inherent difficulty of defining and studying emotions according to verbal reports; however, the conclusions he reaches also reinforce the fact that non-verbal communication through instinctual and emotional patterns of behavior (such as that displayed by animals) is a truer and more authentic way of imparting information about one's essential nature than language is. The intervention of language distances us from our real human nature and from the natural primary rhythms that govern our existence.

The essential and authentic nature of non-verbal communication among animals makes them an obvious choice as subject-matter for poets exploring primitive sub-verbal modes. For the same reason, children also appear in several of Oppen's poems. Children are unsullied by the artificialities of social discourse; like animals, they are more directly tuned to the essential rhythms of life; they have not yet acquired a superego of censorship and repression. This, of course, can make them more volatile individuals than their socially oriented adult counterparts; but in exploring primitive modes and primary states, a poet like Oppen may find in children a valid representation of the essential and primary qualities he wishes to explore. For example, Robert Bly, already mentioned here as a Deep Image poet, and one whose work explores primitive consciousness and primary states, in "Portrait" (a translation of a Spanish poem by Antonio Machado y Ruiz) configures the end of the speaker's life as a setting out to sea in a boat which will never return, and likens the speaker, stripped of almost all worldly possessions, to pure sea children.[18] Bly links the speaker's last departure, the final stripping away of everything physical and the return to a naked and primal state, with what he calls "the children of the sea." Children, like the sea, are identified with symbols of that elemental existence which underlies all life. In this poem, they are stripped of all possessions, at one with the natural rhythms of the ocean — those currents which both carry life and also carry us away from it. Oppen, too, features the ocean and the sea in many of his poems, emphasizing that great tide of elemental life (and sometimes destruction) which is at the source of all being.

Both children and animals are natural choices for a poet like Oppen, who wishes to explore primitive modes. Together with primary images like moon and water, mythic and symbolic thinking, and sub-verbal elements such as spaces, tone and rhythm, they form the stuff of which primitive modes are made. This kind of subject-matter draws the reader closer to experiencing and understanding those elements and basic rhythms which are the undercurrents of language, and which affect the way in which we perceive and employ the spoken and written word.

The primitive elements at work in the poetry of Oppen are expressed through the various modes discussed in this chapter: Oppen's poetry is constructed mainly around primary mythic symbols and Deep Images, and reinforced through gaps and breaks in his syntax. These primary symbols and Deep Images — centering on water, light, stone and sand — as well as his references to animals and children and his unique use of disjointed syntax form the source of Oppen's primitive voice.

Two
Oppen and Language

Poststructuralist thinking has led to current trends which question the reliability of language and its ability to convey a clarity of meaning: there will always be unconscious (or linguistic, or historic) forces at work which cannot be mastered. These trends have been particularly pertinent to the themes dealt with in recent poetry. In a poststructuralist view of language, the signifier drifts away from the signified, Derrida's "difference" disrupts the connection between them and inserts gaps, the semiotic undermines the symbolic, and power systems distort knowledge. Poststructuralist themes decenter the world and the self, obliterate boundaries once held to be self-evident, and resist interpretation. The paradox inherent in Oppen's portrayal of primitive sub- or pre-verbal states through this often unstable medium of language leads to a closer examination of language itself, and to what extent it can define experience. The question of whether language produces experience and meaning or is produced by them has provoked sufficient argument, both from a linguistic and a philosophical viewpoint, to merit attention before examining the ways in which language functions.

In a critique of Husserl's phenomenological approach and his belief that there is an internal sphere of experience which precedes language, Terry Eagleton claims:

> The hallmark of the "linguistic revolution" of the twentieth century, from Saussure and Wittgenstein to contemporary literary theory, is the recognition that meaning is not simply something "expressed" or "reflected" in language: it is actually *produced* by it. It is not as though

we have meanings, or experiences, which we then proceed to cloak with words; we can only have the meanings and experiences in the first place because we have a language to have them in.[1]

The essence of Eagleton's statement is that there are no experiences outside the realm of language; in Eagleton's view, what cannot be articulated is annulled as a meaningful experience at all. Yet there do seem to be experiences which elude or defy a language to express them: one example of this would be the accumulation of learning experience in the life of a child who has not yet learned to speak. Other experiences which appear to elude language are those for which we have no words available: certain experiences arouse in us a sense of foreboding or anticipation, or the conviction that they are significant in a way that we find impossible to express. These experiences often arise from a deep-seated unconscious or emotional state which cannot be put into words because we do not have the words for it: it is a sub-verbal and sub-cognitive state. To say, as Eagleton does, that experience is created by language is to deny that the above-mentioned situations are experiences at all; it is to say that they have no significance unless they can be articulated. Otherwise they cannot be considered meaningful experiences at all. Eagleton's view that language is an integral part of meaningful experience is true for the articulation (or sometimes communication) of that experience, but not for its authenticity. A sub-verbal state may be a valid one which does not depend on language to grant it significance. Julia Kristeva, for example, would argue that our unconscious—the seat of our primary drives—provides a definite "undertext" of valid experience which eludes linguistic representation, but which makes itself felt through rhythm and rupture. The primitive modes dealt with in this analysis of Oppen's work reflect states that are essentially too deep for language, and somehow have to be refashioned through the medium of words in order to be meaningfully communicated. Or as T.S. Eliot explained: the poet must choose words "with a network of tentacular roots reaching down to the deepest terrors and desires."[2] These kinds of words suggest images that are embedded in the primitive levels of experience common to all humankind.

Freud's exploration of the individual unconscious focused on those basic drives which lie below language and must percolate upwards through conscious social discourse by way of dreams and what he calls "parapraxes": slips of the tongue, jokes, misreadings. Freud divided the human psyche into the "id" (the unconscious reservoir of drives which are constantly active and are ruled by the "pleasure principle"), the "ego" (which operates mainly at conscious and preconscious levels, is ruled by the "reality principle" and takes care of the "id" urges) and the "superego" (a partially conscious censor on the ego functions, comprising the individual's ideals derived from familial and social values). Freud's division of the psyche into these three states has brought into focus the existence of basic primitive urges which control much of our lives and must undergo a transformation through the medium of language in order to be revealed, and has spawned a great deal of poststructuralist investigation into the effect of one's primary and subconscious drives on the self's expression in literature.

Both Julia Kristeva and Jacques Lacan have examined and attempted to explain those primary drives which not only precede language but also express themselves in a turbulent underplay of rhythms and energies that can impinge upon and disrupt our social discourse. Julia Kristeva talks about the "semiotic" and the "symbolic" aspects of language, where the semiotic stands for the realm of the unconscious inhabited by our primary drives, and the symbolic stands for conscious discourse ordered by syntax and socially regulated laws. Kristeva uses the word "semiotic" in its Greek sense of "trace" or "imprint," implying that the instinctual drives which inhabit and define the unconscious provide a primary blueprint of experience which both imposes itself on language and is also imposed upon by the symbolic order of articulated discourse. Kristeva uses the Greek term "chora" to define the semiotic drives, which defy linguistic representation:

> Although our theoretical description of the *chora* is itself part of the discourse of representation that offers it as evidence, the *chora* a rupture and articulation (rhythm) precedes evidence, verisimilitude, spatiality and temporality. Our discourse — all discourse — moves with and against the *chora* in the sense that it simultaneously depends upon and refuses it ... the *chora* precedes and underlies figuration and thus specularization, and is analogous only to vocal or kinetic rhythm.[3]

Kristeva emphasizes that the *chora* is not positional, and therefore does not function as signifier or signified; it has significance, but it cannot be linguistically articulated. The semiotic precedes linguistic signification, and therefore has no cognitive function. It is, however, a prerequisite of language. According to Kristeva, "All those various processes and relations, anterior to sign and syntax, have just been identified from a generic perspective as previous and necessary to the acquisition of language, but not identical to language."[4] The primary processes at work in the semiotic are governed by rhythms and can be perceived as a kind of language, though not a linguistically meaningful one. In order to attain ordered meaning, these primary processes must enter the symbolic order of language, where they are repressed. However, the semiotic drives manifest themselves in language, not by signs but through tone and rhythm, and also through contradictions, disruptions and meaninglessness. The semiotic, for Kristeva, is the "other" of language, providing an undercurrent of energies and unconscious drives which ripple through social discourse (and literary texts), threatening the symbolic order and disrupting overt meaning. Kristeva's semiotic, then, is fluid and flowing, undermining linguistic signature and opposed to all fixed signification. It thus provides an essential undercurrent to the realm of the symbolic, which is defined by law and syntax.

The semiotic *chora,* when it filters through into the symbolic sphere of signification, modifies linguistic structures and radically transforms them. The transparency of the signifying chain is disrupted by rhythmic, lexical and even syntactical changes which "transgress" (Kristeva's term) representation by displacing the sign. Kristeva calls the positioning of the sign, or the entry into the symbolic realm the "thetic" and maintains that the rupture caused by the intrusion of the semiotic into the symbolic is most evident in the creative process:

> Though absolutely necessary, the thetic is not exclusive; the semiotic, which also precedes it, constantly tears it open, and this transgression brings about all the various transformations of the signifying practice that are called "creation."[5]

Kristeva makes several references to music and literary works, citing James Joyce and the French poet Stephane Mallarme as examples of writers whose texts are transparently ruptured by the semiotic drives, and who consciously exploit these semiotic rhythms in order to reach a more authentic truth about human existence. Kristeva herself believes that poetic language is one form of discourse which explores the rupture of the symbolic realm through rhythm, tone and "musical" language: "This is particularly evident in poetic language since, for there to be a transgression of the symbolic, there must be an irruption of the drives in the universal signifying order, that of 'natural' language."[6] This "irruption of the drives" through rhythmic distortions in the overt text of poetry is clearly at work in the poetry of Oppen, who employs visual elements such as line breaks and spaces between words as well as tonal elements such as rhythm to reflect the primary forces which manifest themselves in the poetry and provide an underlying, primitive "phonotext" to the overt "genotext" of syntax and signification.

Jacques Lacan, the French poststructuralist who believes that the central concept of human experience is language, talks about the "Imaginary order"—the primary symbiotic relationship—and the "Symbolic order"—the realm of language and conscious social discourse. From the Oedipal stage onwards, the subject is split—divided between desire and the law, banished from the imaginary position of reality into the empty world of language. One signifier implicates the rest, causing a slippery relation between language and reality. We must live, according to Lacan, with the sense of lack, and make do with substitutes; we move in a world of temporary alleviation. These constantly shifting signifiers emphasize our sense of loss and create a dispersal of the self. In addition to the Imaginary and the Symbolic order, Lacan also believes in a third order—that of the "Real." This is the realm of raw experience which cannot be directly accessed; it cannot be processed in a linguistic network. It is a realm of "Otherness," an unmediated, unarticulated state, always at one remove. It is amorphous, ineffable, ineluctable; nevertheless, it intrudes, it is *there*. Lacan's view of the unconscious is that it is an attempt to capture the elusiveness of the Real, to make up for the fact that the Real is beyond language. He claims that it is structured like a language and is also structured by language; for example, the unconscious goes through a process of endless deferral, moving from one image to another by virtue of association, just as language moves through an endless chain of representation and definition, each word or phrase leading to a variety of possible interpretations which in turn are defined by yet more words and phrases, and so on in an endless shift of signification.

Lacan's view of language, then, is that it reflects our sense of loss and alienation from our essential selves — a self which is, to him, inaccessible. He sees the acquisition of language as the entry into a world which severs us from the Real, that unattainable realm which is beyond signification, beyond the symbolic order. Although Lacan believes that the unconscious (that striving to return to a perfect symbiotic state) is created by language, both Freud's theories of the id, with its instinctual urges, and Kristeva's theory of the semiotic, point to the evidence of primary rhythms and drives which underlie language and have an autonomous existence which is made manifest in the metaphors and rhythms of poetic language. These primary rhythms are common to us all, and many poets, whether they are drawing on their own personal experience, or tapping into the "collective unconscious" which belongs to all humankind, attempt to bring these primary states to the conscious realization of the reader through elemental images and rhythms. Lacan's view of the unconscious (a personal, individual well of experience) may be seen as a blueprint of a more universal experience, since one's own personal fears and desires are often mirrored in the unconscious fears and desires of us all. The primitive motifs and the undercurrents of energy made manifest in certain rhythms which display themselves in Oppen's poetry point to the existence of a subterranean energy, a raw experience which Lacan would probably locate within the Real. Contrary to Lacan's theories, there appears to be evidence in the world of poetry that the Real is accessible, although it may be unarticulated in social discourse as we know it. For example, Oppen's depiction of primary states through basic images of stone and fire, elements which are "just there," corresponds, I believe, to Lacan's description of the Real. Social language, as we have seen, is too unreliable and slippery to convey any kind of transcendental meaning, and certainly seems to be impotent to convey those essential experiences which are an unspoken but definitive part of our existence; however, poetic discourse, which searches between and beyond the words, does appear to harness this raw, essential energy and articulate it through different elements in poetry.

Both Roland Barthes and Jacques Derrida take a deconstructionist view of language, casting serious doubts (like Lacan) on the ability of language to convey the true essence of reality. They explain the ways in which language defines, confines and ultimately contradicts and fragments its own definitions, revealing the infinite multiplicity of references in the word chain, the gaps, the definition-by-absence and the ultimate elusiveness of words. In addition, Barthes' term "jouissance" (or "bliss"), which is discovered when we go beyond the overt meaning of a text and unexpectedly "bump against" some unorthodox use of language, should be considered when examining the ways in which Oppen manipulates language. The idea of a "join" or "seam" between two surfaces, which Barthes uses as a metaphor to describe the meeting between a reader's sudden realization of meaning and the naked language of the text, may be compared to the breaks in the poems to be discussed in the coming chapters, where deep primal energies, whether individual to the poet or common to all human experience, burst to the surface and cause what may be described as "a rush of meaning" in the reader. Barthes says that the text of bliss "unsettles the reader's historical, cultural psychological assumptions, brings a crisis to his relation with language."[7] It does appear that Oppen aims to bring about such a crisis, to produce a certain jolt in the reader who encounters "fault lines" or disruptions in the language. Moreover, in defining "jouissance" or "bliss," Barthes grants the term explicit sexual connotations, likening the pleasurable rush of meaning to orgasm. This sexual connotation provides a succinct parallel to the release of generic primal energies which Oppen often works towards in his depiction of primitive states. Barthes makes a distinction between the text of pleasure and the text of bliss, contending that pleasure is derived from the arrangement of words in a text, whereas the text of bliss "always rises out of it like a scandal." He elaborates:

> Here, moreover, drawn from psychoanalysis, is an indirect way of establishing the opposition between the text of pleasure and the text of bliss: pleasure can be expressed in words, bliss cannot. Bliss is unspeakable, inter-dicted. I refer to Lacan, ("What one must bear in mind is that

bliss is forbidden to the speaker, as such, or else that it cannot be spoken except between the lines...").[8]

In making this distinction, Barthes also makes it clear that the primal undercurrents which pulse through a text cannot be pinned down in words: they must be expressed by other means. He joins Lacan and Kristeva in emphasizing those primal undercurrents which surface in the gaps between words and in the rhythmic interplay of language. Both Barthes and Derrida view language less as a clearly defined structure of signification and more as an open-ended movement of elements, all interconnected and none definable in any absolute sense, shot through with endless shades of meaning.

The idea that words can have an "absolute meaning" or significance becomes suspect within the concept of language as defined by Derrida. He uses the term "logocentric" to describe a belief in some ultimate truth or reality embedded in words, the belief in a transcendental signifier, and deftly points out that in order to function as an ultimate truth, that transcendental signifier would have to be placed outside the whole system of language, as an unquestionable point of reference beyond discourse itself. This, of course, is an impossibility, since language must employ its own system of reference in order to discuss itself. The transcendental signifier, therefore, becomes a fiction. This paradox inherent in language — of employing its own terms to talk about its inherent instability — provides an inverse reflection of the paradox Oppen faces: that of evoking primitive elements beyond the grasp of words through the medium of a linguistic system which employs those very words to define them. Still, the words will be shot through with streaks of meaning which are manifested in the gaps and constant shifts between the different linguistic terms. Derrida's critical work "Differance" looks at how words are defined by what they are not, as Derrida dissolves the rigid boundaries between classic binary oppositions (light and dark, male and female, nature and culture) to show how each term inheres within the other and can only be defined as the absence of being "other" than what it is. Therefore, words can not be independent entities at all. This means, as Terry Eagleton explains it:

> Writing, like any process of language, works by difference; but difference is not itself a *concept,* is not something that can be *thought.* A text may "show" us something about the nature of meaning and signification which it is not able to formulate as a proposition. All language, for Derrida, displays this "surplus" over exact meaning, is always threatening to outrun and escape the sense which tries to contain it.[9]

This "surplus of meaning" which Eagleton identifies in language is precisely the existence of an underlying current of signification which the overt meaning of the words themselves does not articulate. A simplified example of this concept can be found in idioms, where the true meaning of the phrase cannot be discovered by interpreting the words one by one. There is a collective, "surplus" meaning, different from the literal one, which gives the phrase an additional significance. For example, when we say about a newly-wed couple that they "tied the knot," we are not talking about joining the ends of two pieces of string or rope, but rather referring to the rite of marriage, a joining of lives. Derrida's point is that the meaning of a text cannot be pinned down in the words of the text; however, there may be traces of meaning which overflow from the text, an additional "shimmering" which surfaces independently of the overt meaning which the words denote. Or as Derrida himself puts it: "and, in the same process, designate the crevice through which the yet unnamable glimmer beyond the closure can be glimpsed."[10] This corresponds roughly to the way in which the Deep Image discussed in chapter one surfaces from the overall content of a poem. It may also be seen as a parallel to the semiotic rhythms of Kristeva and the "jouissance" of Barthes.

The sense of immanent meaning which a text gives off, independently of its linguistic significance, is echoed in Martin Heidegger's philosophical view of language, and is particularly pertinent to a discussion of Oppen's work, since Oppen was influenced by Heidegger's approach to the whole concept of "being." Heidegger claimed that "being" is not an "entity," and that it cannot in any true sense be directly represented in language; in his view, language "reveals" rather than "tells." There is no direct mode in language; it can only hint at reality indirectly. Heidegger discusses metaphor as a means of speaking non-representationally, of "calling into existence." Poetry establishes "being" by means of the word, and therefore language becomes a means through which essentials of existence are evoked. In this respect, like Derrida, Heidegger believes that there is a halo of significance which reflects reality quite independently of the actual meaning of the words themselves. In Oppen's poetry the use of simple, basic nouns reflects this idea: the significance of the small, primary words cannot be explicated linguistically. They are "just there," entities of a basic existence which convey a sense of essential reality going beyond the linguistic meaning of the words in the poetry. Within the context of this approach, the word "stone" in a poem, for example, would not directly represent a lump of hard material, but rather a deep, essential form of "being" or existence. The basic elements of stone and sand, wind and water and fire in Oppen's poetry reflect the simplest and most primary forms of existence, representing the underlying essential state of things.

Like Heidegger, who believes that words cannot represent reality, only reveal it, the Nominalist group of poets also claim that words cannot represent the reality of experience, but for a different reason: they perceive language as inadequate to tell the personal and individual experiences of the poet because the meanings of words are too general to pin down those experiences. In an analysis of Nominalist poetry, Robert Pinsky defines the Nominalist poet as someone who has a "sense of his experience as a stream of unique, particular perceptions."[11] This creates a problem for the Nominalist poet, as Pinsky sees it: if experience is believed to consist of individual, unique moments, then a gap opens up between the lived experience and the language used to express it. The Nominalist view of language sees words in general categories; the words become arbitrary and unreal, unable to capture the moment of the experience. Words, as Derrida points out, carry a multiplicity of meanings, and may go in different directions, conveying different things to different people; they are, therefore, inadequate to pin down the exact sense of a unique experience felt deep in the bones.

Although Oppen would not be considered a Nominalist poet, the underlying concept of Nominalist poetry — that there is a gap between the essential nature of words and that of reality — seems relevant when exploring the approach to language exemplified by Oppen in his portrayal of primitive modes. Since essential reality cannot be directly conveyed through language (in Oppen's poetry even the basic words like "stone" and "fire" go beyond their direct representation), the essential elements must be conveyed through the "music" of the poem — in its rhythms, rhymes, tone and spaces.

The view that words are often misleading and impotent to reveal the essential poetic voice is explored by Marjorie Perloff, who comments on an interview with Philip Levine, during which he was asked if he was trying to create a "language of revelation," and quotes his reply:

> I don't know if I'm trying to create a language. I've never really thought about that. In a curious way, I'm not much interested in language. In my ideal poem, no words are noticed. You look through them into a vision of ... just see the people, the place.

Perloff comments:

> Language, for the poetry that persists in its demand for authenticity, seems to be something of a distraction, interfering as it does with the direct communication between poet and reader; perhaps poetry can dispense with it altogether and go for the unmediated image.[12]

Language here becomes an impediment to the true experience which the poet is trying to convey, whether it be the poet's personal experience or a universal well of images which the reader can tap into. The poet relies on other means to express the essential ideas of the poem: disrupted syntax, sound-text, rhythm. These elements, unlike the words themselves, provide the "unmediated image" with which words interfere. One example of a poem (by Clark Coolidge) using these elements is given by Perloff to illustrate the use of oddly spaced lines and truncated phrases which provide interesting tonal and rhythmic formations. In her commentary on this poem, Perloff discusses "how ideas, lodged deep within the mind, come to the surface of consciousness."[13] In a poem of this kind, the disjointed syntax, the absence of a concrete referentiality between words and phrases, allows for a play of meaning to spark through the poem and bring to the reader's consciousness various associations which tap into an underlying well of universal images, concepts and experience, much like Yeats's spiritus mundi or Jung's collective unconscious. It is not incidental that

Perloff devotes a whole section of her book to a discussion of Oppen's poetry, since Oppen often works in this way with disjointed syntax and (apparently) randomly juxtaposed phrases, precisely in order to create a pattern of experience which underlies the surface association of ideas reflected in the phrases themselves. Donald Davie elaborates on the function of dislocated syntax, rhythm and gap in poetry, saying:

> *Rhythm,* in free verse and metered verse alike, is determined as much by syntax as by lineation.... The rhythm is determined very largely by the spacing and placing of pauses — the pauses of different weights and duration signated by comma, semicolon, colon, full stops, by line ending without punctuation stop, line ending with comma, line ending with colon, and so on.[14]

Language, then, becomes intractable and unreliable as an expression of what lies in the depths of our consciousness, or lodged in the bones and sinews of experience. Our basic intuitions, our deepest sense of what is real and true, must often be conveyed by unlocking what lies between and beyond the words and phrases themselves. The poet must find ways whereby the conscious mind and the deep-seated currents of the unconscious converge to produce a true sense of lived experience. In dealing with primitive modes in his poetry, Oppen chooses to represent metaphorically the need to cut down deeper into language in order to free those primary elements which reveal essential states and provide a purer and more luminous means of communication.

THREE

Oppen's Materials

Oppen's first collection of poems, *Discrete Series*, was published in 1934, the year that Oppen and his wife Mary returned to New York after living in Europe, where Oppen earned the recognition of such poets as Ezra Pound. On their return they joined the Communist party and devoted the next two decades to political activity; as a result, Oppen (believing that committing himself to his art was not compatible with a commitment to the Communist party) stopped writing poetry and returned to it only in 1958, after several years in exile in Mexico. His second book of poems, *The Materials*, therefore marks a new phase in his artistic life, one in which he did not, however, abandon his political concerns, but rather merged them with his poetic vision. This second book of poems investigates the value of the basic elements (or materials) of everyday life, imbuing them with an organic and inherent value which paradoxically goes deeper than their symbolic value: these "materials" are important to human experience because of what they are and not because of what they signify. Burton Hatlen mentions "various forms of solid matter" (such as earth, wood, stone and iron), "the tools (hammers, saws, knives, lathes and other machines) which humans use to shape these 'materials,'" as well as the organic matter of humans, living creatures and plants (flesh, birds, trees and seeds), "the habitations (houses, skyscrapers, boats)," and the human words used to communicate these elements. He goes on to say: "These images constitute the 'materials' out of which Oppen makes his individual poems; and the recurrence of the same set of 'materials' in one poem after another serves to unify the book."[1] By fashioning the poems in *The Materials* around such fundamental images, Oppen creates a poetry both concrete and elemental, using the basic building-blocks of language — mostly nouns — in stark and uncompromising ways.

In the *Collected Poems* (1975), the first poem to appear from *The Materials* is "Eclogue," a term used to define a short poem which is usually pastoral or idyllic. However, Oppen sweeps away any images aroused by the terms "pastoral" or "idyllic," replacing them with sharp, hard images of rock and hunger; at the same time, this poem has an organic quality compatible with a pastoral ode. The poem opens, as several of Oppen's poems do, in a social setting: "The men talking / Near the room's center," and continuing with "They have said / More than they had intended." Already in these opening lines, Oppen clears away the clutter of words to expose what really lies behind social discourse: one's intentions and one's inner thoughts, which are what impel speech into being. In the following lines, he cuts down through the social clatter to a silent place of beginnings: "Pinpointing in the uproar / Of the living-room // An assault / On the quiet continent." The use of the word "pinpointing" echoes images in other poems of funnels, narrowing-down and whirlwinds, all of which imply a concentration inward or downward to a point of origin. This "pinpointing" subtly reinforces the "room's center" of the second line. One is reminded, in the "uproar of the living-room" of Eliot's women in "Prufrock," who "come and go / talking of Michelangelo." There is a sense here of inane chatter which is chaotic ("uproar") but also threatening ("assault") to that "quiet continent" of organic beginnings. It seems significant that Oppen uses no verbs, no words of action, in these lines: "Pinpointing in the uproar / Of the living-room // An assault / On the quiet continent." The focus here is on nouns — "uproar," "living-room," "assault," "continent" — which are more concrete, more fundamental parts of speech than the more fluid and active verbs. Thus the reader has a sense of the static rather than the process; what is being described here is a state of being which underlies the chaotic din of social discourse. This is a place both external and internal, found in one's inner being, preceding speech, but also outside the window of the room, in the great dark sky and in the earth under one's feet: "Beyond the window / Flesh and rock and hunger // loose in the night sky / Hardened into soil." Here is a place defined by the lowest common organic denominator: flesh, the basic stuff out of which animate life is composed; rock, a primary mineral element; and hunger, arising from our most elementary need, the need for food. These elemental concepts are juxtaposed with manifestations of organized society such as the living room and the window, both of which belong in one's dwelling place. Flesh, rock and hunger are to be found outside the social sphere, "[l]oose in the night sky," "tilting if itself to the sun once more," yet they provide the foundations for one's social existence, rooted in the ground beneath our feet, "[h]ardened into soil." Within this elemental, organic sphere one finds the beginnings of life: "small vegetative leaves / And stems taking place // Outside." This is the "quiet continent," the silent space of origins where all creation begins: "— O small ones / To be born!" The use of the word "ones" by Oppen in this last line of "Eclogue" bears noting, for the word signifies both singular and plural; "one" is the most primary of numbers, the foundation for all creation and creativity. One is a number both static and independent, singular in all aspects of the word, yet without it nothing can develop.

"Eclogue" appears to reinforce, but also to refute, Lacan's theories of language. The symbolic order of language, as Lacan sees it, functions as a superstructure imposed on those primary drives which tumble about in the unconscious, yet in this poem it is social discourse, rather than the turbulence of the primary drives, which is chaotic and threatens the "quiet continent" where essential energies lie. At the same time, Lacan's view of language as a force which alienates us from our essential selves seems to be upheld in this poem. Language is described here as "uproar" and "assault," a great noise which threatens that quiet space, marked in the poem by an actual visual space (a long dash in the last line), where the core of existence and of the self begins. In using this concrete marking space, Oppen thus clears away words to present us with a non-verbal concept integral to the theme of the poem.

The poem which follows "Eclogue" in the *Collected Poems* is "Image of the Engine," a poem in five sections. The poem appears to chronicle the "death" of a machine, opening with the lines "Likely as not a ruined gasket head / Spitting at every power stroke, if not a crank shaft / Bearing

Three: Oppen's Materials

knocking at the roots of the thing like a pile-driver" and continuing: "...when the thing stops, / Is stopped, with the last slow cough / In the manifold..." Here we have, indeed, an "image of the engine," coughing its last, about to be stopped for ever. Yet:

> From the idle cylinders will one imagine
> That squeezed from the cooling steel
> There hovers in that moment, wraith-like and like a plume
>   of steam, an aftermath,
> A still and quiet angel of knowledge and of comprehension.

This section has been discussed by L.S. Dembo with Oppen himself, in an interview in which Oppen explains that the idea presented is "the image of man as a machine, with a ghost, the ghost in the machine."[2] Whether this is, indeed, a poem about man and ghost or simply a poem about the final breakdown of a machine, there is a clear movement towards a dissembling and a disintegration, the breakdown of a structure into its basic components. These basic components, all concrete elements, house "a still and quiet angel," and it is only when the engine is dissembled, broken down into its most elementary units, that knowledge and comprehension can be released; when the "voice" of the engine is stilled, the silence of comprehension ensues. There is an echo here of the biblical story of the burning bush, when Moses heard from within the bush which was burning and yet not consumed, the "still, small voice" of God. Both the image of the now silent engine in the poem and the biblical story emphasize the stillness of the moment of revelation, and both imply that only when the object described is reduced to its most elemental state (the engine dissembled into the crankshaft "knocking at the roots of the thing," the manifold, the "idle cylinders," the fire in the bush burning away everything superfluous with a clear flame) does the revelation take place. We are reminded of Barthes' concept of "jouissance," a burst of illumination when a text is split open to reveal a sudden significance, the "still and quiet angel" appearing out of the heap of lifeless components.

In fact, the first section of "Image of the Engine" might be seen as a metaphor for Oppen's poetic technique, as manifested in many of the poems, as he fractures syntax and word order, breaking down sentences into single units, in order to release the non-verbal, underlying knowledge of the text.

Oppen reinforces the sense of stilled activity through his choice of verbs: the poem begins with the clanking and "spitting" of the head gasket and the crank shaft "knocking," and moves through "valves jumping" and the "heavy frenzy of the pistons" — all of these images powerful both from a visual and an auditory perspective — then slowing down in the "last slow cough," and finally leading to the passive participles "stopped" and "squeezed." The final verb is "hovers," conveying the sense of an aura, a word both abstract and concrete, although almost invisible, and silent. The "plume of steam" connects both the elemental concrete image (steam is condensed *water*) and also the abstract image, the "aura of significance." Although Oppen's use of language in this poem is fairly conventional, there is a visual space between the words "plume" and "of steam," conveying, perhaps, that silent moment of knowledge and comprehension which the aftermath of steam reveals; this space creates a non-verbal pause through which underlying significance can surface.

"Population" is another good illustration of Oppen's poetic and linguistic techniques. Since it is a fairly short poem, it can be quoted in its entirety:

> Like a flat sea,
> Here is where we are, the empty reaches
> Empty of ourselves
>
> Where dark, light, sound
> Shatter the mind born
> Alone to ocean
>
> Save we are
> A crowd, a population, those
> Born, those not yet dead, the moment's
>
> Populace, sea-borne and violent, finding
> Incredibly under the sense the rough deck
> Inhabited, and what it always was.

What is immediately evident in this poem is the connection between the ocean and "the moment's populace." Oppen appears to be contrasting the flat emptiness of the sea with the ocean's depth when seen from a collective perspective. This collective population is bound to the ocean; it is "sea-borne," finding the "rough deck" underfoot. In his essay "Not Altogether Lone in a Lone Universe," Burton Hatlen gives his interpretation of the poem, saying that "Population" is

> a poem which makes clear Oppen's sense of the relationship between the human world and the formless but inescapable inhumanity of the sea.... But we do not confront the "flat seas" alone. We are joined together in a community that includesnot only the living but also the dead and the not-yet-born.[3]

This reading of the poem clearly explains the connection between the first two and the last two stanzas, while relating to the sea imagery which features in many of Oppen's poems. However, since Oppen is a conscious craftsman, engaged at once in both portraying the elemental through the simple nouns (those things that are "just there") and also in examining how the poem is articulated through various verbal and non-verbal elements, the poem may also be interpreted as the crafting of poetry, its sources and the elements of which it is composed. In such a reading of the poem, the "we" becomes the poems on the "flat sea" of the page, stark words on the blank paper, while the "dark, light, sound" are the influences which break into the poet's mind and shatter the poem into language. The "mind born alone to ocean" may then refer to the poetic creation in the poet's mind, a creation which has its sources deep in elemental images such as the ocean. Each poem is an entity unto itself, yet belongs within a body of poetry, a "population" of poems, some newly created, some existing already for a time, the "moment's populace" of a whole series of poems, each pinning down a concrete moment of experience. The last stanza reinforces the poetic source of all these poems, ("sea-borne and violent"), many of which violently dislocate syntax and conventional sentence structures, to inhabit the "rough deck" of Oppen's poetic stand. The key phrase in this stanza is, of course, "under the sense," a phrase examined by Randolph Chilton as to its different possibilities of interpretation:

> Here "sea-borne" can mean both "carried by the sea" and "born of the sea," and beyond such punning, the use of "under" is highly ambiguous.

> We might read it in the sense of "under scrutiny" or in the sense of "beneath" (i.e. beneath the sensual level — insensible — a reading consistent with understanding "incredibly" as a modifier of the prepositional phrase "under the sense" rather than "finding"), or simply in the spatial sense of being at our feet.[4]

Certainly the closest reading of "under the sense" in an interpretation of the poem as a reference to poetic sources would be Chilton's idea of the "insensible," or rather a more primary level than that of the senses or conscious experience, so that the poems then evolve from "what ... always was," a deep bedrock of existence which is unchanging and permanent.

Oppen's language in "Population," although more conventional than in some of the later poems, nevertheless evidences those techniques which are his hallmark. Verbs are almost non-existent here, apart from the central word "shatter" and the gerund "finding," both of which pinpoint what Oppen is doing in the poem: shattering language in order to find or reveal the primary substance out of which the poem evolves. The only other verbs are versions of "be" ("is," "are," "was") which reinforce the static fundamentals Oppen tends to explore in his work. In addition, there are no periods in the poem until the end of the last line; this opens up the grouping of phrases, refracting possibilities of interpretation and so defining or "shattering" meaning. Oppen's interest lies in what is and not in what it means. The word "alone" in the sixth line, for example, can apply equally to the mind which is born alone, or to the ocean which is the only element for which the mind is born. Similarly, the word "incredibly" in the second last line may be grouped with "finding" (where it enhances the revelation) or with "under the sense" (to show the unexpectedness of where it is found). And in the last line, the "it" in "what it always was" does not have a definite reference, so that the reader is left with a sense of an all-encompassing, deep-seated continuity and permanence, freed of any specific allusion. These floating words and phrases — "alone," "incredibly" and "it" — form the "dark and light" of the poem, the shades of interpretation, and also the fluctuating movement of the water, while the "sound" is echoed in the two-dimensional tone of "flat," the unevenness of the "r" sound in "rough," and the hard, uncompromising consonants of "deck." Thus we find sub-verbal shadings in this poem which reinforce the refraction of the syntax and allow the essence of the poem to manifest itself.

In "Birthplace: New Rochelle" Oppen sets out a thought that has occupied many poets, writers and philosophers — that the passage of the years leaves its mark on humans, but not always on the basic elements of their surroundings. The primary images of this poem — rocks, the sun's light, stones, ground and the "world of things" — remain unchanged in the face of time (at least in the poem), as opposed to humans, who are stamped by its passing; thus the speaker becomes "an aging man" with knuckles that are "jointed." Oppen uses images of basic concrete elements in the sense that Heidegger described: they are "just there," entities of a fundamental and unchanging existence, self-justifying. These images of rock and ground, "stones in sun" and "sun's light" embody an essential autonomous reality beyond the linguistic signification of the words used to describe them. One of the ideas implied in this poem is that humans justify their existence through procreation, extending themselves in time; primary elements carry a deep, fixed reality of their own. The idea of human extension through procreation is exemplified in the mention of the speaker's father and his daughter: "The house / My father's once, and the ground. There is a color of his / time / in the sun's light" and again in "A generation's mark. / It intervenes. My child, / Not now a child." As opposed to the passing generations of father-speaker-child, the "sun's light" absorbs the memory of the father (and therefore of change), yet itself remains unchanged. Between the lines, "A generation's mark" and "My child," the phrase "It intervenes" shows how the mark of generations interrupts the time passing before and after it, leaving a "ripple" as it were in the ongoing and unchanging flow of time, much as the twisted knuckles mark the speaker's hands. The notion here is that generations of humans both mark and are marked by time, whereas "stones in the sun" are not marked by time, only "suffer" it, as we read in the last few lines:

> My child,
> Not now a child, our child,
> Not altogether lone in a lone universe that suffers time
> Like stones in sun. For we do not.

These lines emphasize a need in humans for the flux of relationships, the need to turn away from being "altogether lone." The world of stones and sunlight exists in a "lone universe," a world of single and singular elements, static and unchanging, the underlying foundation of our existence on this planet.

The speaker in "Birthplace: New Rochelle" (who may safely be assumed to be Oppen himself, since New Rochelle was, indeed, his birthplace) asks himself "I am this?" halfway through the poem. Although there is a question mark at the end of this line, the phrase has no question form, and is not really a question. There is surprise and disbelief here — disbelief at the changes time has wrought. In contrasting the word "this" with the "that" of "Returning to that house" in the first line, Oppen juxtaposes the immediacy implied in "this" with the distancing element of "that," as if the concept of the house and its structure — probably stone — are viewed from far away, spanning space and time, fixed in a way that humans are not; Oppen reinforces this idea by using no verbs in the phrases which describe the father's house and the other "things" in the universe: he states only "A world of things" and "The house, my father's once, and the ground." Without verbs, these phrases act as monuments of presence rather than activity, static rather than moving through time. In addition, "A world of things" and "the house" each take a line to themselves. There is no sentence interaction on either side of them. They stand alone in the poem, primary and immobile, untouched.

It seems relevant that the two longest lines in this poem — "And the rounded rocks of childhood — they have lasted well" and "My father's once, and the ground. There is a color of his times" — are both connected with images of stone. As the rocks and the stone structure of the house last through time, these two lines last longer than any others within the spatial structure of the poem. Thus Oppen reflects, in the visual aspect of the poem, his theme of the endurance of elementary materials throughout time. The use of a dash after "rocks of childhood" is an additional non-verbal sign, a wordless space which gives the reader pause to consider the lasting quality of the "rounded rocks," how they continue to exist through space and time. This idea conveys an underlying paradox inherent in all the elemental images of the poem: they manifest both a monumental presence, but also an unchanging reality which spans time from the past, through the present and no doubt into the future. They are images which both overarch temporality and also provide a fundamental, fixed entity.

In "Myself I Sing," Oppen has borrowed from Walt Whitman's *Leaves of Grass*, otherwise called *Song of Myself*. In this collection of poems Whitman champions the common people, proclaiming himself their symbolic representative. Oppen's poem in a sense questions Whitman's song of human identity, as Oppen himself undertakes an undressing, a shrinking, a reduction, a slipping back through various stages, ultimately to confront and then become one with sand, sky, ocean and rocks. "Myself" becomes merged with the elements — "Their weight is part of mine" — as the final section of the poem tells us:

> And yet at night
> Their weight is part of mine.
> For we are all housed now, all in our apartments,
> The world untended to, unwatched.
> And there is nothing left out there
> As night falls, but the rocks

Outside, there is nothing left but the rocks, all traces of civilization removed; inside, we are all "housed in apartments," boxed away in a pseudo-reality inside an empty skin. The real self has become part of the rocks and stone, has become, in fact, an elemental, primal self.

The poem reaches this conclusion as the result of a question posed at the beginning:

> Me! He says, hand on his chest.
> Actually, his shirt.
>   And there, perhaps,
> The question.

This is the central question of the poem: what constitutes "me"? Is it clothes? The speaker's hand is not actually on his chest but on his *shirt*. Is this, then, a part of "me"? Or is it wagons and tools, elements which are introduced as the poem unfolds?

George Oppen

> Pioneers! But trailer people?
> Wood box full of tools —
> >   The most
> American. A sort of
> Shrinking
> >   In themselves. A
> Less than adult: old.
>
> A pocket knife,
> A tool —

It seems that wagons and tools do not constitute the essential "me," since they indicate a "sort of shrinking in themselves." As the poem proceeds, an image unfolds of a man marooned, who

> No longer looks for ships, imagines
> Anything on the horizon. On the beach
> The ocean ends in water. Finds a dune
> And on the beach sits near it. Two.
> He finds himself by two.

This image presents a man isolated in natural surroundings, no longer searching for signs of other human presences. He has retreated from these, becoming one with he elements in his environment. As the ocean "ends in water" we have the sense of a flowing backwards into the primal, elemental reality of water, sand and rock. In the lines "Two / He finds himself by two," we might ask ourselves "Two what?" The answer to this is left deliberately unclear. Oppen offers possibilities of meaning in unspoken ambiguities provided by the fractured syntax. This is a shifting "two," an unfixing of identity. "Myself" is discovered in this unfixing of identity, which leads to a merging with the elements of nature as "their weight is part of mine." Oppen deliberately breaks down syntax at this point, as man's civilized identity — shirts, tools, houses — is fragmented, and man is divested of these in a return to a primary co-existence with rocks, sand and water. One might argue that "their weight" refers to a human "two," yet the fact that man is "marooned" among rocks and sand seems to belie this. The image of the marooned man is a central one in this poem, indicating human isolation but contact and a certain integration with the elements of nature, as the man imagines "any*thing*" (my emphasis) rather than any*one* on the horizon. He finds a sand dune, sits near it on the beach, a Robinson Crusoe figure who relearns to live with the elements, to become one with them, until "There is nothing left out there / As night falls, but the rocks." Oppen chooses to end this poem without a period, intimating, perhaps, that this return to the natural world and the primal self is an ongoing, flowing state, untrammeled by time, atemporal.

The primary condition, beyond thought and a consciousness of self, is again explored by Oppen in his poem "Workman." This poem sets out three states: first, the often violent and broken aspect of nature; second, the quiet craft of the carpenter, as he fits together pieces of wood to form interlocking doors and window-frames; third, the unbound sea, which has its own "voice." The first two states are juxtaposed in a comparison marked by the word "But"; the third state is an elemental one, free of the limitations of any comparison:

> Leaving the house each dawn I see the hawk
> Flagrant over the doorway. In his claws
> That dot, that comma
> Is the broken animal: the dangling small beast knows
> The burden that he is; he has touched
> The hawk's dumb feathers. But the carpenter's is a culture
> Of fitting, of firm dimensions,
> Of post and lintel. Quietly the roof lies
> That the carpenter has finished. The sea birds circle
> The beaches and cry in their own way,
> The innumerable sea birds, their beaks and their wings
> Over the beaches and the sea's glitter.

It is clear that the sea and the seabirds' existence is different from that of the hawk and its prey, and also different from the carpenter's existence. The first two states depend on the relationship between two interconnected entities (the hawk and his prey, the carpenter and his materials), whereas the third state, with the sea and the seabirds, is unchecked by the mesh of relationships which defines the other two, lacking even an awareness of itself. This awareness of self is strongly evident in the hawk-prey relationship, as Burton Hatlen points out: "For the hawk's world has some oddly verbal overtones, as the 'broken animal' becomes a 'comma,' and this 'natural world' even contains some measure of consciousness: the beast 'knows the burden that he is'."[5] The roof that the carpenter has made becomes humanized as it lies "quietly" on the house, thus taking on the kind of emotional characteristics that we associate with people and their own sense of self. But the sea is unknowing of itself, unaware; its existence is unconditional on other influences. It exists at a deeper, more primary level than that of animal or human consciousness.

"Workman" may be interpreted as a metaphor for the craft of poetry and the experiences a poem offers. Oppen raises this possibility in describing the hawk's prey as "that dot, that comma." Dots and commas are not only visual images of how the dangling prey might appear to an onlooker, but also a means of punctuation. If taken as the latter, we may perceive them as symbols of poetic structure and technique, and the "broken animal" as Oppen's own disjointed syntax. Much of Oppen's syntax is violent and brutal in its breaking down of ordered units of meaning, this broken syntax becoming the "prey" which furnishes the poem's structure. Oppen, of course, is the carpenter — as he actually was at various stages throughout his life, working with the basic materials of wood and metal to make furniture — who carefully shapes the poem, fitting together idea and image to create the finished product, the poetic whole. And finally, what emerges from the structure and the crafting together of the different poetic elements is an underlying energy, endlessly moving against itself like the sea, an unconscious ebb and flow having its own indefinable "cry" or elemental voice. Lacan might call this the Real, since it eludes verbal definition; Kristeva would name it the semiotic: it is the deep essence of poetry which remains elusive and undefined by language or image, but is released by both.

Another poem in *The Materials* which deals with different stages of experience is "Antique." In this poem, Oppen looks at the different ages of human experience and how they both interlock and at the same time are detached from each other. The poem opens with a scene from city life in which an antique saw throws speaker and reader back to an earlier age of simple craft, out of which rises the "thin, thin radiance" of survival:

Three: Oppen's Materials

> Against the glass
> Towers, the elaborate
> Horned handle of a saw
> Dates back
>
> Beyond small harbors
> Facing Europe. Ship's hawser
> On the iron bollard at the land's edge mooring
> Continents of workmen
>
> Where we built
> Grand Central's hollow masonry, veined
> In bolted rails in shabby
> City limits daylight and the back yard
>
> Homes. In which some show of flowers
> And of kitchen water holds survival's
> Thin, thin radiance.

The opening lines "Against the glass / Towers" presents an image of urban modernity, suggesting skyscrapers and perhaps the compartmentalization of office buildings. The word "towers" implies isolation and detachment, the individual disconnected from his surroundings even at the heart of collective urban humanity, and the fact that these are glass towers carries connotations of fragility, transparency and exposure to the gaze of the onlooker. Against the glass towers the "elaborate horned handle of a saw" provides an image of solidity and a bygone craft, fashioned not of man-made material but of the horn of some animal. As the poem progresses, we move back and forth between the two conditions of urban alienation and an earlier age of tool-making and simple crafts: the Grand Central train station of New York is composed of "hollow masonry" and is "vcincd" and "shabby," connoting not only the impermanence of travelers in transit, but also tired old age — old men and women with veined hands — and decrepitude, while the elaborately made saw belongs to an era preceding even the harbors with their iron bollards — iron being an older element than the steel, glass and concrete used to construct the towers — and their moored boats. The fact that harbors are built by the water's edge connects them more directly to the living element of the sea, and the collective isolation of the glass towers contrasts strongly with the collective unity of "continents of workmen." Yet they lead into each other: the harbors have no doubt been used to unload the raw materials for the city's structures, and the glass towers throw the antique horn-handled saw into relief.

The final lines of the poem draw back from the urban scene and focus on the individual homes and back yards, coming to a close with the "thin radiance" of survival defined by flowers and kitchen water. One's basic needs for survival are met here; the kitchen provides food and domestic protection, while the whole scene is illuminated by a radiance, a soft light which lifts the domestic picture out of the realm of the everyday and grants it significance and clarity. One does not need much more in the end, Oppen implies; and although the "thin radiance" also implies a certain fragility, it is an enduring fragility, a simplicity evoked from the most basic lives, which shines out bravely in the face of the urban alienation of the self.

In this poem, as in many of Oppen's others, the syntactical juxtaposition of words without connectors or punctuation offers different possibilities of interpretation through its ambiguity. For example, the phrase "at the land's edge mooring" may simply be an extension of the description of the "iron bollard"; but it may also be perceived as an ongoing phrase which includes the line following it—"Continents of workmen"—where the word "mooring" becomes a gerund which binds the "continent of workmen" to it, thus implying a unity between land and sea, harbor and workman. Additionally, the accumulation of words dislocated from recognizable units of significance in phrases such as "city limits daylight" suggests an image of the drab half-light of city suburbs; but the word "limits" may also be understood as a verb, implying that the city curtails the light of day, thus providing a counter-image to the "thin radiance" of survival.

The last sentence of the poem also features an interesting construction. Syntactically, it should be a continuation of the previous sentence, which would then read: "...and the back yards / Homes in which some show of flowers / and of kitchen water holds survival's / Thin, thin radiance." But Oppen makes a disjunction of the final dependent clause beginning "In which...," and so by divorcing it from the previous sentence causes it to stand on its own as a full, self-sufficient sentence, independent of the preceding one. Thus the "radiance" of survival held by plant life and water becomes detached from, and independent of, the city's limits and limitations. And so the light of survival provides its own small, primary source of illumination, an elemental mainstay against the shabby encroachment of time.

The concept of light and radiance features in another poem from *The Materials*, "The Source." The poem itself opens with a series of statements about the city, the first a questioning one:

> If the city has roots, they are in filth
> It is a slum. Even the sidewalks
> Rasping under the feet.

These lines paint a dismal picture of the city, focusing on depressing physical details: the filth, the slums, the rasping sidewalk. The word "rasping" grates particularly on the auditory imagination, combining a sense of roughness with a jarring sound. The city's roots, if it has any, are in the dirt and concrete under one's feet, and concrete is not conducive to growth. This is a purely physical description. Then the poem shifts, like a camera zooming in (a technique Oppen returns to in several of his poems), to focus on a figure in one of the city's buildings:

> — In some black brick
> Tenement, a woman's body
>
> Glows, the gleam; the unimaginable
> Thin feet taper down
> The instep naked to the wooden floor!

From the dirt and black brick of the tenement building there emerges an image of soft light: the glow of a human body and the sculpture of a woman's foot, the gleam of human flesh. The implication is that here are the *real* roots of the city, in the elemental physicality of human beings. This is a woman's foot, that part of a human body closest to the earth, most "rooted" of all one's limbs. The description of the naked instep touching the wooden floor is balanced against the rasp of shod feet on the sidewalk; there is real contact here, uninhibited by footwear. The cameo of the woman and her naked foot casts a small, soft light in the dark tenement building — not a blinding or dazzling light like a sudden realization, but a soft glow, an illumination, a casting of significance on a seemingly insignificant detail.

The last sentence of the poem leads away from the physical description of the woman's foot to a probing conceptualization of the image in the tenement building:

>   Hidden and disguised
>   — and shy?
> The city's
> Secret warmth.

These final lines work around a paradox: although the woman's feet are naked and exposed, divested of any physical covering, there is a hidden, disguised quality to them — there is both an unveiling and a veiling. The questioning "shy?" implies a possible withdrawal, a retiring into the self. The resulting "city's secret warmth" is thus both elemental and elusive. The "thin feet" are "unimaginable," suggesting, perhaps, that this is an image embodying what Lacan would term the Real: the etching in words of the woman's feet captures, somehow, a sense of "otherness," unmediated, unarticulated, "unthought" even, the significance of the image beyond one's grasp but nevertheless felt.

The structural layout of the poem reinforces the transitions made from one state to another, while the dashes mark these transitions. The first transition — from the hard, drab city images to the soft radiance of the woman's limbs — is marked by the first dash: " — In some black brick / Tenement, a woman's body," and the lines are indented from the rest of the poem; the second transition — from the glow of the woman's body back to the city, but a different city with an intangible warmth — is marked by the second dash and a second indentation of the lines: " — and shy? // The city's / Secret warmth." This final depiction of the city is beyond the tangible; it relates to a warming of the spirit, rather than a physical warmth.

Oppen's manipulation of language throughout the poem follows the thematic pattern, as the initial, structurally recognizable sentences give way to simplified, but more grammatically condensed units containing only key nouns and adjectives without verbs. This gradual stripping-down of the sentence structure to essential key words parallels the "undressing" of the city to reveal the etched foot and the underlying warmth emanating from this luminous image.

Finally, the title of the poem, "The Source," leads the reader to a consideration of the central idea set out here. As the unpleasant urban images fall away to reveal the singular luminosity of the woman's feet, the scene takes on a generic quality similar to the biblical story of the Creation, the light beginning in the dark and generating warmth. This is, therefore, ultimately an affirmative poem, even when clad, as always, in the characteristically unsentimental, stark and uncompromising language that is the hallmark of Oppen's work.

In "Sunnyside Child" we again come across a cameo set in the midst of the city, this time a neighborhood child who stands "preoccupied" on a summer street:

> As the builders
> Planned, the city trees
> Put leaves in summer air in lost
> Streets above the subway. And in this
>
> Achievement of the housed, this
> Air, a child
> Stands as a child,
> Preoccupied
>
> To find his generation, his contemporaries
> Of the neighborhood whose atmosphere, whose sound
> In his life's time no front door, no
> Hardware ever again can close on.

This poem hinges on the elusive and indefinable atmosphere of the city trees in the summer air, an atmosphere which cannot be contained by the "achievement of the housed." Man plans, molds materials, builds streets and subways, boxes everything in and surrounds the preoccupied child. Yet there is an elemental quality about the summer air in the neighborhood; the child has stepped out into the street and senses, beyond the search for his friends, the underlying, unheeding presence of the elements and that indefinite quality which eludes the confinement of human endeavor. The summer trees hold their own seed of life, while the air turns from being part of the "achievement of the housed" to become an "atmosphere" of the neighborhood beyond the capability of man to close it in. As in several other poems, the central figure here is a child, rather than an adult figure; heedless of urban planning, innocent of grown-up ambitions, the child standing in the summer air is more receptive to the natural, primary world around him.

Kristeva's theory of the symbolic and the semiotic may be seen to be paralleled here, in the sense that the overt structures of man's achievement — the streets, the subways — impose themselves on the indefinable neighborhood atmosphere in the same way that the symbolic structures of language impose themselves on the semiotic flux. And yet the air, the sound, the atmosphere are meaningful elements which, like the underlying turbulence of the semiotic, cannot be completely controlled or constrained by the structures imposed on them.

If we look at the structure of Oppen's language in this poem, we find the displacement from line to line of significant units of meaning. For example, the opening lines read "As the builders / Planned, the city trees / Put leaves in summer air" rather than "As the builders planned, / The city trees put leaves / In summer air...." Then, in the second stanza we find: "Achievement of the housed, this / Air, a child / Stands as a child," instead of the more linguistically predictable "Achievement of the housed, this air, / A child stands as a child." These displacements of significant chunks of language parallel the displacement of human achievement by the elements of air and sound, the symbolic by the semiotic, the defined by the indefinable. As in many other poems in *The Materials*, Oppen has maneuvered the concrete materials out of which humans fashion their lives, to expose the underlying elemental materials from which a sense of one's fundamental existence evolves.

Another child appears in "Pedestrian," again a city child, one characterized this time by a naïve wonder. This child, dazzled by the lights of the city stores, is a small figure among tall buildings. As the poem develops, an innate comparison is made between the city lights and a lighthouse, moonrise and by extension, a harbor:

Three: Oppen's Materials

> What generations could have dreamed
> Tis grandchild of the shopping streets, her eyes
>
> In the buyer's light, the store lights
> Brighter than the lighthouses, brighter than moonrise
>
> From the salt harbor so rich
> So bright her city
>
> In a soil of pavement, a mesh of wires where she walks
> In the new winter among enormous buildings.

In fact, the poem traces a regression beginning with the urban shops, moving back through lighthouses (a transitional image, since lighthouses are man-made structures which function by using the element of light) and moonrise (which is natural light, as well as being a mythic symbol — of woman, of the dark side of the self and of the cycle of life) to the salt of the "salt harbor," salt being a basic element and representation here of the sea, of a body of water. The poem closes with a return to the city, but a metaphorical city in a way, for the second to last line talks about the "soil" of pavements; "soil" may be understood in the sense of "soiled" or "polluted," but may also be regarded as "earth," that element in which seeds grow and which produces new life. The use of the word "mesh" in this line describes the network of wires, but also implies an interconnectedness, for this poem in effect describes a dreaming-back (the word "dreaming" appears in the first line) and forward again, weaving back and forward between different states and different times.

There are several ambiguities in this poem which also imply dual movement in different possible directions. The first two lines — "What generations could have dreamed / This grandchild" — may be interpreted as the generations dreaming the grandchild, but also vice versa: the grandchild dreaming the generations. This second possibility would reinforce the sense of dreaming back to one's ancestors. Then the lines "Her eyes / In the buyer's light, the store lights / Brighter than the lighthouses" is ambiguous in terms of what is brighter: the store lights, or the child's eyes? This possible ambiguity has been detected by Burton Hatlen: "yet 'her eyes' are 'brighter than the lighthouses,' brighter than the moonrise over the sea. Or is it the 'store lights' that are brighter than the lighthouses?"[6]

Whichever it is, the intermeshing of possibilities, the one-within-the-other of city life and the element of light is clear. A third ambiguity lies in the third and fourth couplets: "From the salt harbors so rich / So bright her city // In a soil of pavement." These lines raise the question of whether the phrase "so rich" and "so bright" belong to the "salt harbor" or the city. Again, a dichotomy is set up, looking both backwards to the primary materials of life such as water and salt, and also forwards to the complexities of urban living.

A final, interesting phrase in the last line of "Pedestrian" is "new winter." This is a strange coupling, for we usually regard winter as the "oldest" of the seasons, and spring as the "new" season of the year. So once again, as can be discovered through the ambiguities discussed here, indeed permeating this whole poem, is a sense of the old entwined with the new, the ancient with the modern, primary states with states of progress. This poem thus reflects a theme similar to that of "The Source."

Oppen's syntax here follows a characteristic pattern: there are only two verbs — "dreamed" and "walks" — in the whole poem, and only two adjectives — "rich" and "bright" (or variations on "bright"). The poem, therefore, is constructed primarily around nouns, and this gives it a spare, stripped-down quality, with the focus on the nouns: "generations," "child," "lights," "moonrise," "salt," "harbor" and "soil." The richness and brightness of the single two adjectives included in the poem are those defining the objects, which then take on the shining truth of their own existence. As a poet who belonged to the Objectivist school in the 1930s, Oppen believed strongly in this idea of objects embodying their own truth, independent of any outside agent who bestows truth or significance upon them.

One of the last poems in *The Materials* is "Leviathan" (strangely enough, also the name given by W.S. Merwin — a poet with concerns and poetic techniques similar to those of Oppen in several poems — to one of his own poems), whose title intimates something primary and powerful, arising out of the depths. This poem explores the contrast between temporal existence and what Oppen calls, in poem 29 from the collection *Of Being Numerous*, "open time": a dimension of ever-present fundamental existence. The poem opens with a disjointed phrase in the first two lines: "Truth also is the pursuit of it: / Like happiness, and it will not stand." Abby Shapiro comments on the unusual use of syntax and punctuation which produces this enigmatic quality: "Also syntax is fractured in odd ways, and punctuation functions very carefully, selectively joining and separating."[7] For example, the natural syntax to use in the first two lines would be "Truth, like happiness, is the pursuit of it; and it will not stand." By placing "happiness" in the second line, after the colon, Oppen forces the reader to back track to the first line to find the analogy, thus preventing (at least visually) the "ongoing pursuit" of the idea. The split-off phrase "and it will not stand" separates what truth is and what it is not: it does not "stand," it does not belong to that dimension of fundamental "being" of which the "objects" that appear later in the poem are a part. Truth, or meaning (in the postmodernist sense) is constantly shifting, cannot be pinned down, is trapped in a temporal, fluctuating existence.

In the next four stanzas, Oppen gives additional examples of temporal existence:

>Even the verse begins to eat away
>In the acid. Pursuit, pursuit;
>
>A wind moves a little,
>Moving in a circle, very cold.
>
>How shall we say? In ordinary discourse —
>
>We must talk now. I am no longer sure of the words,
>The clockwork of the world.

These lines describe manifestations of a time-locked existence: meaning is being gnawed away by conventional verse, while the fruitless circular motion of the cold wind and the "clockwork of the world" are reminiscent of a dog chasing its own tail. Interestingly, the "verse" of the third and fourth lines takes an active (rather than the anticipated passive) verb: the verse "begins to eat away" instead of "begins to be eaten away." This active use of the verb emphasizes action rather than being, contrasting the often frustrating activity that poetry engages in as it attempts to capture the being-ness of those elements that give it life, but which themselves do not "act"; these elements embody, for Oppen, a mystery of being which lies outside of time and temporal activity. Within the time-locked existence of temporal activity, Oppen is "no longer sure of the words," ordinary discourse being mechanical, clockwork, the coin of a civilization trammeled by the constant need to catch up, to grasp and to pin down. In the midst of all this, "...What is inexplicable / Is the 'preponderance of objects.' The sky lights / Daily with that preponderance." These lines highlight the other dimension of existence, an underlying self-subsistent state of "being" that imbues objects (and all small concrete nouns, for Oppen) with a mysterious presence of their own. Existing in "open time," this is the essential stuff of which poetry is made, always there, inexplicable, lighting up the temporal world. In contrast, "...we have become the present. // We must talk now. Fear / Is fear. But we abandon each other." The end of the poem returns us to mortality, to the fear and abandonment that death brings, reminding us of the importance of being in the present, and sharpening our awareness of that "other," underlying presence which can add depth to our temporal existence.

There is a disdain in this poem for the limitations of social discourse as opposed to the deep, unspoken being that objects embody for Oppen, who after all began his writing from within the Objectivist school. This disdain is underlined in the use of the blank after "ordinary discourse —" as if indicating that mere social conversation leaves an empty space after it. In contrast, there is no punctuation after the lines "...The sky lights / Daily with that preponderance," showing the open-endedness, the ongoing presence of what lights the sky and illumines the hurried and fearful world. We are reminded of the concept of the "still point" in T.S. Eliot's *Four Quartets*, which explores that essential, unfathomable sphere of existence that underlies our own temporal lives and illuminates them, although Oppen's essential state of being is invested in the concrete, rather than the abstract, transcendental state that Eliot describes. This idea will be developed in a later chapter on Oppen's recurring themes.

Ranging through the poems in *The Materials*, then, is an underlying current of primary experience, the essential existence of states beyond and below everyday life. In this body of poems it is often done (though not always, as we see in poems such as "Leviathan") through the medium of craft and tools, the humdrum city life, the common occupations of common people. By focusing on concrete objects and elements — the materials out of which human experience is fashioned — Oppen fosters a perception, and allows an exploration, of underlying, more primary states that might be difficult to fathom without the concrete details which provide a "springboard" of sorts. The perception of these underlying states, therefore, depends on the substantiality of objects — and the components of language — to trigger it, although these states in fact lie beyond the ability of language to capture them. As a result, Oppen must bring into play other elements of language, like the visual structure, dashes and the use (or deliberate non-use) of punctuation, elements not directly contained in the concrete words themselves, in order to release the energies inherent in essential and primary states whose nature often cannot be captured in words alone. For Oppen, the little concrete words do seem to embody a truth beyond the lexical significance, although the expression of this truth would, paradoxically, be almost impossible to explain in the language system to which these words belong.

Four
What Is There

The volume of poems which followed *The Materials* is titled *This in Which,* and is prefaced by two quotations. The first is taken from Robert Heinlein's *The Unpleasant Profession of Jonathan Hoag:*

> "Wait a minute," Randall said insistently. Are you trying to describe the creation of the world—the universe?"
>
> "What else?"
>
> "But—damn it, this is preposterous! I asked for an explanation of the things that have happened to *us.*"
>
> "I told you that you would not like the explanation."

The second quotation is a phrase from Martin Heidegger, and perhaps defines a process which Oppen grapples with in much of his poetry: "the arduous path of appearance." These two quotations sum up, in a sense, Oppen's approach to human experience of the world and the ways in which this experience is perceived and crafted into his poetry. Oppen seldom attempts to explain the "why" of our engagement with the events of history, both personal and political; rather, he is interested in the phenomena themselves and the truths they embody, the "what" of our experience and our existence. Norman Finkelstein contends that Oppen's poems carry political impact, even as he reminds us that Oppen condemns political poets who foreground political issues by writing about them: "Those of us who have seen in Oppen one of the most important poets of our time have often linked our admiration to his ability to embody difficult political issues in a poetry of startling clarity, a discourse that itself forbids answers while continually insisting that questions be asked."[1] Finkelstein is right to call Oppen's work "a poetry of startling clarity"—Oppen himself defined his poetry as "a test of truth"—but Oppen's intent (as seen in the two quotations which preface *This in Which*) has never been to engage actively with political issues in his poetry, since politics, by its nature, is concerned with the shaping of events and experiences in order to produce certain outcomes, to provide "answers" to certain "problems," and Oppen's truth does not lie in the provision of answers. He has always focused on the incidents themselves, the sharp clear images of human experience and the manifestation of truths embedded within them. He does not deal in explanations or philosophical debates; his belief is that one's understanding of the how and why is already inherent in the objects, the situations, the phenomena he chooses to portray. The reader must, therefore,—like Oppen himself—take an "arduous path" to discover the "appearance" of these truths, since they are embedded within the objects, the creatures and the scenes Oppen chooses to present to us in the poems; they constitute a primary core of meaning which can only be revealed by examining the nature of these concrete elements in the poem, their position and juxtaposition within the poem; and their significance is often enhanced by non-verbal means: dashes, spaces and rupture, tone and rhythm, syntactic breaks.

Within the relatively small body of criticism relating to Oppen's poetry, one of the most frequently mentioned poems is "Psalm," a phrase from which provides the title of the collection in which it appears: *This in Which*. As its title implies, this is a poem of praise: praise for a moment of wonder and awe, and the means to express it. The Latin inscription under the title ("veritas sequitur") tells us "the truth follows," and this poem is, indeed, an attempt to reveal the truth of those rare occasions where one seems to have been immersed for a moment in a dimension of experience not normally encountered. In this poem Oppen chooses to write about deer:

> In the small beauty of the forest
> The wild deer bedding down —
> That they are there!

George Oppen

The poem proceeds to focus on small, specific details of description:

>   Their eyes
> Effortless, the soft lips
> Nuzzle and the small alien teeth
> Tear at the grass
>   The roots of it
> Dangle from their mouths
> Scattering earth in the strange woods
> They who are there
>   Their paths
> Nibbled through the fields, the leaves that shake them
> Hang in the distances
> Of sun.

Perhaps Oppen chooses deer for their quiet immobility, their acceptance of the environment in which they live, their embodiment of some deep, true essence of animalhood. Everything about them is minute and clear and precise; their "alien small teeth" cut a clean, nibbled path through the grass. The use of "alien" and "strange" sets this scene of deerhood apart from the everyday and the mundane; the deer are quietly but clearly delineated against the leaves hanging in the "distances of sun." Oppen has captured an essential "moment of being," a primary experience in a wood. However, it is the last verse of the poem which highlights what Oppen is really doing in this poem:

>   The small nouns
>
> Crying faith
> In this in which the wild deer
> Startle, and stare out.

There is a shift here from the perception of an experience to its capture in language, and the poet pinpoints the paradox of language (which cannot pin down in words the complete essence of what we experience, and yet does so through the choice and arrangement of those words), as he refers to the "small nouns" which are employed to convey that experience. Norman Finkelstein says that "language, as unreliable as it may be, can correspond to our perception of reality."[2] This view of language as

Four: What Is There

approximately corresponding to our perception of reality certainly works in this poem, but the language here does more. The "small nouns," for Oppen, embody a fundamental state of being without actually saying what it is; they reverberate with more than what they convey to our cognitive knowledge of them. Thus the last part of the poem encompasses both the essence of the deer, and also the language employed to convey that essence, so that both the deer and the small nouns which frame them in poetic language are "just there." The small nouns also express a faith in the physical world the deer inhabit, by verbally replicating that world.

Oppen's syntax sub-verbally reinforces the poet's sense of awe at the being-ness of the deer. Twice he uses relative clauses to describe them: "That they are there" and "They who are there." The reader expects a main clause to follow, but none does; the normally dependent clauses stand on their own, as self-sufficient and singular as the deer they describe, arousing in the poet (and in the reader) a sense of awe and wonder. In addition, Oppen carefully spaces the lines of the poem so that, from the second stanza on, the first line stands on its own, set apart at the end of the line. This technique gives visual emphasis to the small primary words in which Oppen has so much faith — "their eyes," "the roots of it," "their paths" and "the small nouns," encapsulating in a few concise, concrete phrases the main idea of the poem.

The sense of wonder aroused by the deer in "Psalm" is captured again in "The Forms of Love," a poem which describes Oppen's first encounter of love with his future wife Mary. The poem begins by telling how the two parked in a field beside a lake as the moon was rising. The speaker then remembers getting out of the old car:

> Together, I remember
> Standing in the white grass
> Beside it. We groped
> Our way together
> Downhill in the bright
> Incredible light
>
> Beginning to wonder
> Whether it could be lake
> Or fog

George Oppen

> We saw, our heads
> Ringing under the stars we walked
> To where it would have wet our feet
> Had it been water

These events comprise a personal version of what Mircea Eliade would term a "primordial revelation," where sacred myths or events are re-enacted through ritual repetition in order that man may regenerate himself by reliving the event. Examples of such events might be the Christian ceremony of Communion, where the wafer and the wine represent the body of Christ, and participants thus relive the Crucifixion and the Resurrection of Christ; a more ancient and primitive example can be seen in the Celtic ceremony of Beltane, still practiced in parts of Scotland and Ireland on May Day. (Beltane is a fire festival which also acts as a fertility ritual.) For Oppen, this is a very personal version of a "primordial revelation"; he is concerned here with re-examining a supremely significant event in his life, not in order to dissect it but to realize its primal, revelatory impact on his subsequent life experience. As the poem unfolds, the speaker goes back to a scene of primary importance deep in his primal consciousness; this is borne out by the use of primary images in the poem such as the lake (water), the moon, the bright light and the stars, and also by the description of his car as "that ancient car." We can chart this return to a primal state through words such as "groped," a word emphasizing a sensory rather than a cognitive action, leaving conscious thought behind and entering a world of sensations, and "downhill," which leaves the parked car behind and takes the speaker down to a deeper level of consciousness less structured, less organized, more amorphous than the conscious social level, a realm of fog and wavering water. The fog, usually a symbol of lack of clarity (as in T.S. Eliot's "Prufrock," for example), here becomes the medium for a blurring of boundaries, inducing an undefined state where mystery and awe take over. The wondering pair find their heads "ringing under the stars," as all logical, conscious thought-processes are swept away by the dizzying sensation of being exposed to the elements. Heads normally represent reason, deliberation and the intellect — the cognitive aspects of the self — but here they reel under the light, losing touch with their cognitive selves. The "ringing" suggests the "ring of truth" —

this is a moment of truth for Oppen, a speechless moment of epiphany to deep for language, captured only by the indefinable ringing in his head.

From the phrase "we groped" onward, there are no periods at all, not even at the end of the last line, and only one comma, after the word "saw." This reinforces for the reader a sense of gathering impetus, an inexorable movement towards the illumination of the "incredible light." In this primal moment of revelation, Oppen begins "to wonder / Whether it could be lake or fog / We saw." Now he leaves behind the world of form and structure, where a car is a car and a field is a field, and enters a primordial, protean realm where defining characteristics no longer apply (the grass, for example, no longer green but becoming "white grass"), while elements blend into each other, becoming fluid and organic, where lake becomes fog and fog becomes lake and both are interchangeable, immersing the "we" of the poem in a primal world of awe and wonder.

The title of this poem, "The Forms of Love," may be understood in different ways. On a more superficial level, it may refer simply to the different shapes that love takes on; but at a deeper level it may also refer to the different kinds of love expressed through the images of the poem: the love on a hillside between man and woman — physical and tangible — and also the primary, revelatory love they experience as they immerse themselves in the great organic universe and are embraced by it.

The longest poem in *This in Which* is the eight-section poem "A Language of New York," which was later developed into the group of city poems which comprises Oppen's Pulitzer Prize–winning collection *Of Being Numerous*. "A Language of New York" deals with urban landscapes and our human relationship with the different elements of city life, and sets out New York's "language" as one not of words but of images and objects and the truths they represent. Edward Hirsch talks about Oppen's innate distrust of language and his attempts at a more direct engagement with the things of the world, in order that we may better understand ourselves through them and their "being":

> The human can only know itself through relationship to the non-human and through the faithful attempt to make language escape its self-contained nature.... There can be no reduction of that world, but there can be a naming, a bringing forth of being out of appearance.[3]

Oppen does deal with the relationship of the human to the non-human, but his "non-human" is not only the man-made world of city structures, but often the most primary elements in our environment — the minerals, the rocks and stones and sand, the ocean and the stars. These exist at an even more fundamental level than the manifestations of human habitation such as walls and streets and buildings, and although these primary elements do not appear in "A Language of New York," Oppen does use words like "mineral" and "matter" in the context of the raw materials out of which all animals and inanimate bodies derive. In doing so, he focuses on those elements which connect the human to the non-human, the most fundamental materials common to all things and all people.

Section one of the poem opens in a kind of urban dream-world, full of dream-images:

> A city of the corporations
> Glassed
> In dreams
> And images —
> And the pure joy
> Of the mineral fact
> Tho it is impenetrable
> As the world, if it is matter
> Is impenetrable.

The fact that the city is "glassed in dreams" evokes a sense of fragility, as the dreams are protected by glass, but are also exposed, transparent. Glass also reflects, showing, perhaps, that these dreams and images reflect us back to ourselves and therefore constitute something of their human makers. But what gives us "joy," unadulterated and "pure" (does this mean the dreams and images are then impure because they are not impenetrable but transparent?) is the "mineral fact." This is an interesting phrase, for a "fact" is objectively real and brooks no argument or speculation; it is basic, fundamental, indisputable, essential and impenetrable. "The mineral fact" thus both embodies and also reinforces the underlying essentiality of the elements upon which we build and live our lives.

Four: What Is There

The opening phrase of the poem — "A city of the corporations" — is also interesting. The word "corporations," in its urban context, refers to businesses or companies; but "corporation" also means "body," evoking corporeality, physical matter. Already the city landscape is being defined in terms applicable equally to humans and also to the most basic organic unit. The fact that Oppen later uses the word "matter" — albeit as a verb, but Oppen is known for his ambiguous bending of syntax, and "matter" is also a noun — reinforces the notion that this poem may also be dealing with those fundamental elements (a kind of elementary blueprint) that connect the living and the non-living. If this is so, then the dash after "images" can function as a dividing line, below which the lowest common denominator of our existence — the mineral, the matter — is to be found.

Oppen's innate doubts about the adequacy of language to convey real experience can be seen throughout "A Language of New York," even in section one. The syntax is quite blatantly fractured here in the last four lines, a puzzling juxtaposition of phrases which do make sense eventually, but not grammatically. The jumbled language may be seen as a reflection of the jumble of the urban landscape (even though this was almost certainly not a conscious intention on Oppen's part), but the fracturing of ordinarily coherent phrases also creates cracks in the logical meaning through which the underlying truths, connected to one's intuition rather than to the orderly expression of language, can surface. This is not the notion of "jouissance," which is sudden and revelatory, but a gradual "unpuzzling" of the juxtaposed fragments, a rearrangement of ideas which creates not a logical pattern of meaning but a deep sense of underlying significance, an intuition of being and presence

Oppen continues to treat the paradox of language (how it can and cannot convey experience) in section four of "A Language of New York." This poem examines the different frameworks within which words function, comparing everyday social discourse with a more creative and poetic use of language. The opening lines of the poem take a cautious approach to language, relating to words as untrustworthy units which may defeat one's purpose and intention:

George Oppen

> Possible
> To use
> Words provided one treat them
> Like enemies.

Looking at words in this way implies that they may block our way, frustrate intentions and work against us; in the following lines an additional way of looking at words is introduced:

> Not enemies — Ghosts
> Which have run mad
> In the subways
> And of course the institutions
> And the banks.

Here we have words as "ghosts" — insubstantial, not the small, concrete words that provide the foundations for meaning, but rather wraiths that dissipate when we try to grasp them, or perhaps taking on lives of their own, multiple identities which fracture any unity of meaning. These words are of the kind used in slogans, in commerce, in slick everyday discourse. Oppen's own language becomes looser too: phrasal verbs like "run mad" instead of a more concise one-word verb, and the intrusion of the phrase "of course" add little in the way of precise, exact meaning.

The latter half of the poem sets out an approach to language which Oppen himself adopts, using small, individual words — the basic building-blocks of communication — to construct meaning:

> ... If one captures them
> One by one proceeding
>
> Carefully they will restore
> I hope to meaning
> And to sense.

Capturing words implies locking them into some sort of framework — the poem, for example — or placing them within a structure, so that they become like the stones of a house, laying the foundation on which to build. The words must be taken "one by one," as small concrete units, each placed carefully in the poem in order to achieve meaning. It is interesting to note Oppen's own careful phrasing of the words:

"proceeding," for example, may refer to "one" (the person using the words) or to "them" (the words themselves), so that we have a double, interlocking possibility of interpretation; the poet proceeds with the structuring of the poem, but the words also advance the meaning through their accumulation and interlocking possibilities. Similarly, the word "carefully" can relate both backwards to "proceeding," but also forwards to "they will restore," so that we can see how the individual words come together to provide different webs of meaning. Oppen's syntax, too, is carefully structured; beginning the poem with "Possible / To use / Words" rather than "It is possible / To use / Words" reflects an economy of words, taking only the essentials of language to work with. And his use of the active verb "they will *restore* ... to meaning" rather than the more passive "They will *be restored* ... to meaning" (my emphasis) gives more power to the words; they activate meaning and sense, rather than being activated by meaning. Oppen could also have used the word "restore" as a causative verb, and told us what they restore to meaning and sense, but he uses "restore" as a reflexive verb, making the word more self-contained. Thus Oppen restores power and substantiality to the basic units of language, those small units which he believes embody an autonomy of being. The word "restore" may also be perceived as "re-store" or "store again," thus implying that meaning has lost its accumulation of possibilities and the poet wishes to give back to meaning its richness and variety through the power of the small, individual words.

Oppen's preoccupation with the capacities and incapacities of language appears in several of his poems. One or two of these poems explore, either in an overt or a circuitous way, the verbal and sub-verbal facets of language, the obvious and the obscure in words. "Penobscot" is one of those poems which touches, at least towards the end, on the sub-verbal aspect of the articulated word. "Penobscot" deals with the way in which children engage with their surroundings; as individuals who have not yet acquired the abstract reasoning faculties of the adult mind, they are more directly attuned to the primary rhythms of life and therefore have access to elemental dimensions of existence less easily accessible to their adult counterparts. The first part of the poem presents children of the "early countryside" who sit on the back steps of their house and talk together.

The steps lead to the "locked room / Of their birth / / Which they cannot remember," these phrases indicating a slipping-back through time and consciousness to a pre-natal, pre-conscious state which is primal and unmediated. The words "early" and "back" and the birth they have forgotten emphasize this return to a sub-verbal and pre-verbal dimension of experience.

The poem continues:

> In these small stony world
> In the ocean
>
> Like a core
> Of an antiquity
>
> Non-classic, anti-classic, not the ocean
> But the flat
>
> Water of the harbor
> Touching the stone
>
> They stood on —

This "core of antiquity" is the heart of an elemental dimension defined by stone and ocean, and it is both "non-classic" and "anti-classic," so that it cannot be identified by any temporal division into eras; it is beyond time. Yet children can make of this atemporal and intangible state a tangible reality, defined by the "flat water" and the "harbor touching the stone" on which they stand.

The next lines of the poem introduce the world of adults who will not violate, but also cannot penetrate this atemporal world accessible to the children:

> I think we will not breach the world
> These small worlds least
> Of all with secret names
>
> Or unexpected phrases
>
> Penobscot.

The "we" of adulthood cannot violate the "small worlds" and the ability of children to tap into an "illud tempus" of sorts through their primary contact with the fundamental elements of their environment. These

Four: What Is There

"small worlds" are reduced to an even more essential and fundamental level by being "least of all," and their "secret nouns" and "unexpected phrases" add to the sense of veiled significance and mystery which they embody. The "unexpected phrases" intrigue the speaker, as indeed they do Oppen, who may himself be defined as a poet of the unexpected phrase. Oppen has, more than once, mentioned "the greatest mysteries of all" represented by the small words — how less can mean more, how the "small worlds" and the strange names like Penobscot may hold the most significance and inspire the most awe. There is a probing in these lines of the meaning of language, how some words (like names, for example) have no linguistic function or significance but carry an aura of meaning nevertheless, which is the sub-verbal capacity of articulated sounds. In the light of this notion, the whole poem now becomes an exploration of an elemental sphere beyond the immediate, beyond the tangible, beyond the spoken, but still accessible to the primary self unmediated by language, to the sensitive and the curious.

This poem contains two dashes. The first one is followed by "I think..." and heralds a section of the poem set apart from what comes before and after the second dash, which occurs after "unexpected phrases." This section between the dashes returns the reader to the reasoning processes of the speaker's conscious mind, as he deliberates over the significance of the involuntary, unmediated "small worlds" of stone and sea and secret names. It is as if the adult, reasoning mind is barred by the dashes from entry into a world accessible only to the innocent, open minds of children. Yet there is a paradox here. It is Oppen the adult who has managed to unlock this world through the use of poetic images and a language which releases something beyond its own capacity to define.

In "The Founder," Oppen creates a figure who may be contrasted with the child in "Penobscot." This is a man suffering from the malaise of contemporary society, a man who prefers to lie in bed because he cannot deal with the day before him. The poem juxtaposes this man with the natural, simple village he has founded:

> Because he could not face
> A whole day
> From dawn

George Oppen

> He lay late
> As the privileged
> Lie in bed
>
> Yet here as he planned
> Is his village
> Enduring
>
> The astronomic light
> That wakes a people
> In the painful dawn.

The "he" of the poem — presumably the founder of the village — cannot face the light of day and what it holds for him, and stays in bed, while the village he planned carries on its existence both day and night under the fading light of the stars and the coming light of dawn. "Dawn" is a key word in this poem; it appears in the first stanza as the light the founder cannot face, and in the final stanza as "painful" to the people. Who are "a people" in the last stanza? Are they the socially sophisticated, the "privileged," living a supposedly civilized life? Or are they the simple village people? The poem does not provide a clear answer, but the village endures nevertheless. The poem plays between the constructions of man — the houses of the village — and the people who built them and who perhaps live in them. What endures is the embodiment of man's dreams and plans, the houses (presumably made of stone, if they are "enduring") in the rural setting.

The dawn is painful because it throws into relief the reality of those living in an environment they have created but cannot face. The start of the day, the beginning light, casts their so-called socially advanced lives back at them. The man lies late, as the "privileged" do; but he is privileged only in choosing to say indoors in bed, away from the light. He is not really privileged at all. The stars and sun, primary sources of light and a fundamental necessity of our existence, make the civilized man look paltry and weak, even in his achievements.

"The Founder" is one of Oppen's more conventional poems from the point of view of structure and use of language. There are no fractured lines, no disjointed syntax, no dashes or spaces; but there is an interesting division of the lines. There is one single line which contains a single word: "Enduring." Visually and conceptually, this single-word line stands out as the hinge on which the poem turns. In contrast, those lines with most words — "Because he could not face" and "Yet here as he planned" — both have to do with man's social activity, what he does and does not do with his day; perhaps Oppen (consciously or subconsciously) feels that the more we say, the more words we use, the less power we have and the more fragile we are. On the other hand, the lean, one-word line reflects the spare, lean but hardy endurance of the village.

The use of the word "astronomic" to describe the dawn light is unusual. We would expect to find "astronomical" instead, but since this would rupture the rhythm of the line, the word has been shortened. But if we understand it as "astronomical" it takes on interesting meanings. In its original sense it refers to the light of the heavenly bodies — the stars, the moon, the sun — but it is also used in a contemporary sense to mean "enormous" or "very great," beyond our control or grasp. This latter meaning of the word grants the light an intensity beyond man's power, no matter what schemes he has planned and executed. The overall significance of this poem then, its Deep Image if we like, is of a light that throws into relief the fundamental difference between the impotence of man in latter-day society, indolent and weak-minded, and the enduring materials of the environment he has helped to create but cannot face.

One of the most primitive of the poems in *This in Which* is "The Occurrences." This is a poem that is concerned with the most primary and fundamental elements of our lives — the most basic components of language, the essentials of nature, our ancestral origins (both cultural and personal), the simple human body — and the way in which they come together to create a total immersion in the "now." This "now" of the poem is depicted as a vital presence at the heart of our human experience; it is the "now" of being, or as Heidegger would describe it, "Being-in-Presence." The three stanzas of the poem follow a pattern of concrete images from nature set out in the first stanza:

> The simplest
> Words say the grass blade
> Hides the blaze
> Of a sun

George Oppen

> To throw a shadow
> In which the bugs crawl
> At the roots of the grass

This develops into a moving image of personal and collective ancestry which arouses an emotional response in the speaker:

> Father, father
> Of fatherhood
> Who haunts me, shivering
> Man most naked
> Of us all, O father

The sequence closes in a revelatory experience triggered by the images of the previous two stanzas:

>   watch
> At the roots
> Of the grass the creating
> *Now*   that tremendous
> plunge

The "tremendous plunge" entails great risk; it demands a willingness to divest oneself of the complexities of language (accepting the "simplest words"), the trappings of one's social and civilized lives, clothes, (becoming the "most naked"), one's past (the one who "haunts me") and one's plans for the future, in order to experience the fundamental roots of being, to submerge oneself in the essential present moment; in the second stanza, the speaker's personal father shifts to become the original father, a "father / Of fatherhood" (Adam in the Garden of Eden?) suggesting a collective, primal ancestry and perhaps original sin, the implication being that these must be shaken off in order to produce a different Creation: the "Now." It is not made clear in the text who is the man "most naked of us all"—is it the "father of fatherhood" or the "me"?—and we are not sure who is "shivering," but it does not really matter. All these must be put aside in order to take that "tremendous plunge."

    The text of this poem moves from the reasonably conventional syntax and punctuation of the first stanza into a final stanza devoid of punctuation and composed of a strange juxtaposition of phrases. The phrases are suspended on the page—"watch," "*Now*," "that tremendous plunge"— as time must be suspended in order to experience that "*Now.*" The single-word lines at the beginning and end of the stanza are the only ones in the whole poem without capital letters, indicating, perhaps, the lack of division and closure, and thus reinforcing the sense that this stanza deals with a concept which cannot be fully captured within the confines of time or language, although it is defined by both. In a way, it is a concept comparable to T.S. Eliot's "still point," described in the first of the *Four Quartets,* "Burnt Norton"; this "still point" pivots on the meeting of past, present and future, yet exists beyond temporal reality. Perhaps Oppen, in contrast to Eliot, would emphasize that his "*Now*" takes the simple stuff of everyday experience and infuses it with infinite significance, whereas Eliot's "still point" is lifted out of temporal existence into a realm both spiritual and mystical. For Oppen, the "*Now*" of this poem is a single revelatory moment held in a single concrete image, in this case the shadow on the roots of the grass.

The visual setting-out of the poem on the page leaves a gap in which the italicized "*Now*" appears, and this visual structure parallels Roland Barthes' concept of "jouissance," that moment where the text gapes open and a sudden rush of realization bursts through. Oppen's way of laying out the words in the last stanza allows us both to "see" and to experience that realization. In fact, the whole poem is an attempt on Oppen's part to capture in language — whether in the "simplest words" or in non-verbal ways — an experience which is ultimately beyond language and beyond man's ability to conceptualize. Norman Finkelstein also makes this point, as he draws the reader's attention to the word "hides" in the poem:

> Oppen's use of the verb "hides" in the third line seems to indicate that simple words obscure the complex natural relationship that they supposedly represent.... To experience immediate events directly is to preclude the possibility of language, which by its very nature is a mediating power.[4]

The poem does appear to deal with a direct experience which can be sensed, but not thought out or articulated. In a way, too, this experience recompenses human beings who are willing to take the risk, to strip themselves down to the bone, as it were, and face their fears, the things that haunt them, everything that leaves them shivering and exposed.

In addition to the concrete images presented in "The Occurrences" (the sun's shadow and the bugs crawling about at the roots of the grass), there is an overall Deep Image here which permeates the whole poem. It is the image of a diver who, eyes closed and near-naked, plunges into the water, immersing himself in a sea of sensations as a whole new dimension of experience, existing under the surface of the everyday world, reveals itself to him.

An additional poem which deals with the inadequacies of language to capture one's true and essential experience of the world — as do almost all of Oppen's poems, but not always overtly — is "The Building of the Skyscraper." Hugh Seidman believes that "Oppen is distinguished from his other contemporaries in his commitment to an intensely personal moral vision and yet, paradoxically, by his detachment from the sentimentality of morality through 'objective clarity.'"[5] Perhaps Oppen is not so much concerned with moral vision as with acts of belief, but it is certainly true that he works hard to produce a poetry of hard clarity, indeed devoid of sentimentality, which attempts — through the medium of the words themselves — to deal directly with aspects of experience which will illuminate our understanding of the self and the things of the world.

"The Building of the Skyscraper" is a poem about an underlying essential presence, a substantiality of being, which is vast and overwhelming to human consciousness. It is also a poem about what poets and poems do. Oppen uses an urban industrial image to introduce his theme, and links it to language:

> The steel worker on the girder
> Learned not to look down, and does his work
> And there are words we have learned
> Not to look at,
> Not to look for substance
> Below them. But we are on the verge
> Of vertigo.

The steel worker has learned "not to look down" because then he will not be able to do his construction work effectively, and in the same way we have learned not to look below words to find substantiality. There are two ways to interpret "look at" in the fourth line; one way is in the sense of "observe" (as with the steel worker), and the other is in the sense of "notice" (as with words). We do not "look at" the words we use; we toss them off carelessly, inanely, without looking below them to the essential substance which the words may obscure. But sometimes we teeter on the edge of words, sensing subconsciously the great depths beneath. The words themselves are flimsy and superficial, but underneath is an essential "being-ness" which, once sensed, might overwhelm us with a force that cannot be contained in, or by, language.

The next part of the poem relates to the task of the poet:

> There are words that mean nothing
> But there is something to mean.
> Not a declaration which is truth
> But a thing
> Which is. It is the business of the poet
> "To suffer the things of the world
> And to speak them and himself out."

As Oppen sees it, the poet's job is not to talk about the "things of the world," but to release them in the poem, to "speak them ... out." This is a difficult task; it is a truly "arduous path of appearance," and the poet carries that burden when undertaking it. Although Oppen was Jewish, there is a Christian feel to these lines; they embody something of the burden Christ carried and the truths which He felt committed to tell. The word "suffer" in "to suffer the things of the world" is used both in the sense of "tolerate" and also in the sense of "bear"; it is not easy. In fact, the whole phrase rings faintly of the Christian crucifixion — the taking on of a burden by the poet that is too hard for the ordinary man to carry. Like radiation, this task entails a painful exposure which can damage the self if not mediated through image and poetic device.

In the last stanza, the poet provides the kind of image which can carry this tremendous underlying sense of the presence of things:

> O, the tree, growing from the sidewalk —
> It has a little life, sprouting

> Little green buds
> Into the culture of the streets.
> We look back
> Three hundred years and see bare land
> And suffer vertigo.

We suffer vertigo when we see "bare land," when we expose ourselves directly to what is beyond the image. We can only grasp the significance of "being"—in the things of the world and in ourselves—by perceiving it through an image such as the clear, plain image of the tree and its "little life" at the side of the road. The tree in fact grows *out of* the sidewalk—it has pushed through the cement laid down by men, made its "arduous appearance" with its small green buds. In essence, it has overcome the trappings of civilization—the bricks and cement of the road, the "culture of the streets"—with its simple presence. And now we all "suffer" at the end of the poem, the poet by taking on himself the things of the world and exposing them through the image, and the rest of us as we read the poem.

If we look at the phrase "But a thing / Which is" we find it appears exactly in the middle of the poem, and is therefore a statement upon which the whole poem turns. By ending the sentence with the word "is," rather than adding an object, Oppen makes it more emphatic, empowers this static verb of existence with added significance. In addition, he prefaces the image of the tree with an "O," a poetic device adopted in several other poems. This "O" captures an empty space and endows it with meaning as well as introducing an exclamation of wonder and awe at the little tree growing out of the sidewalk. The dash at the end of the line acts as a non-verbal signal that this image is important to the poem as a whole.

One of the last and best-known poems in *This in Which* is the ambitious sequence "A Narrative," which in many ways sums up the themes dealt with in this collection of poems. The final section, number eleven, appears in full on the cover of *George Oppen: Man and Poet,* probably because it embodies the fundamental issues with which Oppen is engaged: "being" or "presence," our consciousness of that "being" and the ways in which it can be articulated. This last section of "A Narrative," as opposed to many of the

Four: What Is There

previous poems in *This in Which* that focus on the particular detail, takes a much more universal view of the world around us and our experience of it; there are no streets or subways here, no steel scaffolding or glass towers, no minute blades of grass. Here we have the "all-encompassing river of our substance" and the open space of the sea. The phrase "river of our substance" works on different levels, both physically and conceptually. From a physical point of view, it is both fluid and solid, both "river" and "substance"; from a conceptual point of view it links both the natural world of matter and our notion of the self's existence on this planet: the river is "*our* substance" (my emphasis). Our view of human existence within time and space therefore becomes fluid and flowing; we are carried along by our experience of the world, which includes the concrete (the "silt"), the process ("erosion") and the larger pattern of life ("the earth's curve"). Oppen asks us to find happiness in that moment of consciousness that arises from "knowing" the great flow of deep, elemental energies in the universe, a state in which we, our world and a sense of time are all encapsulated:

>River of our substance
>Flowing
>With the rest. River of the substance
>Of the earth's curve, river of the substance
>Of the sunrise, river of silt, of erosion, flowing
>To no imaginable sea. But the mind rises
>
>Into happiness, rising
>
>Into what is there.

This is a river both concrete and abstract, a river of "substance" following the earth's curve, carrying silt, but also flowing into an unimaginable sea, one we cannot conceive of. Where this river leads, like our own future, is unforeseeable, and Oppen may be stressing here that future and past, although contained in our experience of the world, become inconsequential at that moment of consciousness — the most we can achieve — which is born of "knowing" the existence of those fundamental energies embodied in river and sea and wave, whose "being" is not contingent on any other element, whose enduring qualities are part of the nature of their existence, intrinsic to what they are. But let the poem tell it:

George Oppen

> The marvel of the wave
> Even here is its noise seething
> In the world; I thought that even if there were nothing
>
> The possibility of being would exist;
> I thought I had encountered
>
> Permanence; thought leaped on us in that sea
> For in that sea we breathe the open
> Miracle
>
> Of place, and speak
> If we would rescue
> Love to the ice-lit
>
> Upper World a substantial language
> Of clarity, and of respect.

That moment of consciousness is our knowledge of the "being" embodied in river and sea, where "thought leaped on us," where love and happiness reside, a fundamental mainstay against the vulgar discourses of our everyday shuffling existence; here is our sense of the underlying and elemental forces of being which can be raised up into the cold, unfeeling and unthinking, historically and politically oriented lives we lead on a day-to-day basis, conferring a "substantial language of clarity and respect." This language is not a verbal one, not a language of social discourse and half-truths and dogma, but a deep and unspoken language of understanding and acceptance. Interestingly, the moment of consciousness which triggers our understanding is a sudden and vital revelation, captured in the word "leaped." We are flooded with the realization of "the open / Miracle // Of place" which leads us to a new vision of the world in which we live. This paradoxical "open miracle of place" stresses not only the boundaries of the space we occupy, but also the limitless, "open" dimension of the miracle, one which stretches our imagination beyond the confines of physical existence.

It is ironic that Oppen speaks of the Upper World — and capitalizes it — as representing our social lives, as if "upper" somehow meant "superior" instead of the obviously superficial sense in which it is used. The Upper World is "ice-lit," imbued with a cold light, frozen (as opposed to the warm "glow" or "gleam" of the woman's limbs in "The

Source"). In contrast, when the mind "rises / Into happiness," we find true superiority, paradoxically superior because this is, in fact, a more elemental state: the mind is rising into "what is there."

The syntax of the last seven lines of this poem is rather difficult to follow, since there is no division of clauses or phrases (apart from the one comma after "place") and we find one phrase tumbling into another and then into the next. This gives the sense of an on-going "flow," and although syntactical clarity may have been forfeited, there is a clarity of rhythm and tone, like the wave's "noise seething / In the world." This is the "substantial language" of which Oppen speaks, and which reflects the ever-present, primary energies of "being."

"A Narrative" fittingly draws together Oppen's leading concerns as set out in *This in Which*. In this poem, he takes a magnifying glass to the flux of human lives in all their aspects — social, personal, urban, collective, political in a way — and pinpoints the scenes (city office buildings with their glass windows, the steel worker on the scaffolding), the moments (stumbling down a grassy slope under the stars, seeing the deer as if for the first time), the objects (a tree growing at the side of the road), all the concrete particulars that may bring to the surface the underlying truths and significances of our existence. It is often a hard task, demanding a hard, clear choice of words which must convey more than they mean, for those underlying truths cannot be apprehended through language alone. Oppen does believe that words embody meaning, but it is not always a meaning that can be articulated, and it is indeed an "arduous path" — for both poet and reader — to grasp the unarticulated truths that words may embody and that make our lives significant, teaching us something about our perception of ourselves and the world we live in. This belief in ulterior truths which are often veiled and obscure, but not altogether unavailable to us, makes for a poetry which is ultimately affirmative, and which reflects Oppen's own affirmation of life. As he tells us himself, he derived a great deal of pleasure from his life, and defined this positive feeling about his life experiences "by the word 'curious' or, as at the end of 'A Narrative,' 'joy,' joy in the fact that one confronts a thing so large, that one is part of it. The sense of awe, I suppose, is all I manage to talk about."[6] And in *This in Which*, Oppen does, most definitely, "manage to talk about" it, and in doing so, conveys to the reader the awe and the wonder of small things, little details, moments of sudden clarity; in short, the basic stuff of our lives and how it all fits into the greater pattern of existence.

Five
Cityscapes

Of Being Numerous, Oppen's best-known and most-discussed collection of poems, and the one for which he won the Pulitzer Prize in 1969, is a sequence poem in forty sections, each section an individual poem but together comprising a coherent body of work which presents and examines images of the city and its people. The poems portray New York city life and Oppen's exploration of its various manifestations such as doorsteps, bridges, glass and steel structures, buses and subways, brick walls. In many of these poems, Oppen picks out the fine details, the concrete images, the small cameos of daily urban life, examining them minutely, deliberating over their significance within the larger pattern of things, finding in a study of these objects and situations the possibility of discovering and knowing our own selves, using the collage of individual buildings within a cityscape as a metaphor for the individual and his place in the greater collective of humanity. At other times Oppen takes us behind the façade of the city, beyond the streets and the buildings to a more elemental mode of existence which underlies urban life. He does this through the use of primitive imagery emerging from the constructions of glass and steel, and also by cutting through the din and bustle of urban humanity to a deeper primal silence where a clarity of understanding is possible. Oppen thus portrays city structures of glass, brick and steel as the concrete "language" of urban life, beneath which lies a fundamental level of existence — beyond truth and falsity, beyond logic and reason, beyond individual experience — which encompasses us all.

David McAleavy argues that Oppen's approach to a "dark world" through imagination, intuition and emotion "lead[s] Oppen to affirm a fundamental but only partially knowable 'real' world, which is not the 'true' world. The terms 'true' and 'false' no longer apply to this 'real' world."[1] McAleavy claims this "dark world" prohibits clarity, adding: "The intellectual, however, *needs* clarity." Yet the knowledge of this only partially-perceived "real" world — what Lacan also calls the "Real"— surely provides a clarity of some sort, or at least an illumination to the self of the self's experience of, and in, the world.

However, since the "real" world is, as McAleavy says, "only partially knowable," Oppen must find correlatives within our own everyday experience which will open up to us an intuition of a deeper, more elemental mode of existence which can be glimpsed, if not completely grasped. Oppen does this by juxtaposing the different small details in his cityscapes, and re-evaluating them in the light of a larger pattern, often evoking awe and wonder in both himself and the reader.

Oppen employs language in the same way that builders use building materials, constructing the shape of his poetic ideas as an artifice composed of individual units — words, phrases, spaces and dashes. In referring to Oppen's way of working with language, Henry Weinfield says about this series of poems: "Although its method is disjunctive and associational, this is always in the service of clarity and cohesion which could not otherwise have been attained."[2] The juxtaposition of word and image within a poem is, as Weinfield says, often disjunctive, but still functions like the bricks and steel rods in a city building, each of which is a separate item, but heaped each on each produce together a coherent whole.

In fact, Oppen appears at times to work self-consciously towards an overriding metaphor of creativity (without using any single, specific metaphors), informing his poems — whatever the overt subject-matter may be — with a sense of their own unfolding, or at least implying the possibility that his images contain a poetic frame of reference. In *Of Being Numerous* this possibility is paralleled by several others, which function in conceptual pairs sequentially as concrete materials, individual people and single images, leading to structures, collective humanity and poetic integration.

Of Being Numerous evolved, at least in part, from the shorter sequence "A Language of New York"; this is borne out by the patterns of urban imagery in "A Language —" which recur in *Of Being Numerous*. The thematic link is further verified by the repetition of whole chunks of language, as we see in the second poem of the forty-poem sequence, almost all of which is lifted from the first section of "A Language of New York." This second poem has an addition of four lines at the beginning:

> So spoke of the existence of things,
> An unmanageable pantheon
>
> Absolute, but they say
> Arid.

Otherwise, the two poems are identical except for the spacing of the last two lines, and an additional comma at the end of the second to last line of the second poem in *Of Being Numerous:*

> Tho it is impenetrable
>
> As the world, if it is matter,
> Is impenetrable.

The added first four lines reflect on "the existence of things," defined as "unmanageable," "absolute" and "arid." These lines link up to the worldly "matter" of the last two lines, matter which is "impenetrable." This impenetrability of the basic existence of things in the world is what makes it "unmanageable" for most of us; we prefer transparency, dissectability, the knowledge of what makes things what they are. "Absolute" and "impenetrable" are too final; they demand a certain amount of faith to accept them as they are. This is why the existence of things is an "unmanageable pantheon," "arid." But Oppen does not necessarily concur with the idea; he tells us: "*They say* / Arid" (my italics). The fundamental being of all things, their absolute existence, is only "arid" to those who cannot see farther than the superficial structure, whose vision ends, as Joe Keller in Arthur Miller's *All My Sons* says, "at the building line."

The addition of the comma after "matter" in the penultimate line picks out the phrase "if it is matter" and asks us to consider the possibility that it may not be. If the world is *not* matter, however, what is it?

Perhaps this is a different world, the world of Jacques Lacan's "Real," which is impenetrable in the sense that we cannot fully grasp it, cannot fully comprehend it, although it exists both beyond and within the real world of our everyday lives.

In poem number three, the next in the sequence, Oppen describes an initial experience, and the attendant sensations, of coming into the city:

> The emotions are engaged
> Entering the city
> As entering any city.
>
> We are not coeval
> With a locality
> But we imagine others are,
>
> We encounter them. Actually
> A populace flows
> Thru the city.
> This is a language, therefore, of New York.

Here, coming into the city (it seems for the first time) engages both the emotion and the imagination, but not the intellect. The speaker — we may safely say Oppen, for Oppen does not deal in persona in his poetry — does not have thoughts or ideas about the experience, but does have feelings, and his imagination is aroused by the sight of others around him. One's imagination works pictorially, bringing pictures into the mind, and so the experience of entering the city takes place at a more visceral, sub-verbal level than that of the intellect, which demands language to express itself. The initial experience is slightly disconcerting, as the speaker is "not coeval / With a locality" — he does not yet feel at home, as he imagines the others do, until he encounters them. Then the individual experience merges with that of others, and "a populace flows / Thru the city." The phrase "a populace" is interesting, because it combines both singular and plural, both the individual "a" and the communal "populace." The last line gathers this flow of people into a "language" of the city, a discourse of humanity, as it were. It is a sub-verbal language, deriving from the emotion and the imagination and the flow of people (we are reminded of Kristeva's semiotic flow and flux), rather than from verbal utterances. It is physical and concrete, manifested in the inhabitants rather than in the abstractions of words and semantic phrases.

As the people flow through the city, so do the lines at the end of the poem flow into each other. The line "But we imagine others are" at the end of the second stanza flows into the "We encounter them" of the next stanza, and the "Actually" at the end of the lie flows into "A populace flows" in the following line. Oppen also cuts away at the words themselves, using "thru" instead of the more usual "through" (and in the previous poem cutting "though" down to "tho"). This may be an arbitrary device of Oppen's, but in shortening these words he is, in a way, diminishing them, "castrating" them, showing that language, unlike the "matter" of poem two, is not "impenetrable"; language becomes flimsy, the solidity of words weakened. There does seem to be an implicit suspicion here of the power of language to reflect our experiences of the world — better to rely on the more "real" emotional and, paradoxically, imagined perception of ourselves and our interaction with others.

Poem number seven contains the title phrase of this body of poems, and presents one of the major themes of the collection:

> Obsessed, bewildered
> By the shipwreck
> Of the singular
>
> We have chosen the meaning
> Of being numerous.

The idea of shipwreck is a recurring image in Oppen's poetry, sometimes coupled with a "bright light" ("the bright light of shipwreck"); here the "bright light" is missing, being replaced by the phrase "of the singular" to form the notion of individual foundering, losing one's bearings, encountering insurmountable obstacles, perhaps even hidden obstacles. The lighthouse, another recurring image in Oppen's work, is also missing, leaving the focus on the wreck itself. The opening adjective "obsessed" raises the question of whether we are obsessed by the idea of individual shipwreck or by the need to avoid it; whichever is intended, the coupling of "obsessed" with the phrase "the shipwreck of the singular" implies the difficulty of dealing with individual disintegration or calamity. The option set out in the last lines is to lose ourselves in the many, either to be together in our trouble or together in order to prevent the threat of shipwreck.

The last two lines may be perceived as either negative or positive: in the negative sense, we lose our individual identity, becoming swallowed up in the urban masses of humanity; in a more positive sense, we may find comfort in the tribal collective, in the idea that "united we stand, divided we fall." Oppen is not quite as blasé as this, however; referring back to poem number three, the meaning of "being numerous" may signify that we become part of the "flow" of the urban population, part of a larger system which generates a source of energy that can keep us afloat. Interestingly, Oppen does not say "We have chosen to be numerous" but "We have chosen *the meaning of* being numerous" (my italics). The significance of being numerous gathers us into a collective humanity much like the collective unconscious of Jung, where a set of images or situations, common to us all and subconsciously recognized by us all, provides an underlying network of experience which links us together.

Oppen uses the word "singular" rather than "individual" in this poem, in the sense of being single but also singled out, which implies, paradoxically, being noticed, but also being detached from others, isolated, and therefore weakened. As in several other poems of Oppen's, Eliot's Prufrock is a shadowy background figure here — Prufrock as an individual who singles himself out from those who indulge in the superficial chatter of social gatherings; unable to communicate with others, he flounders in a sea of self-doubt. Oppen may be taking a more positive view than Prufrock does of the "numerous" as representing a body of people whose identity is a communal one, who form a "language" of the city, a deep, unspoken expression of the collective self. This is reflected in the phrase "we have chosen," as each individual "shipwreck" is also an experience we all choose to share in.

Some critics have commented on the poems in *Of Being Numerous* as an attempt to voice the function of the poet within contemporary society, where political issues often take over language discourses. Eric Mottram, for example, says of poem number seven: "It is the poet's function now to know his singularity within 'man's way of thought' (*CP*, p. 152), the language, and his own particular experience. That triad is the only possible way to hold to the singular."³ Oppen, I think, would prefer his own singular, "particular experience" to be merged with the collective experience, since he directed so much of his energy throughout his life towards helping the masses, and identified with their social plight. Oppen's is, indeed, a singular voice, but the underlying and unspoken concerns which manifest themselves in the particulars of his poems are those he shares with all people. This is what makes him so different from poets like Eliot and Pound, his contemporaries and (at least in Pound's case) his fellow poets.

Poem number eleven, like poem three, also talks about one's encounter with urban landscapes and the interaction between perceiver and perceived. The poem opens in light, a light which picks out small concrete details and illuminates them with something of their own existence in time and space:

> it is *that* light
> Seeps anywhere, a light for the times
>
> In which the buildings
> Stand on low ground, their pediments
> Just above the harbor
>
> Absolutely immobile,
>
> Hollow, available, you could enter any building,
> You could look from any window
> One might wave to himself
> From the top of the Empire State Building —

The light in this poem "seeps"— it permeates the little city scenes, gathers them all in a moment of illumination which brings awe and wonder. This feeling of wonder is deep-seated, rising into our consciousness from deep in our being because we see, physically, the concrete elements of the city that surrounds us — the shapes of buildings against the sky, the stones of the pavement, the contiguity of street and harbor, the suddenly opened door; and in seeing them physically we perceive in them, at a deeper sub-verbal level, the manifestations of our own existence. The "light" of the first line may derive from a physical source such as sunlight, or a street lamp, but it is also "*that* light" which is "anywhere," so that it becomes a particular kind of light, residing in the buildings themselves, a self-illumination. And these buildings also reflect ourselves; we can wave to ourselves, get in touch with our selves through them, they are "available," they may be entered.

After the description of the buildings, the next part of the poem tells about the poet's attempt to make them meaningful:

> Speak
> If you can
> Speak

There is a difficulty here: the encounter with the urban landscape produces feelings of awe and wonder, but it is hard to speak of it. These lines present the functional inadequacies of language and the laborious task of the poet to articulate the impact of what our eyes see. Our sense of wonder derives from an unarticulated, even unconscious response to our surroundings and the small actions — standing in front of a building, getting off a bus — which may trigger that response.

The next part of the poem sets out an individual response to an encounter in and with the city: a girl coming home from work on the bus, whose heart is "suddenly filled with happiness." This sets up a similar response in the speaker:

> I too am in love down there with the streets
>   And the square slabs of pavement —
>   To talk of the house and the neighborhood and the docks
>   And it is not "art"

Here is a singular experience (the speaker's), which merges with the girl's experience to produce a joint sense of happiness. The speaker too is in love "down there," the "down there" implying a deep fundamental response, existing below and beyond the power of language to capture it. Oppen's aim in this poem is to unlock that fundamental, visceral response in the reader rather than create an artistic composition which will explore the significance of that response. Therefore the poem talks about the buildings and the harbors themselves, without making an "art" of it. Oppen wants direct engagement and direct emotion, not self-conscious poetic discussion about it. Therefore it is not the poem which creates a sense of awe, but the city itself as we experience it deep in ourselves — although that experience is aroused in us *through* the poem.

Oppen uses four dashes in this poem; like the spaces in other poems, these dashes have a non-verbal function, allowing the images of the poem to impact on the reader. Likewise, Oppen separates out the lines "Speak // If you can // Speak" from the rest of the poem and from each other, to produce a hesitancy, a careful deliberation over each word. The images of the poem *will* speak, but not through long strings of language and complex lines; each will speak through itself and its own occupation of space.

Unlike almost all of Oppen's other poems, this one begins in the middle of a line and without a capital letter, giving the reader a sense of being caught up in the middle of the phenomenon of physically and emotionally experiencing the city images. This device also allows for a sense of continuation from the previous poem, significant because *Of Being Numerous* is a series of texts about the place of the individual (person or poem) within the collective (humanity or body of poetry.)

In a seemingly odd deviation from his urban theme, Oppen describes the lifestyle of a primitive culture in poem twelve, which has no mention of urban images whatsoever. After a brief quotation, the poem continues:

> They made small objects
> Of wood and the bones of fish
> And of stone. The talked,
> Families talked,
> They gathered in council
> And spoke, carrying objects.
> They were credulous,
> Their things shone in the forest.
>
> They were patient
> With the world.

David McAleavy maintains that this kind of primitive society is "untenable" in Oppen's eyes, and is introduced only as an imaginary vision quite incompatible with the contemporary urban life he sets out in *Of Being Numerous*.[4] Oppen himself concludes this poem by reinforcing that idea:

> This will never return, never,
> Unless having reached their limits
> They will begin over, that is,
> Over and over.

This kind of primitive life is not feasible as a possible alternative to the contemporary urban lifestyles described in other poems in this collection, unless life has gone as far as it can go: "having reached their limits." It belongs in a different time frame altogether. Yet Oppen's primitive realities are not diachronic; they are synchronic. They offer a contemporaneous alternative *within* the heedless shuttling back and forth among urban diversions, a different, underlying reality, not bound by human consciousness or thought or language, a reality which can be sensed at certain moments in our lives, triggered by small details such as a momentary grouping of people, the outline of a tree in a street, the rush of air as a bus goes by. These singular moments kindle a deep-seated response which is sub-verbal, subconscious, visceral. They allow us to tap into a reality which is available, at certain moments, to us all, if we are sensitive to its possibilities, a shared experience which may bind us as individuals to a collective experience. Oppen's poetry attempts to disclose those revelatory moments by using ceratin concrete images which may jolt us into discovery, allowing us to share in an experience which somehow validates the fraught and often heedless realities of everyday city life.

The people of once-upon-a-time described in this poem are contrasted with the city people of contemporary times in different ways. Here, there are families who sit together to discuss their concerns, who take council from each other, who do much more together than simply "encounter" one another. They live in harmony; they are "patient / With the world." The rhythm of their lives is slower, more deliberate than the fast pace of the city, with its buses and subways and jostling streets. They make more of their lives, with less. There is none of the teeming uncertainty so peculiar to the lives of many urban dwellers. And yet, though this poem presents a primitive system very different from the city lifestyle described in other urban poems (basketball games, subway rides, shopping), there are several elements which appear in both. The primitive society makes objects of wood and stone and bone, reminding us of the horn-handled saw in "Antique" (*The Materials*), as well as the stone of buildings and pavements; the objects in this primitive society "shone in the forest" like the woman's limbs which "gleam" in "The Source." In this way, Oppen makes the connection between the different primary realities, one unattainable today because the cycle of time makes it impossible, physically, to go back, the other accessible within the framework of the "now" of urban living. He even tells us this in the line preceding his description of the primitive society: "and it is the same world." And so there is a tension set up in Oppen's simultaneous belittling and empowering of the common everyday elements of city life: they cause "shipwreck," they make us insensitive and superficial, yet they can offer, at sudden moments, a glimpse of a more fundamental sphere of reality which casts significance on the mundane events of our lives.

Poem number thirteen in the sequence carries on from number twelve, in the sense that it takes up the possibility of going back to the "beginning" where people lived a communal life based on the gathering of families to discuss the issues of their everyday existence. This poem is identical to poem number two in the short sequence "A Language of New York," where Oppen portrays the mindless superficiality of urban living and an urban population who do no more than skim the surface of experience, and also of language. Those who are "unable to begin / At the beginning" are ironically called "the fortunate," perhaps in the sense that they do not live deeply enough to feel real pain or pleasure, but only experience the ready-made:

> Unable to begin
> At the beginning, the fortunate
> Find everything already here. They are shoppers,
> Choosers, judges;... And here the brutal
> is without issue, a dead end.
>   They develop
> Argument in order to speak, they become
> unreal, unreal, life loses

> solidity, loses extent, baseball's their game
> because baseball is not a game
> but an argument and difference of opinion
> makes the horse races. They are ghosts that endanger
> One's soul.

This is a description of the inanity not only of mindless routine and cheap thrill, but also of a mode of discourse used solely for betting and disagreeing. It is not only life which loses "solidity" and "extent"; it is also language, and communication through language, both of which are bandied back and forth without furthering any kind of understanding, acceptance or authentic interchange of ideas.

Baseball and horse races are the only reasons for language to exist at all in this kind of life, where everything depends on taking sides, opposing others, widening gaps instead of closing them. "Communication" has become an alienating force, driving the horses perhaps, but also driving people away from each other until they become "ghosts that endanger // One's soul." The word "ghosts" echoes poem number four in the sequence "A Language of New York," where *words* are ghosts, insubstantial and flimsy. This will all "come to the end / Of an era," reflecting back to the "brutal ... without issue, a dead end," implying that there is not only a finality about the urban human condition, but also a lack of continuity, no real ongoing dialogue between people themselves or between people and history. There will be no lasting mark left.

Oppen turns away from all this to consider ways of extending oneself beyond the two-dimensional aspects of mindless shopping and betting, concluding the poem with the phrase "First of all peoples" and musing on the possibility of distancing oneself from it all. Perhaps he is thinking of his own Jewish heritage when he talks about "first of all peoples," and the possibility of going back in time to a distant past that was more primitive but more authentic, a time of desert tribes and a sense of community. Perhaps he implies a stepping out of the cycle of time altogether, not in a physical but in a spiritual sense, drawing on inner resources deep within us to create more authentic modes of communication which are not time-bound in the sense that a baseball game or a horse-race is time-bound.

Five: Cityscapes

This poem begins both with a small letter and also in the middle of the line, as if it carried on from poem twelve, pitying those who are "unable to begin / At the beginning" because they and their experiences of the world are too "small" to be given a capital letter. The three dots in line four, "Choosers, judges,... And here the brutal" suggest, in a visual way, that these kinds of people are no more than dots on the horizon of human experience. This "littleness," this lack of significance, is emphasized in the fact that from line six to the middle of line twelve there are no capital letters and no periods, giving this section of the poem (which describes the baseball game and the horse-races) a sense of inane chatter, without closure or beginning. And Oppen is constantly looking for beginnings, going back and down into our most primary experiences to find authenticity and meaning.

The next poem in the series, number fourteen, chronicles Oppen's memory of war companions, who have remained with him long after the war experiences are over. Since Oppen's poetic voice is so personal and direct in most of his poetry, it seems safe to assume that this is an autobiographical account of his own experiences and not the mediation of another speaker's voice through the words of Oppen. Although the landscape described in the poem focuses strongly on the destructive aspects of war hospitals, "blasted roads" and "ruined country," the memory grants power to the figures who feature in it, even when Oppen cannot remember all their names. These figures both become individualized within the collective humanity of the city, and constitute a united "force" and presence in the city landscape:

> How forget that? How talk
> Distantly of "The People"
>
> Who are that force
> Within the walls
> Of cities
>
> Wherein their cars
>
> Echo like history
> Down walled avenues
> In which one cannot speak.

These war companions of Oppen's now "echo like history," providing an extension of the present into the past. They are "that force," a deep unspoken bond of lived and shared experiences which goes beyond speech to a place "[i]n which one cannot speak." They take both speaker and reader back and down into the personal and collective origins of sub-verbal (and subconscious) recognition. Theirs is a primary bond of the spirit, unspoken and unspeakable because words cannot frame it, a mythic sense of community.

When Oppen asks "How forget that?" he links the personal with the collective, in the sense that the question relates to the lieutenant whose name he has forgotten (and Oppen seems to reproach himself for this), but also to the collective memory which is passed down through history and is often submerged in the trivial routines of everyday urban life. Perhaps Oppen is thinking here of his own Jewish oral tradition, which kept alive the significance of certain rituals; perhaps this is a reference to what Eliade calls the "illud tempus," that "other time" where sacred myths were created and enacted. Certainly there are elements of myth in the kind of war experiences Oppen remembers: the courage and heroic endurance of his war-fellows recalls the great mythic figures such as Hector and Achilles. This seems to be borne out in the repetition of the wall motif in this poem: "Within the walls / Of cities" and "walled avenues" are both reminiscent of the great mythic walled cities such as Troy, and perhaps also Jerusalem.

It is significant that what "[e]cho like history" in this poem are the cars, rather than the men themselves; cars are vehicles which transport us through space, but may also be seen in the context of the poem as vehicles which transport through time, linking present with past, "this time" with "that time," the present concrete city landscapes and the great mythic landscapes of human origins. The visual form of the last four lines of the poem bears this out, as the lines contract and then swell out again, reinforcing the idea of a mythic force which comes to a point in the city and then swells out again through time, regaining momentum.

If poem fourteen works diachronically — ranging from past to present — poem seventeen in the series works synchronically, moving from temporal surfaces to an underlying depth. This is borne out in the first two and last two lines:

Five: Cityscapes

> The roots of words
> Dim in the subways
> There is madness in the number
> Of the living
> "A state of matter"
> There is nobody here but us chickens
> Anti-ontology —
> He wants to say
> His life is real,
> No one can say why
> It is not easy to speak
> A ferocious mumbling, in public
> Of rootless speech.

The first two lines introduce the words "roots," "dim," "subways," whereas the last two lines mention "ferocious mumbling," "public" and "rootless speech." These lines imply that the roots of words — the sources of communication and signification — lie below the surface at a deeper level, irrational and anti-logical (but strangely substantial), in the dim depths where structure and shape melt away and things are felt in the *bone;* on the surface, in public, speech becomes rootless and rambling, inconsequential. Like many of the other poems in *Of Being Numerous,* this one also deals with the insubstantiality of superficial urban discourse, language used for argument and haggling; it is not *real.* The "public" becomes an indiscriminate conglomerate of urban humanity, existing as a hustling mass on the surface of an experience which lacks impact and significance for the individual. It is unreal. "Us chickens" is a phrase which may take us back to William Carlos Williams' "The Red Wheelbarrow," but is just as likely to be an ironic description of an urban population scratching at a mindless existence: a state which is "anti-ontology," which defies a sense of being. Like the heedless urban society of Eliot's "Prufrock," the people of this poem drift through their lives, engaging in the kind of empty discourse that leads nowhere. And like Eliot's Prufrock, the "he" of this poem also feels that somewhere, just beyond his grasp, is a reality which is implicitly significant but cannot be explained in logical terms. This person feels his life is real, but cannot put it in to language: "It is not easy to speak." The Real cannot be explained, cannot be delineated; one cannot say "why," because it cannot be put in rational or logical terms. This reality can be sensed at a visceral level, but not articulated. And even if it could be, it would become lost in the "ferocious mumbling ... [o]f rootless speech."

Unlike poem fourteen, the individual here bears a significance which threatens to become inundated by, and lost in, the collective. This collective is embodied in the phrase "madness in the number / Of the living," which may be interpreted in different ways. One way is to see it as the loss of one's sanity through a consideration of the innumerable masses of the city; another way to understand it is that urban multitudes create an aura of madness by their very number. Oppen, as a Jewish poet, may even be hinting here at the destructive madness of the collective, as exemplified for example in Nazi Germany.

Several of the phrases or word groupings here reflect the poem's theme of empty versus significant language. The phrase "a state of matter," for instance, becomes an example of "rootless speech," a phrase empty of significance, just words with no fathomable meaning for the ordinary individual. In the last three lines, there are different ways to group the phrases: if we take "It is not easy to speak" together with "A ferocious mumbling" we get Oppen's perspective as a poet who finds it difficult or loathsome to engage in superficial babble. However, "It is not easy to speak" may also be seen as an autonomous line — it is separated from both the previous and the following lines by a blank line — declaring that it is not easy to speak the sub-verbal language of the "real"; the "he" of the poem *wants* to say his life is real, but cannot. There is also a comma after "A ferocious mumbling," so that "in public" goes with "rootless speech" rather than reading "A ferocious mumbling in public"; this emphasizes the idea that rootless speech belongs in the public domain. The roots of speech are embedded in the real, the subsurface, the nonverbal.

The overall tone of this poem is staccato, suggesting the mindless jerking of a puppet existence for "us chickens." Of the only two commas appearing in the whole poem, the first one comes after "His life is real," giving the reader pause for a moment to consider the significance of this

Five: Cityscapes

phrase. Perhaps if the mindless urban crowds were to pause in their lives for a moment, they might find it possible to tap into that deeper dimension which is unarticulated and elusive, but which would grant a greater significance to their everyday existence.

Poem number twenty-two in the sequence is a short poem, different from almost all the other pieces in the series in that it is much more abstract; it is a poem about writing poetry. It talks about the need for clarity, echoing the last two lines of poem number eleven from "A Narrative": "a substantial language / Of clarity, and of respect." There are only four lines in the poem:

> Clarity
> In the sense of *transparence,*
> I don't mean that much can be explained.
> Clarity in the sense of silence.

Oppen relates here to clarity and transparence (as he does in a later poem in this collection) as concepts which cannot be fully grasped or explained; poetry must speak directly through the ether, as it were. In order to do so, there is a need for silence — a doing-away with language and the voicing of ideas, which can only cloud or diffuse the essence of the poem. Oppen conveys in this short poem the necessity of going below and beyond the words; he believes in allowing an image to resonate through, but also beyond, its depiction, to move the self at bone level, to be absorbed by the blood, and not necessarily to be reshaped in language. (Of course, this is the ultimate paradox of this kind of poem: in order to convey the idea that language is inadequate to convey certain ideas or perceptions, language itself must be employed in some form or other.) This is a pivotal poem in the series, and perhaps in Oppen's work as a whole, implying that the images of the cityscapes, like the moment of looking down at the street from the dizzying height of a skyscraper or the outline of a body in a tenement room, but also those single important unvoiced moments in our lives — all these have a hard, clear impact of their own which "speaks" without words, which eludes language as its organizing force.

If poem twenty-two equates clarity with silence, number twenty-three presents the semi-madness of "vocabularies" and the jargon of the media:

> "Half free
> And half mad"
> And the jet set is in.
> The vocabularies of the forties
> Give way to the JetStream
> And the media, the Mustang
> And the deals
> And the people will change again.

These ever-changing social labels, each displacing the previous mode of discourse, are juxtaposed with core organic material:

> Under the soil
> In the blind pressure
> The lump,
> Entity
> Of substance
> Changes also.

There appears to be a parallel here between "the people," molded and changed by shifting social patterns of speech and the "entity of substance" which is also changed. Both are affected by pressure — the social pressures of fashionable jargon for the people, and the "blind pressure" of the earth's crust. Yet there is a radical difference between these two, and the difference lies in the presence or absence of consciousness. Randolph Chilton comments on the last lines of Oppen's "Myself I Sing," saying:

> Beyond individual apartments, beyond any assertive "Me!," beyond consciousness itself lie the rocks, emblems of pure existence, which in the absence of all else ties us together. Moreover, the rocks suggest another bond among us — the bare fact of the enduring common environment in which we find ourselves.[5]

The changes in the "lump" of "substance" are "blind," having no sense of their changing. The "blind pressure" creates new landscapes, effected by elemental energies, taking place over eons of time, whereas social changes are effected through vocal channels of persuasion, enticement,

Five: Cityscapes

self-consciously changing "vocabularies," a labeling of intentions. It is a superficial change, constantly replacing itself and constantly being replaced. Oppen's use of capital letters in "JetStream," and "Mustang" emphasizes this labeling, naming and packaging each social fashion. In contrast, the soil and the lump represent solid content rather than empty jargon; these are real, fundamental changes rather than the superficial changing of names and labels.

Oppen uses two different verb tenses in his descriptions of change: "And the people *will change* again" (my italics) and "substance / Changes also." The future tense in the first phrase implies a shift, a break from one time and one form of jargon to another, while the present tense in the second phrase implies a gradual, on-going, ever-with-us evolution. There is a difference between the brittle patterns of social change and the slow, fundamental processes of the earth's formation. People will abandon and adopt new vocabularies in an artificial and self-conscious manner, whereas organic change is natural and "blind" and knows no consciousness of itself. These differences are reinforced by Oppen's use of language in this poem: the middle section is characterized by minimal, spare, noun-based phrases, in contrast to the diffuse and wordy phrase of the first stanza.

The poem's last stanza brings together the self-conscious changes in social dialogue and the blind, unconscious changes in the earth's crust. We are presented here with the girls who attend parties held in various rooms of city apartments, after which:

> The girls
> Stare at the ceilings
> Blindly as they are filled
> And then they sleep.

This final stanza depicts the party girls *after* the party, disengaged now from the party chatter and the social chit-chat, emptied out by talk. Now, in their beds, they have entered a world of silence, staring blindly at the ceiling, being replenished and finally falling asleep. Falling asleep entails losing consciousness of the self and allowing deep organic processes to take over — muscle relaxation, the regulation of the heart-beat, the rearranging of one's experiences through dream sequences: all those physical processes that are essential to one's well-being. And so Oppen intimates to the readers that true organic change does not take place as a result of shifts in patterns of social dialogue and social fashion, but at a deep fundamental level far below consciousness and language.

Poem twenty-five, like number twenty-three, also juxtaposes two different conditions, but this time diachronic rather than synchronic. Oppen considers the "strange" blend of old and new, old and young, past and present in the poem:

> Strange that the youngest people I know
> Live in the oldest buildings
> Scattered about the city
> In the dark rooms
> Of the past — and the immigrants
>
> The black
> Rectangular buildings
> Of the immigrants.
>
> They are the children of the middle class.
> "The pure products of America—"

The quoted line here is from William Carlos Williams' poem "To Elsie," from *Spring and All* (1923); Oppen's borrowing of this line not only shows an affinity with his colleague Williams, but also enriches the theme of his own poem. The continuation of the line from Williams' poem tells us: "The pure products of America / go crazy–," as Williams portrays a series of ragged American characters, pursuing adventure and finding themselves hemmed in by circumstances, all straining after a bygone pastoral countryside, the ideal America of once-upon-a-time. Oppen's poem portrays the young living in the old; he finds this "strange," a contradictory blend of what was and what is. For Oppen, the past appears to be less inviting, less satisfactory than the imagined bygone scenes of Williams' poem: here there are "dark rooms / of the past" and the old buildings are "black." The young people in Oppen's poem, the speaker implies, are making their lives in the present, searching for the Dream in the checkered culture of a modern America, sloughing off the past, as the last lines tell us:

Five: Cityscapes

> Investing
> The ancient buildings
> Jostle each other
> In the half-forgotten, that ponderous business.
> This Chinese Wall.

For these young people, the past is "half-forgotten, that ponderous business"; they appear to be solely occupied with their present lives, "pure products," still innocent, naïve, full of vision and desire, not yet contaminated or compromised by social pressures such as those described in poem twenty-three. Yet they form a "Chinese Wall," a human chain of living "stones," creating the modern version of a monument ancient and monolithic. Oppen juxtaposes the words "that" and "this" in "*that* ponderous business" and "*[t]his* Chinese Wall" (my italics), thus both distancing the past and also making it current and actual.

In the short stanza "Investing / The ancient buildings / Jostle each other," the short individual phrases may be combined into different semantic units. The word "investing" may be coupled with the previous line "The pure products of America" to indicate the young people's effort to live their American lives; if this is so, then the "ancient buildings" are those that "[j]ostle each other." On the other hand, the word "investing" may relate to the "ancient buildings," in which case it is the young population who "[j]ostle each other." The different possibilities in the coupling of these phrases invites a comparison with the way the stones in the Chinese Wall fit into each other in different ways. Like the stones, the phrases in the poem link both backwards and forwards, both in space and in time. And so Oppen, in this poem, blends past and present, not only historically but also in the sense that one's origins, one's ancient and primary past, are embedded in an urban present of jostling human lives. This is achieved both through the content of the poem, and also in the primary image of the great stones of the Chinese Wall.

In poem twenty-six, Oppen again raises questions about past and present, history and temporality and our human consciousness of both. The first part of the poem examines the concept of chronological time, talking of the poet's "metaphysical sense [o]f the future," one's "denial [o]f death" and the individual life as one part of the chain of generations.

George Oppen

Oppen analyses one's sense of continuity as a single life within the span of many single lives which make up a generation. This sense of one's temporality and the consideration of suicide as a manipulation of that temporality, or of death as the boundary between the generations, leads Oppen to eschew one's "metaphysical" consciousness of time and suggest, as an alternative, "the great mineral silence":

> Street lamps shine on the parked cars
> Steadily in the clear night
>
> It is true the great mineral silence
> Vibrates, hums, a process
> Completing itself

Against this is juxtaposed the

> Power and weight
> Of the mind which
> Is not enough, it is nothing
> And does nothing
>
> Against the natural world,
> Behemoth, white whale, beast
> They will say and less than beast,
> The fatal rock
>
> Which is the world —

Oppen implies that one needs a certain fundamental clarity of mind to conceive of "the great mineral silence," which is an underlying hum, a natural process that completes itself constantly and is not bound by time. The "power of the mind" cannot adequately fathom the "natural world," that great cycle in which the elemental beasts, the "white whale" (reminiscent of Moby Dick), live out their lives untrammeled by a consciousness of themselves or of time. The clarity of mind of which Oppen speaks is similar to the clarity of the street light shining on the cars, and it allows one to see more:

> O if the streets
> Seem bright enough,
> Fold within fold
> Of residence ...

Five: Cityscapes

> Or see thru water
> Clearly the pebbles
> Of the beach
> Thru the water, flowing
> From the ripple, clear
> As ever they have been.

Here is the clarity both of light and of water, throwing the pebbles into sharp, clear outline, illuminating fundamental elements that are there, always, for us to see in the ever-present moment that is the suspension of time. Oppen's acquaintance with the writings of Heidegger seems to be demonstrated here; Heidegger's work on the nature of existence within time tells us:

> Everyday Dasein ["being there"], the Dasein which takes time, comes across time proximally in what it encounters within-the-world as ready-to-hand and present-at-hand. The time which it has thus "experienced" is understood within the horizon of that way of understanding Being which is the closest for Dasein; that is, it is understood as something which is itself somehow present-at-hand. How and why Dasein comes to develop the ordinary conception of time, must be clarified in terms of its state-of-Being as concerning itself with time — a state of Being with a temporal foundation. The ordinary conception of time owes its origin to a way in which primordial time has been levelled off.[6]

One's consciousness of time, the occupation of the "power of the mind," flattens out that "primordial time" in which the great mindless beasts and the small pebbles have their existence; the "clarity" comes about when one is able to shake off a sense of time and immerse oneself in an ever-present "now" which is both constant and fundamental, and also suspends temporality, whether capturing the urban image of the cars in the light of the street lamps or the natural image of the pebbles in the clear water.

The phrase "fatal rock" harnesses the underlying oppositions of the poem, combining "fatal" (a consciousness of one's mortality, and therefore time-bound) and "rock," a fundamental image, elemental, primordial, one of Oppen's favorite images to represent "being-there." Together, they are "the world." Oppen knows we cannot shake off the shackles of time—generations see themselves in the spectrum of time, living their lives, doing and dying, considering the self's place in the world, and sometimes engaging in a metaphysical consideration of that self and of the concept of time—yet would want to open our eyes to a "clarity of silence," to sweep away conscious, analytical thinking in order to sense, deep in one's being, that "primordial time" where existence is self-evident and self-sufficient, free of all temporal consciousness, part of the great mineral "hum." This is where real generation, or rather *re-generation* of the self takes place.

The underlying oppositions of this poem—our time-bound, conscious selves as opposed to the fundamental, time-less "ever-presence" of natural entities—is evidenced in the choppy syntax of "The power of the mind, the / Power and weight / Of the mind which / Is not enough, it is nothing" as against the flow of "or see thru water / Clearly the pebbles / Of the beach / Thru the water, flowing / From the ripple, clear / As they have ever been." There is an immanent clarity in the phrasing of the last stanza, a smooth flowing movement to these lines, which is lacking in the truncated syntax of the former stanza.

Introducing the last stanza is the phrase "Fold within fold," an image which rejects the linear concept of time and replaces it with convolution, an on-going, internal self-renewal. Even in Oppen's use of the semi-archaic "thru" (rather than the more conventional "through") in "see thru water" we may find, in addition to his favoring minimalistic word forms such as "tho," a usage that folds past into present, that leads us down into the water to the sea-floor and the pebbles underneath. With this image, Oppen allows the reader to leave temporality behind and be immersed in a dimension of experience where time stands still in a crystal moment of clarity and recognition.

Poem twenty-seven is a prose poem about poets, the choices they face when writing poetry, and the existence of simultaneous, but very different, dimensions of experience. Poem twenty-eight presents the finished product of poetry, the tightly packed layers caught in the poem, and the light that comes off the text to expose both its origins and the beginning of a new understanding:

Five: Cityscapes

> The light
> Of the closed pages, tightly closed, packed against each other
> Exposes the new day,
>
> The narrow, frightening light
> Before a sunrise.

The "new day" in this poem presents the reader with something fresh but also fearful, the "narrow frightening light" at the break of the day, at the dawning.

Here the written text, layered, produces an awakening to something elemental, a recognition of the source or origin which sheds light on the understanding of one's experience. The poetic experience is paralleled with the daily, mundane doings of one's life, the forces of experience marshaled throughout the day and also through the pages of the written text, all those revealing a primary source of light which both illuminates and threatens because it reveals: it strips us bare. Our experiences are thrown into stark relief by the recognition of their elemental origins. Oppen here digs deep into those unconscious beginnings which give rise to an awareness of both our life's experiences and also of the poetic experience.

The poem is structured in such a way that it reflects the idea presented therein: the long middle line ("Of the closed pages, tightly closed, packed against each other") squeezes the words against each other like the pages of the text. In contrast, Oppen opens and closes this poem with the minimal lines "The light" and "Before a sunrise," to pinpoint our attention on the source of illumination. A short poem about itself and the poetic experience unlocked by its own text.

Poem number thirty-five, like number twenty-seven, also traces back to origins. It begins and ends as if in the middle of a deliberation, bracketed between a series of dots conveying a sense of being in transit, on a journey of recognition:

> ... or define
> Man beyond rescue
> of the impoverished, solve
> whole cities

George Oppen

>   before we can face
>   again
>   forests and prairies...

The previous poem (number thirty-four) is about women, plural and uncapitalized, while this one is about Man, a term both individual and representative, capitalized. "Man," therefore, embodies both the singular and the collective together, reminding us of the title of this collection, *Of Being Numerous;* as a result, the term "Man" becomes a more universal and all-embracing concept. Man is defined here as being beyond the "rescue of the impoverished"; or perhaps, in a different reading of the lines, Man is defined, comma, and is also beyond rescue. It appears that this stanza may be interpreted both ways. And what does Oppen mean by the phrase "Solve / whole cities"? Does he imply that we must solve the riddle, or formula, of what cities are? Or is he using the word "solve" in the sense of dissolving, of unraveling or disentangling them from our lives? Whichever is the case, Oppen seems to be telling us that we must understand the city in order to go back in time to a more primitive and natural state defined by forest and prairie. With the city entangled in us, we cannot face nature because we have usurped it.

Forest and prairie in this poem become emblematic of our origins, of who we once were. We cannot face these origins until we understand how we have removed ourselves from them. Only then, when we can admit and accept them, can we define ourselves, define the singular and collective, where we came from and who we are. Man is impoverished by being estranged from what he once was — simpler, less polluted (in all senses of the word) by the empty desires and empty language of urban cultures, by the lack of which Lacan speaks. We have to solve the riddle of who we have become in order to be rescued.

In this poem, the city is set against the forest and the prairie, and is consequently seen (in contrast to some of the other poems in *Of Being Numerous*) in a negative light. "Solving" the city implies problem and entanglement and complexity, as opposed to the simplicity of the forest and prairie. The forest, in fact, is a particularly primary image — originary, secret, often holding the key to solving riddles; it is the stuff of fairy tales, throwing into relief the innocence of Red Riding Hood or Hansel and Gretel, and also of myth, for example in the case of the sacred grove at Nemi. (Fraser's *The Golden Bough* presents Nemi, the sacred grove of the goddess Diana, as a place of regeneration and fertility, and is similar in pattern to the myth of the Holy Grail, in which Lancelot, who roams the forest, comes upon a city whose king is dead, and who is crowned as his replacement. Lancelot also features as the Quester in the later Holy Grail legend.) Oppen's poem may also be re-examined in the light of the Quest: beginning and ending as it does in the middle, we have a sense of being caught up — in an experience, a deliberation, a journey — in which, to be rescued from impoverishment, we must "solve" the city, find the key to the regeneration of the self. Only when we know what we lack, can we go back to that originary state, that "illud tempus," that sacred grove to understand and replenish ourselves.

Towards the end of *Of Being Numerous,* there is a fourteen-section poem called "Route," a sequence within the larger sequence framework of the whole collection. This sequence poem is prefaced by a phrase from Lu Chi's *Wen Fu* which says "*the void eternally regenerative.*" These words reflect a thematic idea running through the whole of this mini-sequence: that regeneration is brought about by being emptied out. This idea is implicit in the first section of "Route":

> The sources
> And the crude bone
>   — we say
> *Took place*
> Like the mass of the hills
> "The sun is a molten mass." Therefore
> Fall into oneself—?
> Reality, blind eye
> Which has taught us to stare —

Just as the process of aging is "not ours," we are also dissociated from "sources" and "crude bone" which, according to the poem, simply "took place." This phrase is italicized and therefore emphasized, as if we played no part in the forming of those elements; they simply happened. Yet the poem tells us they "took place," occupied their space in the spectrum of time; this is a more active term than the passive "happened." They seem somehow firmer, the sources and the bone; they have more presence than humans, who are simply caught up in the swing of time. The phrase "The sun is a molten mass" presents a powerful image; having been confronted with this, we are asked if the consequence is "fall[ing] into oneself–?" There is a sense of collapse here, an implosion of sorts, the inability to control who we are.

In the light of these ideas, reality becomes a "blind eye" which has "taught us to stare"—uncomprehendingly, it is implied. We gaze at reality and try to make sense of it; but we are blind, or reality makes us blind. We must train ourselves to look, not at "reality" in general, but at the small, sharp details (like "your elbow on a car-edge," an image from the next line of the poem), and make sense of our existence through those clear, sharp images, the "crude bone" of our lives, the basic stuff of which our experience of reality is made up. When we do so, when we train ourselves to focus on the single, primary moments, we empty our minds of conscious thought and logic and strip ourselves to the bone, as it were; we enter a sub-conscious and sub-verbal level at which we have a naked perception of how things really are. At this moment in time, when time itself is frozen, we gain a sense of stability, like bone and hills, in the flux. Once we perceive this, once we empty ourselves of worry, despair and concern, once we stop looking at how time moves inexorably onwards and freeze the moment, we may achieve a clarity of sorts. This is Oppen's avowed and implicit aim in writing poetry, as he states at the end of this section:

> I have not and never did have any motive of poetry
> But to achieve clarity.

In this poem, as in many others, Oppen captures a time-frame in an image, and works his poem around it to achieve the clarity he wants to convey to the reader.

The central part of this poem is full of dashes, abruptly truncated phrases, and a question mark which appears exactly in the middle of the poem, at the end of the twelfth line. (There are twenty-three lines in the poem.) One has a sense that this deliberating and questioning does not lead anywhere; the question is not answered but, like the other fragmented phrases, hangs in the air. In contrast, the last two lines of the poem make a firm statement; like bone, like hills, they are set out as a fundamental notion, a base truth underlying and emphasizing Oppen's primary poetic aim.

Section four of "Route" opens with a concept which runs through many of Oppen's poems — the juxtaposition of clarity and transparence with impenetrability. The poems which refer to "matter" often talk about its impenetrability, in the sense that it is solid and therefore reassuring, and present; but there is a clarity about transparence which is lacking in the "solid" matter presented in the poems. Section four of "Route" deals with these concepts, which recur frequently in Oppen's work:

> Words cannot be wholly transparent. And that is the
>   "heartlessness" of words.
> Neither friends nor lovers are coeval...

The outcome of words not being wholly "transparent" is that their opacity makes them "heartless." They are opaque both in the sense of not being capable of reflecting much, but also of not being accessible to one's understanding. As friends cannot exist together with lovers, neither can words exist together with true perception.

In opposition, the sea anemone which appears in the following lines is both transparent and porous, allowing dreams to pass through it and absorbing the sea water:

> The sea anemone dreamed of something, filtering the sea
>   water through its body,
> Nothing more real than boredom — dreamlessness, the
>   experience of time, never felt by the new arrival,
>   never at the doors, the thresholds, it is the nature
> Native in native time ...
> The purity of the materials, not theology, but to present
>   the circumstances

The sea anemone experiences dreams and water at a sensory level: it is an almost fetal image of the dreaming embryo absorbing and floating in the amniotic fluid of the womb, a pre- and sub-verbal image. Everything about the sea anemone is primary and organic: it is one of the more basic forms of life, it is protean, and it dreams. This is significant because dreams themselves belong in the subconscious at a much more rudimentary level of the self.

In contrast, boredom in this poem is, in essence, defined by a lack of dreams and by an over-consciousness of time. It is not experienced at doors and thresholds, both of which allow one to pass through. The "nature / Native in native time" becomes an image of the primitive, whose experiences of life are primary, and through whom time flows onward, unobstructed. In this state, one experiences one's being at a deep, organic sub-verbal level where the heartlessness of words means nothing, because language has no function at such a level. This is where the "materials" come to have a purity, a clarity, a transparency; they "present the circumstances," their manifestation is enough to justify their existence. Or, in other words, they are "just there." Here, perhaps, is where Oppen's concept of solidity and transparence coincide. There is no need for doctrines or theology to explain them: they are self-explanatory and self-justifying. Words, in contrast, can never be self-explanatory entities, since they will always be the stuff of which doctrines and theologies are composed; words exist as a means to an end, and not as an end in themselves.

It is interesting to note that Oppen puts the word "heartlessness" in single quotes in the poem. Perhaps he is thinking of words with no heart, like the ghosts of words in section four of "A Language of New York." But he is almost certainly using the word in the sense of being impervious to one's surroundings, as opposed to the sea anemone which accepts and absorbs the sea water and can then dream. Language — words — prevents this acceptance of others and the world around because it is, ultimately, self-centered.

The visual structure of the poem also emphasizes certain words. "Words" stands out at the beginning of the first line because there is a space under it in the following line; similarly (although not exclusively) with the word "Nothing" in the middle of the poem. This device reinforces the blankness of both "words" and "nothing." In addition, the poem becomes progressively less structured as it follows through its idea. It begins with the closure and finality of a period after "words" (which

Five: Cityscapes

themselves close off accessibility to understanding in the context of these lines). The lines continue with several instances of three dots, interspersed in the middle lines by a series of commas signifying continuation, but in the case of the dots, an unspecified continuation. Finally, the poem ends with no punctuation whatsoever, thus leaving it open and "accessible." In this way, the poem's theme of accessibility and of openness is reflected in its syntactical structure. Perhaps the quote which prefaces "Route" becomes once again relevant in this context, with its "eternally regenerative" void which is bottomless, never-ending, open, accessible?

The next-to-last section of "Route," number thirteen, takes a look (in the opening image of the obsolete Department of Plants and Structures) at man's failed and subsequently abandoned attempts to construct, to manifest his power through urban planning blueprints. In his planning, man digs up the earth to make way for the foundations of buildings and the lying of pipes, regardless of what lies beneath the surface:

> Department of Plants and Structures — obsolete, the old name
> In this city, of the public works
>
> Tho we meant to entangle ourselves in the roots of the world
>
> An unexpected and forgotten spoor, all but indestructible
>   shards
>
> To owe nothing to fortune, to chance, nor by the power of
>   his heart
> Or her heart to have made these things sing
> But the benevolence of the real

The ancient footprints of animals, the remains of past cultures (spoor and shard) are disregarded; likewise, man has interfered in natural processes by "ow[ing] nothing to fortune, to chance," not in order to glorify them or make them "sing" but to impose his will on the earth. However, all those attempts, those plans to build and construct, have failed:

> Tho there is no longer shelter in the earth, round helpless belly
> Or hope among the pipes and broken works
> "Substance itself which is the subject of all our planning"
> And by this we are carried into the incalculable

Oppen must have intended the reader to catch the double entendre of "plants"—not only in the sense of industrial buildings, but also in the sense of "planting." Man has "implanted" himself in the earth, but has succeeded only in becoming "entangled" in a way he did not intend. His attempts have failed because "there is no longer shelter," there is no more hope, all is broken. We have appropriated "substance" for our own planning, and it has been our downfall — our hope and our strength have disintegrated together with the "broken works," and the "round helpless belly" offers no redemption: the earth has been exposed and is therefore helpless. We have been caught up in the mesh of time which works its own changes, and we cannot control or plan it further because it is "incalculable."

A reading of this section of "Route" can be enriched by looking at the final section in the poem's sequence, in which we find out that man's dreams only take him so far, and when they dissolve or "deconstruct," we are faced with the real. Coming back to this section of the poem, we find "the benevolence of the real"—the real substance, the actuality of the elements that make up our world, independent of our own plans and dreams: what is really there under our feet and before our eyes. To see and feel that fundamental force, to sense its presence and have that moment of understanding and acceptance, may be our salvation. Rather than "entangle ourselves," in a physical sense, in the roots of the world, we can recognize the elemental forces present in our world without imposing ourselves on them. Laying aside our conscious desires to leave our mark on the world is a way to achieve awareness, which can only come about when we divest ourselves of the constant need to assert the self. The "eternally regenerative" void mentioned in the preface to "Route" comes to mind again; clearing away that kind of consciousness which is self-consuming leaves room for natural regeneration rather than artificial destruction. Shelley's Ozymandias, his manifestations of power and glory eroded away by the desert sands, also comes to mind within the thematic context of the poem.

The phrase "hope among the pipes and broken works" arouses associations with "pipe dreams," those often futile visions and desires we have which never come to fruition because they are not viable. The language throughout this whole section is also, in a sense, unfulfilled; many of the sentences are left incomplete, floating phrases which do not link up with each other to form complete semantic units, like the uncompleted works of the Department of Plants and Structures, like our uncompleted plans and dreams. The "real" lies beyond all these, beyond the power of language to encompass its fundamental nature. The "old name" of the Department has outlived its function; corroded and deflated by time, it has lost its power and significance. As has language, in many ways.

Hovering over all the poems in "Route" is the introductory comment about the void; this void may be interpreted in different ways, all of which are relevant to the thematic content of "Route" as a whole, and in fact to the wider spectrum of Oppen's work. Much of his poetry struggles with the great gap between what we encounter in the world and how we can — or cannot — articulate our perceptions of that world. The gap between words and the things they name, the gap between what we can grasp and what lies beyond our grasp, the gap between our reality and the Real of which Lacan speaks — Oppen's poetry steps into these gaps and finds them productive and regenerative, for out of them he spins his poems.

The second to last poem in *Of Being Numerous* is a five-part poem titled "Power, the Enchanted World." It explores different kinds of power — social, political and verbal — which are deconstructed and destabilized. Exploitation through different kinds of power is pitted against empathy with other human beings: the first section describes the crowded apartments in poor neighborhoods of the city, the second leads into the third section which delivers a criticism of global war, while the fourth section discusses graffiti slogans — all of these disturbing to those who are sensitive to the plight of humankind. Section five sums up the case against power:

> Power ruptures at a thousand holes
> Leaking the ancient air in,
> The paraphernalia of a culture
> On the gantries
>
> And the grease of the engine itself
> At the extremes of reality
>
> Which was not what we wanted
>
> The heart uselessly opens
> To 3 words, which is too little.

In this last section, power is divested of its power, as it were. Cracks have appeared in what had previously seemed to be an airtight structure, and the "ancient air" has come in. By "ancient air" Oppen may have been thinking of the winds of the past, which have undermined modern power structures: the simplicity of former cultures seen to be stronger and more stable than the poverty-stricken and war-torn present; but "ancient air" may also be a representation of the underlying natural forces of the universe which overcome and destroy man-made power. The jumble of slogans, reflecting contemporary culture, glares out at us and reminds us of the trivialization of language in the service of social and political power discourses, and the engine-grease propels machinery to the limits of man's capabilities. This, the poem tells us, is the "last frontier" of modern urban reality, and it is not "what we wanted." Man's ultimate vision was not intended to be a power-driven world which would stretch reality to breaking-point and be threatened by simpler, more fundamental forces over which he has no control.

The last two lines of the poem, with the word "heart," seem to refer to love, whether for humanity in general or a particular individual, and imply that love is "useless" when belittled in words. Language in its different aspects has been made suspect throughout the five sections of this poem — in the talk of justice in section two which leads only to war, in the graffiti of section four and in the "paraphernalia of a culture / On the gantries" in this section. Empathy and love are to be sensed biologically, deep in one's being, sub-verbally; the heart should not be betrayed at the conscious level by empty talk.

This poem is composed of four pairs of lines with a single line after the third pair. It is not made clear what this single line — "Which was not what we wanted" — refers to. Does it relate back to "extremes of reality"? Or to the "paraphernalia of culture"? To the ruptured power? Or to all of these? The implication in this poem is that we all, ultimately, seek for true empathy and not power. We want to sense a common bond with others and not be engaged in power discourses, Oppen seems to be saying. And if we look again at the four pairs of lines, we find that in the first three pairs the second of the two lines is shorter, but in the last pair the second line is longer. Yet the line says, "which is too little." This line embeds one of the paradoxes of language: the more words one uses, the less one manages to encompass. It is ironic that Oppen chooses the number "3" rather than the word "three," as if, in *counting* the words, he implies that, in the end, words do *not* count.

Edward Hirsch talks about those issues of clarity and the distrust of words within an urban framework that are among the leading themes evident in *Of Being Numerous:*

> The quest in his work is for clarity in relationship,... For this reason Oppen treats language with circumspection and distrust, questioning the ability of words to escape their current debasement and once more render up what is "out there," to again "name" the world.[7]

Together with the concept of the individual as part of a greater tribal collective, these themes permeate the body of poems that makes up *Of Being Numerous*. Oppen sets out a way of looking at our contemporary urban culture which offers a counterpart to the loneliness and triviality of that culture, a way to see beyond the superficialities of the urban lifestyle and its projected expression in newspapers, advertising and slogans to a deeper and more actual reality "out there," which speaks of itself without words, through clear, hard images and sudden glimpses of a different dimension of experience. These concrete images of the city hold a silent primary power, often comprised of basic materials such as stone and mineral. They resonate with an elemental energy of their own, and with a clarity that goes beyond verbal definition. Juxtaposed with these single, clear images, the jargon of the media — language used for persuasion and dissension — is emptied out of significance, becoming like the biblical "tinkling brass and cymbals," a kind of language static which interferes with our perception of fundamental energies embedded in the images of urban reality and our experience of it. In order to understand, or at least be able to tap into, this underlying primary dimension of experience, we must divest ourselves of our social consciousness, of the ruling ego; we must put ourselves on hold and then we may see what is out there to be discovered. Once we do this, we can exchange the anonymity of the urban collective for another kind of anonymity which erases a consciousness of the self, but allows each of us to become one with the great primary life-forces which underlie our social existence and can link us to each other, and may "speak" to us through objects and images even when they cannot be rendered in verbal terms.

Six

Light and Water

The short collection of poems which followed *Of Being Numerous* was published in 1972 and titled *Seascape: Needle's Eye*. It marks a shift in Oppen's writing, although some poems bear a resemblance in format and writing style to *Discrete Series*. The poems in *Seascape* let in more light than those in *Of Being Numerous*, are more fragmented in some cases, and are even less syntax-evident. Many of them sound like odd fragments of a lost text, and appear on the page like pieces of paper blown about in the wind, puzzling both in intent and also in content on a first reading, phrases flapping against each other apparently at random. Replacing the city imagery in *Of Being Numerous* is a poetry of the outdoors, of sea and cloud and different shades of light. The primary images are, for the most part, natural elements: water, wind, fire. They are spare poems, reticent to the point of silence sometimes, according to Mark Perlberg in a short review of *Seascape*; Perlberg is dubious about Oppen's reticence: "For even the poet who is attempting to bring his reader news of the incommunicable — and I do not think that this is what Oppen is about — must do so in words which cancel silence." Within this context of language, Perlberg observes that Oppen "seems wary of patterns of rhythms, of connections, of the music a poem can make."[1] In contrast, Eleanor Berry claims that "the more recent poetry is concerned with language, music, song, the poem" and compares the imagery of previous collections with the "new" imagery of *Seascape*: "An imagery dominated by hard, unitary objects, typified by rock, has given way to an imagery of the liquid, of light[.]"[2] Oppen's poetry, to my mind, *does* deal constantly with the incommunicable — or at least, incommunicable in words — making use of elements that are non-verbal, such as rhythm, gap, tone and the music of the lines. With reference to Oppen's later poetry, David McAleavy writes:

> [W]e meet a crafted style which uses the form of the letters, the words, the writing on the page to indicate manipulations of sound, pace, cadence, etc. (the oral-aural forms). Form marks form. Furthermore, style and content reinforce each other and form itself seems to create meaning.[3]

This interplay of form and meaning which McAleavy notes is, I think, true of all Oppen's work, and not only of the later poetry. Sub-verbal aspects of language such as gaps between the words are employed more extensively in the poetry written after *Of Being Numerous*, but the sub-verbal is always evident in one form or another throughout the spectrum of his work. If there is silence in Oppen's work — and I believe there is — it is often the silence of the sub-verbal, a meaningful silence, more significant than the words used to circumscribe it. Oppen seems to be warier of words than he is of music and rhythm; his poetry on many occasions produces a strange music, atonal and not always harmonious but, like the eerie calls of whales, essential as a means of communication. What ultimately comes across in the poems of *Seascape: Needle's Eye* is an often wild landscape in which we may find our most elemental existence as beings stripped of ego and a consciousness of the self, but more fundamentally attuned to the deepest rhythms of the universe which we all inhabit.

The first poem from *Seascape* which appears in the *Collected Poems* carries the long and enigmatic title "From a Phrase of Simone Weil's and Some Words of Hegel's." The French philosopher and activist Simone Weil, in many aspects of her life and beliefs, seems to have complemented Oppen's own. Both were Jewish, both active in the Communist movement (although Weil later became disillusioned with Communism, as she saw it transform itself into dictatorship), both engaged in manual labor — Weil in agriculture and factory work, Oppen as a carpenter — and both had a seeming distrust of words, especially when used for political ends. Weil's comment, "A mind enclosed in language is in prison," illustrates this distrust of words, particularly for political purposes. She felt deeply that humanity had been uprooted from those foundations that nurture the soul; her political philosophy was explained in her book *The Need for Roots*.

Although we are not told which of Weil's phrases appears in the poem, its main theme would, it appears, match her own concerns. The first half of the poem juxtaposes elements of the natural world with human nature:

> In   back   deep the jewel
> The treasure
> No   liquid
> Pride of the living life's liquid
> Pride in the sandspit wind this ether this other this element all
> It is I or I believe
> We are the beaks of the ragged birds
> Tune of the ragged bird's beaks
> In the tune of the winds

Oppen, in this first half of the poem, sets up an opposition between the natural elements and human dogma; the "I believe," which stabs at reality, intrudes into the natural environment and disrupts its basic pulse. Perhaps Oppen is thinking here of Charles Olson, who, in discussing Ezra Pound's "ego system" refers to the ego as a beak: "though the material is all time material, he has driven through it so sharply with the beak of his ego...."[4] This section of the poem presents the elemental pulse of nature — its liquid, its air, its fire — disrupted by the "I" and the "I believe." These lines seem to indicate that our consciousness of our selves, what we feel and think and say, tunes out the music of the natural universe, what the natural world has to "say" to us, without words, through its fundamental rhythms. The poem's own rhythms bear this out: compare the outpouring of "Pride in the sandspit winds this ether this other this element all" with the stabbing motions of "We are the beaks of the ragged birds / Tune of the ragged bird's beak." The "pride" of the "living life's liquid" and the "sandspit wind" carry an intrinsic grandeur, particularly when juxtaposed with the strutting quality of "It is I or I believe." In addition, there is a sense here that the "ragged birds" are blown about by the wind, and thus Oppen cleverly appropriates the natural elements and turns them into the "winds" of ideologies.

The two enigmatic opening lines of "In   back   deep the jewel / The treasure" frame the poem as a whole, setting a perspective from which we may view the natural environment and our place within it: the deep elemental pulse of the universe is a "jewel," but not easily accessible to the human world of self-assertive beliefs and political creeds. It is "[i]n," "back" and "deep," at the heart of the natural world, pulsing far below our ego-conscious selves. The centering of the conscious self on political dogma flares briefly, but ultimately does little to right social imbalances; it is

> Like a fire of straws
> Aflame in the world or else poor people hide
> Yourselves together   Place
> Place where   desire
> Lust of the eyes the pride of life and foremost of the storm's
> Multitude moves the wave belly-lovely
> Glass of the glass sea shadow of water
> On the open water no other way
> To come here the outer
> Limit of the ego

There is a shift here in the phrase "Lust of the eyes," as the poem swings away from the greed of "seeing and wanting" to a panoramic beauty of landscape which delights the senses, heightened by the musical alliteration of "[m]ultitude moves," "belly-lovely" and "sea-shadow." (My emphasis.) The last lines break over the reader like waves, creating in this poem a Deep Image of vivid sensory experiences tumbling below the ego-conscious self and the ragged shreds of dogma. But there is "no other way" to be immersed in this tumble of the senses except by straining to "the outer / Limit of the ego"; this last line brings the reader back to the beginning of the poem and the "In   back   deep the jewel" of the first line, each word separated by a long space, by "this ether" perhaps, each dissociated from the other as we must dissociate ourselves from the ego, from the words of dogma, in order to hear the "music" of the universe. Like Kristeva's semiotic, the underlying "language" of the natural world speaks to the unconscious mind beneath the ego-centered, ordered self, providing an essential, undulating music to those who can put the ego aside and hear it, who can free themselves from the "mind enclosed in language" and the doggedness of wordy creeds. As Michael Bernstein puts it: "there tugs an equally strong sense of the limitations in any one man's mind or language, limitations that severely restrict how much of that larger world he can honestly (again, that unavoidable word) grasp."[5] Oppen does appear to believe — and this thread runs through much of his poetry — that one's grasp of much of the universe "out there" cannot be adequately clothed in language; still, his poems shimmer with a sense of what the natural universe is like, its rhythms, its sensual beauty and its undulating power. And yet this poem seems to evidence a struggle on the part of Oppen, as he fumbles for the language to best convey what cannot, in essence, be conveyed in words — that paradox of communicating *through* language what is impossible to communicate *in* language. Oppen's struggle is manifested in the opening three lines of the poem: "In   back   deep the jewel / The treasure / No... " The "No" seems to be a denial of the previous two lines, as the poet attempts to capture that elusive, deeply moving beauty of the landscape, yet knowing that it cannot, ultimately, be pinned down in a word or phrase. It can only be conveyed through the overall tone, auditory imagery and rhythm of the poem.

    This pushing against language, butting at the words to find the phrase which can capture the impact of experience, is prominent in Oppen's work, particularly in *Seascape*, where the landscapes seem often to overpower the senses. In "Animula," for example, the poem is prefaced by a phrase from the writings of the Roman emperor Hadrian, written before his death: "animula blandula vagula" or "little pale soul wandering." Indeed, what pervades this poem is a sense of the smallness, the fragility of the human self before the great narrative of the landscape, and the difficulty of capturing its effect on the poet in words. The poem plays with images of light and dark (quoting from the middle of the fourth line):

                                      Air of the waterfronts black air
                Over the iron bollard   the doors cracked

Six: Light and Water

> In the starlight things the things continue
> Narrative   their long instruction and the tide running
> Strong as a tug's wake   shorelights'
>
> Fractured dances across rough water a music
> Who would believe it
> Not quite one's own
> With one always   the black verse   the turn and the turn

The juxtaposition of light and dark is played out here in the "starlight things" against the "black air" and again in the "shorelights' / Fractured dances" which leads into the "black verse." In the following lines, this "black verse" is again contrasted with an image of light in water:

> At the lens' focus   the crystal pool   innavigable
> Torrent torment Eden's
> Flooded valley   dramas
> Of dredged waters

Now the "black verse" concentrates, through the image of the camera, into the "crystal pool." What seems to be implied here is the inadequacy of the "black verse," which is opaque, to reflect the play of light on the water, or perhaps the inadequacy of words to illuminate the frightening beauty of the night scene: the rough tug of the water and the fractured prism of the shorelights. The turning of the "lens' focus" then becomes the poem's attempt to delineate more sharply the harbor images and the "crystal pool" which is nevertheless "innavigable," perhaps because the pool cannot be navigated by the language of the poem. If this is so, the previous lines "Not quite one's own / With one always" may be seen as the inadequacy of the poetic self to fully absorb, embody and master one's experience of the natural universe. It is as if the "crystal pool" is a reservoir of one's sub-verbal, primary and elemental experience of the external world which is "innavigable"; one cannot dredge up into one's consciousness this experience, which is too deep to be addressed at a conscious level. The "crystal pool" combines primary elements of hard mineral and flowing water, the fundamentals of the natural world in the same way that our deepest protean experience of what is around us underlies our conscious perceptions of that world.

The poem closes with an image of the small, fragile self in the midst of the moonlit landscape of water:

> And out to sea   the late the salt times cling
> In panicked
> Spirals at the hull's side sea's streaks floating
> Curved on the sea little pleasant soul wandering
> Frightened
> The small mid-ocean
> Moon lights the winches

"Spirals" throws us back to the turning of the lens in the previous section of the poem — is this, perhaps, the reason for being frightened? That one's soul — poetic or otherwise — cannot capture the fragments of one's life experiences? Or is it simply that the sea overpowers man in so many ways? Oppen's recurring use of the image "bright light of shipwreck" comes to mind. However we choose to interpret these lines, the pervading Deep Image of this poem is of dark punctuated by light, and of the small self bobbing helplessly on the shifting sea of the landscape. This Deep Image comes across also in the visual structure of the poem, as the fractured phrases bob on the surface of the page, like the dancing lights on the surface of the water, like little bits of experience coming together to make "a music," the music of the poem itself.

In "West" the central image is, again, one of light, this time the light of poetic truth. Michael Heller talks about Oppen's "exploration of reality by creative effort,"[6] and "West" is a good example of this poetic exploration. The poem struggles with the truth of experience as depicted in poetry, and the voicing of that struggle becomes more evident here than in almost any other poem by Oppen, although the difficulty of voicing experience strains through a great deal of his work. Oppen eschews much of his poetic writing as soon as he has written it; sentences trail off in a series of dots, the lines are sprinkled with question marks, and the intrusion of the words "yes" and "no" raises doubts in his mind and in the poem about the efficacy of what he has just said. "West" unfolds the process of attempting to depict natural landscapes and creatures and one's experience of them, the deepest impact, the imprint they make on one's perception of the world and the engagement of the self with external reality. The poem reads almost like a stream-of-consciousness text, phrase flashing into phrase in dream-sequence, as Oppen grapples with the words, precariously picking and unpicking the phrases, juxtaposing and discarding in his search for an apt and true expression of that "rare poetic / Of veracity that huge art whose geometric / Light seems not its own...." That poetry of truth seems to inhere in the element of light; it is, according to a later line in the poem, "[t]ransparent as the childhood of the world." Paradoxically, then, the poem depicts, through the words, the idea that the truth of experience is sensory and cannot be linguistically defined; it eludes words, it is present in the element of light and sound, in the primary world of children whose sensory experiences constitute a truth which demands no language to verify it. At the end of "West," children become the inheritors of experience; they are "[n]ew skilled fishermen," whose dexterity manifests itself in an engagement with reality at the purest sensory level. Theirs is an implicit acceptance of the veracity of what they see, hear and feel, without the need to define its significance in words. But the poet's art, the truth of what he sees and feels, involves a creative struggle with language in order to explore it. Or as another poet, Denise Levertov, puts it: "his craft is involved in a desperate struggle with the intricacies of his sense of life. His poems are essentially of process, not tasteful art-objects"[7] This struggle which Levertov also detects in Oppen's work makes for a dynamic poetry, rather than the kind of still-life painting or decorative vase that Levertov seems to be thinking of when she mentions "art-objects." In spite of having grown up in the Objectivist tradition, with its poetry of sharp, clear objects and images, Oppen's poetry is full of struggle.

In "Song, the Winds of Downhill," Oppen reverts to a theme which occupied his attention in many of the poems from *Of Being Numerous*: that great gap between "sophisticated" social dialogue and the essential language of poetry. Although this poem does not deal directly with physical landscapes of light and water, it does grant to poetic language a stark, essential "light" of meaning, in the sense that it illuminates without stating or verbalizing. The poem takes the reader "downhill" to the elemental roots from which poetry derives; Oppen implies that the poet must divest himself of the "wealth of parlance" in order to reach that simple, essential place where poetry begins. This poetic space is described by Oppen as "impoverished," as opposed to the "wealth" of common discourse; but its poetry derives from a clearing away of cluttered language and social posing:

> "out of poverty
> to begin
>
> again"   impoverished
> of tone of pose that common
> wealth
> of parlance

Having rid himself of the social elements which impose themselves on everyday discourse — tone of voice, affectations of speech — the poet can fashion the poem out of those simple, "poor" words (as opposed to the lush "parlance" which is empty of any essential meaning) that are the basics of the poem:

> Who
> so poor the words
> *would   with   and*   take on substantial
> meaning   handholds   footholds
>
> to dig in one's heels   sliding
>
> hands and heels beyond the residential
> lots   the plots

In describing the small words (which are shrugged off in common discourse as being "poor" in significance) as "handholds" and "footholds," the poet restores substantiality to them: they become concrete units on which the poem is hooked, and which poet and reader can grasp in order to further an understanding of what the poem says, therefore providing a framework for the fabric of the poem: "it is a poem // which may be sung / may well be sung."

There are several sub-verbal reinforcements here of the idea that poetry is created out of the small, seemingly insignificant words which nevertheless take on substance within the poetic framework. First, Oppen uses the visual element — the spacing of the words — to give emphasis to the notion of words as handholds and footholds which the reader can grasp in order to reach an understanding of the poetic idea: the words "meaning," "handholds" and "footholds" themselves are each strategically placed on the page, like individual pegs on a mountainside, which can be used both in order to stop the sliding into inanity and also in order to realize the structure of the poem. The little words like "would," "with" and "and" are italicized to make them stand out visually and separate them from the rest of the poem, thus giving them emphasis. As opposed to the autonomous spacing of these little words, the phrases "of tone of pose that common / wealth" and "sliding // hands and heels beyond the residential / lots" are squeezed into one breathless phrase, to give a sense of the uncontrolled "sliding" of everyday loosely used language. In addition, the syntax is fractured at points in the poem, where the "essence" of the small words can leak through, for example in the lines "Who / so poor the words / *would   with   and* take on substantial/meaning." We have to read these lines carefully, more than once, in order to separate them out into units of meaning: the "Who" seems to ask a question, the answer to which is "the words"; and although the words are "so poor," they answer to "Who" rather than to "which," thus taking on the status of living beings rather than objects. Finally, the last two lines draw our attention to the fact that what is being created by those small, concrete "foothold" words is the foundation for the poem — a poem which sings rather than speaks, which derives from a sub-verbal poetic melody that the small words constitute. The importance of the small words is again highlighted at the end of the poem, in the repetition of the phrase "which may be sung." With the addition of the word "well" to the phrase repeated in the last line, ("may well be sung"), the meaning of the phrase is heightened; "well" is a word carelessly used in everyday language (for example, "He may well be late"), but taken literally, with its proper meaning restored, it turns the poem into something which may not only be sung, but sung "well."

What Oppen appears to be doing in this poem, as he carefully draws the reader's attention to the autonomy of the small, often ignored words, is to grant power and substantiality to those simple units of language that are important simply because they embody their own existence in the poem, and not because they represent something else. Oppen views the little words as the basics, the elemental foundations on which poems are structured, creating a primary mode of language very different from the syntactically sophisticated but often superficially significant language of social texts and discourses. His poetry thus becomes stark and uncompromising, each word standing only for its own primary reality. In his discussion of this poem, Michael Heller notes the lack of metaphor and links it to his own view of poetry:

> What is given up ... is the analogical mode in language where image and symbol stand as metaphors for *another* reality. Because of this, Oppen's work seems like a kind of first poetry, ... by virtue of the sheer unaccountability of its construction.[8]

This stark, concrete quality in Oppen's poetry is one of the elements that makes it primary, in the sense that the language is fundamental and essential, functioning in the same way that the primary colors of red, blue and yellow provide the basic spectrum for all other shades and hues.

Oppen's use of starkly concrete phrases is again seen in the second of "Some San Francisco Poems," titled "A Morality Play: Preface." The poem opens with the image of a woman lying on a bed, looking at the speaker with "naked eyes"; Oppen takes up this image both to reflect and also internalize the light on the hills and water of the surrounding landscape:

> Beautiful and brave
> Her naked eyes
>
> Turn inward
>
> Feminine light

and then later in the poem:

> The ocean pounds in her mind
> Not the harbor leading inward
> To the back bay and the slow river
> Recalling flimsy Western ranches
> The beautiful hills shine outward

Six: Light and Water

    Sunrise   the raw fierce fire
    Coming up past the sharp edge
    And the hoof marks on the mountain

    Shines in the white room.

Here is a transformation of the external into an inner light and beauty which shines out; the etched loveliness of the landscape, independent ("The beautiful hills shine outward") and externally autonomous, is nevertheless drawn inward to coalesce in "feminine light." There is a Deep Image here of external and internal patterning: an essential, internal light that is an integral part of the woman is also discovered in the external landscape. As the "great loose waves" of the sea become the ocean which "pounds in her mind," recalling the rolling and swelling emotions of love (for this is a love poem, as we are told previously in the lines "'Love' // The play begins with the world"), so does the sunrise transform into the "raw fierce fire" of the woman's passion. Thus the "play begins with the world" and gathers itself inward to be embedded finally in the "naked eyes."

    There is a primal quality to this whole poem, which goes on to say "Provincial city / Not alien enough // To naked eyes // This city died young." Oppen appears to mourn a once-vibrant city which has "died young," as he attempts to recapture something of that original, uncontaminated quality that still resides in the primally sensual self. The "[p]rovincial city of hill and harbor, not alien enough," seems to embody a quality familiar to the "naked eyes" which reflect the primal sensual self. As the fire, the ocean and the hill embody all that is primary in the landscape, the light in "the naked eyes" embodies all that is stripped and primary in the self. Each is autonomous in its own integrity, and each mirrors an elemental quality in the other. The language, too, is stripped down to honed phrases, each image presented singly and clearly like the hoofprints on the hillside, each a shining fragment like the sun's rays striking on the water, like the glint of ripples reflected — perhaps even physically — in the woman's naked eyes.

    In poem number four of the San Francisco poems, called "Anniversary Poem," Oppen deals with the onset of old age and coming separation, and yet paradoxically this is a poem of return to beginnings, both individual and collective, all that is primary and fundamental and originary. In a way, Oppen goes back to our First Garden, "where everyone has been":

> "the picturesque
> common lot" the unwarranted light
> Where everyone has been
> The very ground of the path
> And the litter grow ancient

There is Biblical imagery here, imagery of the Creation — the "unwarranted light," and later in the poem, beginnings:

> Let grief
> Be
> So it be ours
> Nor hide one's eyes
> As tides drop along the beaches in the thin wash of
>   breakers
> And so desert each other
> Lest there be nothing
> The Indian girl walking across the desert, the
>   sunfish under the boat

The imagery of "the Indian girl walking across the desert" is somehow tribal, reminiscent of the Children of Israel crossing the Sinai desert, and the "sunfish under the boat" takes us back to the Creation, the light of the newly created sun leading to the appearance of the oceans and marine life, and later the creation of Man who built his own sea-going craft. The world unfolds in these lines, as the layers of human experience accumulate, each arising out of the manifestation of the previous layer; the poem, too, unfolds from our "first stories":

> How shall we say this happened, these stories, our
>   stories
> Scope, mere size, a kind of redemption

And:

Six: Light and Water

> Time and depth before us, paradise of the real,we
>   know what it is
> To find now depth, not time, since we cannot, but depth
> To come out safe   to end well

Our first stories—the art of story-telling, beginning with the Garden and developing from oral tradition into the written tradition of literature and poetry, among other texts—tell of the "paradise of the real" and come full circle to "end well" in a "kind of redemption."

The end of the poem discloses an inability to speak: "We have begun to say goodbye / To each other / And cannot say it." In these final lines the approach to one's lifetime experience is synchronic rather than diachronic—"depth, not time"—an ending where we "cannot speak" but, paradoxically, return to our personal origins, searching under layers of individual experience to Lacanian beginnings where speech is absent.

This poem evidences a going-back in time to beginnings, both universal and personal, yet it is synchronic in the sense that the beginnings are embedded in the ending. Interestingly, the only word with a line to itself in the poem is "Be," capitalized; this pinpoints for the reader the simple, encompassing sphere of one's personal and individual, but also collective and universal experience. As in other poems, Oppen punctuates his key phrases with spaces, for example, the words "to end well," preceded by a space which draws the reader's attention to the weight given to the phrase.

Number ten, and the last of the San Francisco poems, called "But So as by Fire," works around contrasts—of dark (or shadow) and light, fire and water (there are pools here), small and vast, the real and the reflected, the temporal and the atemporal, surface and depth. Oppen begins by describing a woodland scene, the tender plant-life underfoot providing a superficial layer over bedrock:

> The darkness of trees
> Guards this life
> Of the thin ground
> That covers the rock ledge

He emphasizes the quiet peace of the place in: "The beauty of silence /

And broken boughs // And the homes of small animals." There is a sense of reverence here, reminiscent of "Psalm," the young lives of plants and animals enhanced by the poet's attention to them. This "first life" as Oppen calls it, will both embody and reflect light, will have a "[h]idden starry life" which is "not yet / A mirror," like the frail human life portrayed in the second part of the poem:

> We have gone
> As far as is possible
>
> Whose lives reflect light
> Like mirrors

The poem appears to be constructed around the idea that the natural and fleeting — plants, small creatures, frail human beings — nevertheless mirror something essential, fundamental and timeless. The lines "We have gone / As far as is possible" imply limitation and a sense of being timebound, yet the fragile lives of those human creatures embodied in the "We" reflect an essential light which goes beyond the temporal.

Line seven — "The beauty of silence" — is central to the poetic idea expressed in this poem, that of communication at a deeper level than sound and voice. It reminds us of the Eliadean concept of primary symbolic constructs which embody the "illud tempus," that "other time." Eliade's mention of the archaic symbol of light emerging from shadow is reproduced here in the lines "To be afraid / Not of shadow but of light," and although Oppen is probably looking ahead here to his own frailty and to the approaching end of his life, the image of light and shadow is reminiscent of the primitive symbol existing in human thought long before language came along to give it shape. The idea of light emerging from shadow provides a symbolic link with what Eliade calls "the deep sources of life," contrasting with linguistic constructs which cannot communicate "deep structures of reality." So the primary and mythic symbols in this poem — fire and water, shadow and light — tap into a primordial state which is both sacred and atemporal, accompanying human life in all its fragility and limitation.

The title of this poem, "But So as by Fire," suggests a baptism of sorts, an entry into a new and different state. Once more, it may be that

Six: Light and Water

Oppen is thinking of his own approaching death and, paradoxically, a baptism marking his exit from, rather than entry into, life; but it may also be a baptism into that primordial, sacred time, embodied in the symbols of rock and fresh water, light and shadow, which lie beyond the temporal and are therefore unaffected by time.

The last poem in the collection *Seascape: Needle's Eye* is called "Exodus"—a fitting title for a poem which both closes the collection and looks beyond where one has been to where one is going. The poem works around mythic symbols which are at once culturally personal and at the same time universal: cloud, fire, the desert. It presents the story of Exodus, the long trek of the Jewish people out of Egypt and into the Promised Land and, through that story, a significant moment between Oppen and his daughter. Again, as in "But So as by Fire," there is a sense of tapping into an Eliadean "illud tempus," a primordial "other time," quite dissociated from historical time and personal lifetime and yet pertinent to that personal lifetime.

The poem begins with a meditation on children:

> Miracle of the children   the brilliant
> Children   the word
> Liquid as woodlands   Children?

Here, children are both a "miracle"—like the miracle of the pillar of cloud by day and the pillar of fire by night which guided the Children of Israel through the Sinai desert—and also "brilliant," perhaps in the sense that they give off a kind of light which illuminates for adults something of the world that is denied to older, more socially constrained people. Children are socially artless, and in that sense "untainted" by norms and social expectations; they are direct, unmitigated, socially naïve; perhaps the "light" they give off arises from this fact. The word "children" is also described as "Liquid as woodlands," creating a sense of the word itself dissolving, language disintegrating, leaving only the "brilliance."

The next few lines of the poem describe a story-telling incident between father and daughter:

> When she was a child I read Exodus
> To my daughter   "The children of Israel...."

George Oppen

> Pillar of fire
> Pillar of cloud
> We stared at the end
> Into each other's eyes   Where
> She said hushed
> Were the adults   We dreamed to each other

This story-telling seems to provoke the breaking open of a different form of communication, one not dependent on vocal interaction. The word "hushed" intimates a lack of sound, and the state of dreaming implies communication through symbols rather than articulated language. Oppen and his daughter interact on a deeper, more fundamental level than that of speech; perhaps it is implied that this form of communication is more accessible to and with children, and that may be why children are described in this poem as "brilliant." The poem ends with this emphasis:

> Miracle of the children
> The brilliant children   Miracle
> Of their brilliance   Miracle
> of

There is a tentative quality to this poem, evidenced in the series of dots, question marks, gaps and the open-endedness of the last line. Language appears ultimately inadequate here to convey the poet's experience with his young daughter. The unfinished ending implies that there is much more to be said but language cannot say it, for the experience goes much deeper than language can go. The reader him or her self must fill in those blanks.

This last poem in the collection turns away from the landscapes of the previous poems (except for the mention of the desert), from the concerns of old age, to look at both past and future, to communicate one's roots, to continue tradition by handing on to one's children the mythic and cultural past. The poem looks both backwards and forwards, both internalizing the external but also externalizing the internal, carrying and sharing one's most fundamental sense of life at a level too deep for words.

In conclusion, *Seascape: Needle's Eye* features poems of water and

Six: Light and Water

light, the light both physical (the dazzle of sun on the ocean, the light of stars, a primary source of heat) and metaphorical (the light of a feminine body, the brilliance of children), as if there is an internalization of physical light at the end of this body of Oppen's work. In these poems, light becomes a primary symbol, a fundamental and essential source from which all life radiates outwards, but which also illuminates from within.

SEVEN

Into the Eyes of the Tiger

Oppen's penultimate collection of poems, *Myth of the Blaze,* gathers up the themes of previous works — stark landscapes, a railing against social injustices, and the deep-rooted human fear of loneliness and estrangement; these poems are peopled by the elemental figures of fishermen and shepherds, Man Friday, the primal Tyger and ancient tribes, pitched against highways and ditches, lynch gangs, theologians and the hangman who "comes to all dinners" (in "Semite"). Appearing and disappearing in the poems, like swimmers in a stormy sea, are the collective stories of human history: Adam, who "named the animals," Romans and barbarians, the shipwrecked survivor who leaves a message in a bottle, and the ancient wanderer. Oppen fuses all these into a poetry which takes a hard look at our shifting world today and exposes, through its cracks, the fundamental and the constant which have kindled it into being, and against which it often struggles. *Myth of the Blaze* also develops an idea which carries strongly into Oppen's last collection of poems, *Primitive:* that of the craft of poetry itself, and how it is fashioned from the images which are presented in the poem. One can sometimes see the poem unfolding from the lines as one reads, noticing itself and bringing its emerging creation to the attention of the reader.

The poem which bears the title of the collection — "Myth of the Blaze" — deals with names and naming, and with the savage, modern "Theatre of the War" which gives way to a different kind of savagery, the pure animal instinct of the tiger. The poem begins with what Michael Davidson explains is a memory of World War II,[1] and ends with the "blaze of the tiger." Although the poem's title contains the word "myth," Oppen did not, in any systematic way, draw on universal myths, according to Eliot Weinberger: "Uniquely among American poets, there are almost no mythological references and no myth-making, no exotica, no personae, only one or two passing historical references, and almost no similes in his work."² Weinberger is correct about the mythological references and the exotica, and about the fact that the speaker in the poem is almost always Oppen himself, but I believe that Oppen did draw on certain types of myth as originary sources of an elemental power which exerts its influence on the primary self. "Myth of the Blaze," however, begins with a demythicizing of war, its blaze of glory and heroism debunked, and subsequently turns away to a different kind of "blaze," that of the primitive forces in the theatre of our experience which sear our senses on exposure to them. This kind of experience, which blazes into our consciousness, is epitomized in the Tyger (a reference, it seems, to Blake's Tyger and its raw magnetic power, although Oppen also spells it "Tiger" later in the poem).

Oppen's description of his war experiences in the poem ends with

> ... the secret taste
> of being lost
> dead
> clown in the birds' world

This choice of words and images conveys a sense of how war mangles not only body but spirit, leaving the soldier spreadeagled like a clumsy clown; there is both ridicule and pathos here. The image pins down man's futile attempt to emulate the free power of creatures in the natural world and to harness it for his own ends. Man's control of flying machines, for example, is no more like a bird's flight than his hunting-down of fellowmen is like the tiger's fiercely elegant stalking of its prey. Oppen then muses on the significance of names: "what names / (but my name) // and my love's name to speak"—and goes on to talk of primal experiences, referring obliquely to the First Garden and Adam's naming of the animals:

George Oppen

>   into the eyes
>   of the Tyger   blaze
>   of changes ... named
>   the animals   name

The coupling of names and animals suggests the Garden of Eden and the animals' primal quality, their pure strength and instinct. Adam's naming of the animals leads Oppen into a consideration of naming and its purpose:

>   giving
>   them darkness the gifted
>   dark tho names   the names   the "little"
>   adventurous
>   words   a mountain   the cliff
>   a wave are taxonomy I believe
>   in the world
>   because it is
>   impossible

There is a contrast here between the gift of darkness and the gift of names in "the gifted / dark *tho* names" (my italics): the former is boundless, whereas the latter sets limits by its naming. The idea of names brings Oppen to reiterate a favorite theme of his, that the "little" words are the most important; here, the "little" words are the primary features of the landscape: the mountain and the cliff— these are basic, rock-hard words. Yet the idea of names is "impossible"; names of words, especially the "little" words, cannot be used for any purpose of reference (for example, classification), but only as integral units that refer to themselves. In the same way, implies Oppen, our direct experience of the world — looking into the eyes of the tiger, as it were — cannot be classified either, only felt powerfully at a sensual level. This is played out in the rest of the poem (which I quote fully):

>   the rain barrel flooding
>   in the weather and no lights
>   across rough water illuminated
>   as the narrow

Seven: Into the Eyes of the Tiger

>   end of the funnel what are the names
>   of the Tyger   to speak
>   to the eyes
>
>   of the Tiger   blaze
>   of the tiger   who moves in the forest leaving
>
>   no scent
>
>   but the pine needles' his eyes blink
>
>   quick
>   in   the shack
>   in the knife-cut
>   and the opaque
>
>   white
>
>   bread each side of the knife

The reader is left at the end of this poem with the conviction that there is no way to classify the moment of experience — its impact, its sharp delineation on one's senses, its autonomy of being (and Oppen may conceivably be relating a near-death experience here — he was badly wounded in the war). Just as the tiger leaves no scent, experience leaves no classifiable imprint. The moment of the rain barrel spilling over (the life spilling out?), the moment of the knife slicing through bread (the wounding?) — these moments are "the narrow end of the funnel," which is the pinpoint of dramatic impact, the sharply and deeply felt moment of interaction with natural forces.

As in several other poems, "Myth of the Blaze" contains no punctuation whatsoever, apart from the occasional set of single quotes. There are no ordinary commas, no colons or semi-colons, no question marks, no periods. This allows for a free-flow from one subject to another, as the poet's thoughts slide (like the shots in some war films) almost in dream-sequence through a spectrum of poetic ideas. The lack of punctuation also allows for a play of light and dark — the blazing eyes of the tiger, the "rough water illuminated" juxtaposed with "the gifted dark" — to ripple through the poem unhindered.

As mentioned before, Oppen (unlike many of his contemporaries) does not draw on the great, well-known mythic figures such as Oedipus,

Ulysses and Helen of Troy; however, *Myth of the Blaze* does explore origins of different kinds: the poet's own personal origins, those of the Jewish people, the mythic origins of humankind in general (what Paul Lake calls the "mythopoeic realm"[3]), and also how his poems unfold from generic images. In "Semite," for example, Oppen compares mythic and poetic sources:

> what art and anti-art to lead us by the sharpness
> of its definition connected
> to all other things this is the bond
> sung to all distances
> my distances neither Roman
> nor barbarian the sky the low sky
> of poems precise
> as the low sky

Art deals in the definition of things common to us all, which from a bond across time and space ("sung to all distances") in the same way that mythic elements provide us with universal origins. Oppen relates also to his own historical origins, being "neither Roman nor barbarian" but Semite. The common bond of universal sources spans distances, just as the "low sky of poems" also bridges space, seeming to bring the sky closer. Oppen then proceeds to set out an almost-pictorial image of how poetry spirals up and outwards from its poetic origins:

> ... sun's light
> on the sills a poetry
> of the narrow
> end of the funnel proximity's salt gales in the narrow
> end of the funnel the proofs
> are the images the images
> overwhelming earth
> rises up

These poetic sources, like mythic sources, contain the images that "overwhelm[] earth," images of sea winds ("salt gales") and later in the poem, of gardens and forests: "...poem born // of a planet the size // of a table-top / garden   forest." The dual upward-downward movement of the radiating poem and the universal bonding through common origins is echoed not only in "the low sky" and "the narrow end of the funnel," but also in the following lines: "of the foxhole what is a word a name at the limits / of devotion / to life," where the foxhole, burrowing down into the earth, is juxtaposed with words which are stretched to their limits in the service of revering life. These images of expansion-contraction are repeated once more towards the end of the poem, where Oppen makes reference (as in several other poems) to the world of the media, which brings images of global suffering into our domestic lives:

> ... whereupon murder
> comes to our dinners poem born
> of a planet the size
> of a table-top
> garden   forest

As the whole planet shrinks to become a table-top, universal suffering becomes personal and individual, and also functions as the basis from which the poem grows. The images of garden and forest carry mythic elements of origin (the Garden of Eden, the Sacred Grove) which once again provide both those common bonds we all share, and also the poetic origins on which Oppen draws constantly for his poetry. As in much of the later poetry, this poem is self-referential: as Oppen fashions the poem from its basic elements (simple, concrete units of language, basic images of sea and forest) he writes this poetic fashioning into the lines, so that the poem talks about itself as it is being actualized.

At a sub-verbal level, this poem is structured to reinforce the connection "to all other things" through both the lack of punctuation and also the arrangement of the lines. Since there is no punctuation whatsoever in this poem (an increasingly obvious technique in the later poems) — no commas, periods or capital letters — each idea is connected to the other without the artificial separation that such punctuation would enforce on the content and structure of the poem. In addition, the lines are arranged in such a way as to bind them to each other, one line flowing into the next without interruption, so that the physical and the poetical structure of the poem provides an ongoing connectedness. For example, "to lead us by the sharpness // of its definitions connected / to all other things," each of which spans two lines that are bound together through the ongoing meaning of the phrases. Again, in the lines "in the narrow // end of the funnel the proofs // are the images / overwhelming earth // rises up" the logical arrangement of the phrases would be "proximity's salt gales in the narrow end of the funnel," "the proofs are the images," "overwhelming" and "earth rises up." Oppen indicates the logical grouping of phrases by the use of the singular verb "rises" to show the reader that this verb agrees with "earth," in order that the reader understand that "earth" belongs not to the adjective "overwhelming" but to the verb which follows in the next line. With this technique, Oppen creates a web of meaning from one line to the next, illustrating in the syntactical structure how "all things" are connected. In doing so, he gives emphasis to the nouns, those more concrete and primary elements of language which he favors most, by placing many of them at the end of the line, so that the reader is made aware of the bones or infrastructure of the poem. Finally, the only two words in the poem which are given their own space within the line are "garden" and "forest," thus individuating these two primary images which embody origins both universally mythic and poetic: mythic because of their connotations and poetic because out of them the poem is born. The flow of words here, the underlying and unhindered movement which propels this poem, highlights what Kristeva would term the semiotic nature of poetry, which breaks the symbolic order of language and its ordered laws of syntax, grammar and punctuation to release a poetic energy quite different from consciously-organized thought shaped into words.

In "The Lighthouses" the reader again finds the interlocking of lines, a technique noted by Rachel Blau DuPlessis:

> In Oppen, the reader experiences a forward pulse of language.... This pulse is ur-syntactic, seeking connectedness, yet a-syntactic because suppressing certain conventions for connection: "That most complex thing of syntax, of those connections which can't be dealt with outside the poem but that should take on substantial meaning within it [Power interview, p. 198]."[4]

Seven: Into the Eyes of the Tiger

In "The Lighthouses" the juxtaposition of the end of one line with the beginning of the next in the same line creates a sustaining music in the poem, what Oppen calls here "the cadence the verse // and the music essential." This musical cadence is the unfolding of the poem from elemental sources: the sources of Oppen's own heritage (once again we have the phrase "neither Roman nor barbarian"), sources of light (the lighthouse) originating from the ocean, images of small fish (minnows) and the "seed sprouting / green." The radiating outwards of the poem from its elemental origins is a "joy of escape":

> ... in loyalty
> to all fathers or joy
> of escape
>
> from all my fathers I want to say
>
> yes and say
> yes the turning
> lights
>
> of oceans in which to say what one knows and to
> limit oneself to this

The poem begins in the ocean, "in which to say what one knows": the light of the poem originates from elemental images of water, illuminating the dangers of "rock-pierced coasts," which may be seen as the populated spaces where people live, as opposed to the often lonely, primitive spaces into which the poet retreats to find the images for the poem. Oppen claims that the return to origins is a "flight":

> the structures ... silver as the minnows' flash miraculous
> as the seed sprouting
> green at my feet among a distant
> people therefore run away
> into everything the gift
> the treasure is
> flight

As the poet reaches back towards the elemental sources which "light up" the poem and provide the "music essential" and the cadence, the structure of the poem falls away to reveal the primal images from which the poem originates:

> ... now the walls are
> falling the turn the cadence the verse
> and the music essential
> clarity plain glass ray
> of darkness ray of light

The "ray / of darkness ray of light" may be taken as a reference to the flashing light of the lighthouse; but it also carries connotations of the Creation, of light created from darkness. This poem, then, radiates both outward and backward; there is an escape back to origins, culminating in the Creation images of the last two lines, and yet a movement outwards from the source of the poem, through the structured layering of the lines, to its own fully fledged appearance as "the cadence the verse" at the end.

Syntactically, this poem functions (as do many of Oppen's poems) mainly on the basis of nouns; verbs are almost non-existent here. This creates an elemental, concrete foundation on which the music of the poem is played. Since nouns are the bones of language, their predominance anchors the poem to the elemental images they represent: fathers, lights, oceans, minnows, flash, seed, feet, walls and rays. Oppen visually reinforces the central primary image of light by twice giving the word "lights" a line of its own; these are the only one-word lines of the poem. The first mention of lights comes at the end of a three-line stanza; the repetition of the word gets not only a line, but a complete stanza, to itself. The fact that Oppen makes frequent use of double spacing throughout this poem also emphasizes the sense of loneliness: the spacing highlights a singling out, an objectification which makes the word or line a "thing," so that the lines take on an aloneness in the space of the page. Consequently, a certain tension is set up in this poem, deriving from the set-apart lines: those fragmented noun phrases which nevertheless, taken together, produce the "cadence" or flow of the poem. Thus we have both fragmentation and synthesis, reflected not only in the content (the piecing together of the poem) but also in the structure and arrangement of the language used.

Seven: Into the Eyes of the Tiger

In "Confession" Oppen once again goes back to primary sources, this time through memory. The title of the poem implies that the poet is going to reveal something that has been secret and hidden, and he does uncover a prior state of sorts. The origins he explores in this poem are at once personal and temporal (moving backwards through his own personal life to before childhood), universally temporal (humankind's mythic origins) and also, in a Lacanian sense, psychological (peeling away layers of consciousness so that he immerses himself in a pre-conscious state devoid of any personal landmark). He begins in the present:

> "neither childhood
> nor future
>
> are growing less" guilts   guilts
> pour in
>
> to memory things leak I am an old ship
> and leaky   oceans

This present is fraught with debility and frailty; his memory is flooded with guilt and his passage through life no longer watertight. He is compensated — paradoxically, since his metaphor is that of a ship on the ocean — by the knowledge that he has plumbed the depths, reached down into that elemental place where the personal, historical and universal has its origins:

> ... but to have touched
> foundations...
> I come to know it is home a groping
> down a going
> down middle-voice the burgeoning
>
> desolate   magic   the dark
> grain
> of sand and eternity

Oppen's phrase "middle-voice" emphasizes that this "groping down" into a primary place of beginnings entails the unburdening of one's voice, because the "dark grain of sand and eternity" is a pre-verbal state, a silent primal sphere which is desolate and dark, but also magic.

George Oppen

The images which Oppen chooses for this poem are the primary elements of water and sand. They are the fundamental materials out of which the physical world is fashioned, as well as being mythical symbols of origin. In addition, water as amniotic fluid is associated with a human being's personal beginnings in the womb, while sand carries connotations of the desert and Jewish tribal origins. These fundamental origins are echoed in the more prosaic "bilges," "keelson" (the crossbeam of a ship's keel) and "cellars," all of which denote foundations, the underlying structures of ship and house (although the cellar may also house one's guilt). These images anchor the poem as it were; they provide stability and depth.

Once again, Oppen uses no punctuation in this poem. There are no commas or periods to hinder the flow of the poem, which is at once the endless movement of the water, the ongoing flow of time, and also the creative flow. The poem ends with the word "eternity," also unpunctuated, so that the concept of eternity as endless continuity is reinforced by its lack of closure as a final phrase in the poem. As in "The Lighthouses," the lines of "Confession" flow into each other, creating a sense of the flow of water and time alike. There is a sense of flux in this poem (as in many of Oppen's poems) created by the double backward-forward connection between phrases, for example: "as all this becomes strange // enough // I come to know it is home...." Here the word "enough" may belong to the previous line, so that the phrase reads "as all this becomes strange enough"; but the word "enough" may also be read in the sense that it is enough "to know it is home." These different possibilities of combination open up the syntax, free it of limitations, of meaning in the same way that the ocean is not bound by any limitation of movement.

The two lines before the last dislocate the words from each other by spacing them apart: "desolate   magic   the dark / grain." In using this technique, Oppen gives them a certain independence from each other, an autonomy of meaning, a visual concreteness which focuses on them as basic building-blocks of language. In fact, the primary sphere of origins which concerns Oppen in this poem is defined by these attributes: desolate, because the source is singular, individual and separate from everything else; magic because it generates creativity; and dark because it precludes memory and experience.

Seven: Into the Eyes of the Tiger

The poem "To the Poets: To Make Much of Life" once again juxtaposes a present reduced by old age with an underlying point of genesis that is not time-bound but rather an immediate, ever-present sphere of being that generates poetic expression. The central image here is of the poem hewn out of elementals:

> the poem
> discovered
> in the crystal
> center of the rock image

For Oppen, the elemental images of sand, water and (in this case) stone represent indubitable and unfathomable sources of poetic creation and expression. These images generate poetic power and propel the poem into being. For the poet, the point of genesis signified by the rock and the crystal illuminates and sustains the temporal process, even in old age:

> "come up now into
> the world" the need to light
> the lamps in daylight *that passion*
> *the light within*
> *and without* (the old men were dancing
> return
> the return of the sun)

Oppen plays with the concept of light in these lines; there is internal and external light, but there is also natural (elemental) and artificial light. The need for artificial light (the lamps) is done away with because there is both external, natural light (the sun) and also the inner light generated by poetic activity. With "the return of the sun" we find "the old men dancing" and although this may be a simple reference to coming back to the world after the dark of night time, it is surely also an expression of the way in which a poet can bring into his temporal present that illumination which has its source in the elemental images of rock and crystal which are "always there," and from which the poem originates. Norman Finkelstein describes the poem as "a celebration of old age, particularly the old age of poets, and the means by which the antimonies of political action and contemplative art can be, if not resolved, at least memorialized in the poem."⁵ He goes on to quote the latter part of the poem:

> and image the transparent
>
> present tho we speak of the abyss
> of the hungry we see their feet their tired
>
> feet in the news and mountain and valley
> and sea as in universal
>
> storm
> the fathers said we are old
> we are shriveled
>
> come.

Certainly the phrases "the hungry" and "their tired feet" do seem to indicate social and political concerns, but in my own reading of this poem Oppen's principal concern is not to celebrate old age, but rather to celebrate those unfathomable poetic beginnings originating in the elemental image of the "crystal in the rock," which enlightens the poet's temporal existence. Oppen reveals to the reader how a poem comes into being, originating from deep, ever-present primary origins and coming into being through the temporal activity of writing these origins into the poem as primary images; even in a poet's old age these primary images may still activate, or discover the poem. Significantly, both the first and the last word in the poem is "come," as the poem itself emerges from elemental beginnings to make its way into the world.

Looking at the structure of this poem, we find that the image of the poem "discovered in the crystal / center of the rock" comes exactly in the middle of the poem, with nine lines preceding it and another nine lines following. This gives the image of the rock a centrality from which the poem radiates outwards; everything leads up to it and is derived from it, so that it becomes a primary hinge around which the poem revolves. The word "image" in the lines "in the crystal / center of the rock image // and image the transparent // present" functions as both verb and noun; the poem and the rock image then "image the transparent present," showing how the poem originating "in the crystal center of the rock" is reflected in the "transparent present" of the poem's existence. The phrase "crystal center of the rock" is in itself an interesting image, since a crystal denotes both light (a leading motif in the poem) and also the genesis of cluster, reflecting how the poem clusters around, or grows out of, primary material.

The theme of basic images which give rise to poetry, coming from a deep sub-verbal space into the conscious mind and world, is again taken up in "Two Romance Poems." Here Oppen juxtaposes sound, sense and scene, exploring the interaction between them and their relationship in the poem. He starts with the difficulty of pinning down poetry in words, seeing his desk (presumably a writing desk) as the enemy, blaming it as the saboteur of his writing, so to speak; the next stanza introduces a primary image of sea and sand and light:

> something wrong with my desk   the desk
> the destroyer, desk is the enemy
> bright light of shipwreck beautiful as the sea
> and the islands

A certain tension is set up here between these two stanzas, contrasting the desk as destroyer with the ship as destroyed; perhaps what makes the shipwreck "beautiful" is that it has been broken by the elements (sea and wind), and so acts as a fitting parallel to the way in which Oppen "breaks" language with the help of elemental undercurrents, using spacing and an often unorthodox grouping of words to set free these underlying currents. This fracturing of the language is what causes the "bright light" of the poem. However, there is a difficulty; the poet cannot articulate the essence of the poetic experience (which derives from elemental images such as the sea and the islands and the light): "I don't know how to say it / needing a word with no sound." What he *can* convey is "the pebbles shifting on the beach the sense / of the thing, everything, rises in the mind / venture   adventure." Unable to pin down the creative experience in words (which are verbal units and therefore inadequate to deal with sub-verbal experiences), he represents "the sense of the thing" through a primary image: that of pebbles on the shore, with their clicking and tumbling sounds, elemental. Through the image of the pebbles, "everything [ ] rises in the mind," and he is able to bring the poetic experience out of the unconscious, sub-verbal depths into his consciousness, and express it. Yet he can only "say as much as I dare," and what can be told is reconstituted in a simple, concrete scene:

> ... power
> of the scene I said the small paved area
> ordinary ground except that it is high above
> the city, the people standing at a little distance
> from each other, or in small groups
>
> would be the poem

Here is the final, pictorial representation of the poem: a little cluster of people, loosely grouped, on a concrete surface somewhere in the city. Just as "everything rises in the mind," coming up into consciousness, so the poet rises up to survey the scene. And this little scene — representing what *can* be said — also represents, in a way, the poem itself, made up of words which are separate from each other like the people, or grouped in small phrases, such as "the desk," "adventure," "Again!!" and "would be the poem." And so the scene is the poem; it is what one *sees*. The *sense* of it derives from the elemental images of sea and pebbles, shifting on the sand. The poem ends with:

> ... no heroics, obviously, but
> the sadness takes on another look
>
> *as tho it mattered, in a way*
> "smoke drifts from the hills"

So this is an ordinary, unheroic depiction, infusing perhaps the sadness of city life with something deeper and more elemental which transforms it. The word "mattered" in the second to last line, and the last line itself, together seem to sum up the gist of the poem; "mattered" suggests "matter" — the physical elements in life, the objects and the people in the depicted scene — while the "drifting smoke" of the last line, sensed and seen but formless and evading containment, is an apt metaphor for the poetic experience which is sensed but not easily pinned down in words. Matter, it seems, is what matters.

Oppen reinforces the content of this poem through several sub-verbal techniques. First, he plays with the words "venture" and "adventure," following them with the phrase "say as much as I dare." We find Oppen daring to say more, as he sets out with "venture" and then takes it a little further to become "adventure" ("ad-" here meaning close to, adjacent, therefore coming nearer to the "venture"), so that we see how the words "dare" to say more: aren't adventures full of daring actions? Thus Oppen builds on the words in order to take them to their limits. Oppen also uses spaces significantly here; in addition to the space between "venture" and "adventure," there are several other spaces in this poem. The first one comes in the first line, after "something wrong with my desk," and seems to indicate that what is wrong is that the desk prevents the poet from writing, so that the space becomes a visual blank, reinforcing the implication that nothing is getting written down. The second space comes after "I say all that I can," implying that what the poet *can* say is in the words, but also in the spaces which "open up" the poem. Here the space (as opposed to the one in the first line) becomes a pregnant pause, to allow something beyond words to express itself. An additional space appears after the lines "would be the poem / If one wrote it," and this space depends for its significance on the conditional clause "If one wrote it" (that is, the poem), telling the reader that the poem is expressed not only in the writing of the words but also in the spaces between and beyond language, in the same way that the concept of an individual, or pair, or group (like those depicted in the city scene of the poem) is defined by the people's proximity to each other, but also by the spaces between them. Finally, the central word "Again!!" is flanked by a double space, one on either side of the word: "What one would tell / would be the scene Again!! power // of the scene." In this case, the spaces serve the purpose of making the "Again!!" stand out in all its doubleness: two spaces, one on each side, two exclamation marks, and a word which means "once more." This duality emphasizes the double perception at work in this poem: the perception of the mundane (the everyday physical scene) and the poetic perception (suggested by the Deep Image of the sea and the pebbles). Indeed, this whole poem sounds and looks like the shifting pebbles, as phrases knock against each other, drift from one line to the next and lie scattered across the page. It is a poem about how deep elemental sounds and images surface through visual and aural patterns and through a momentary scene in ordinary lives that is also, somehow, shot through with significance.

The last poem from *Myth of the Blaze* to appear in the *Collected Poems* is "Res Publica: 'The Poets Lie.'" Its title implies that this will be a poem about the public domain and its representation (or misrepresentation) by poets. In fact, the poem ranges among several topics: the public and the private or personal life, social and poetic language, the "thing" and the naming of it, the falsity of words and their inability to capture or project the true significance of what they are supposed to be representing. The complete poem runs thus:

> words, the words older
> than I
>
> clumsiest
>
> of poets the rain's small pellets   small
>
> fountains that live
> on the face
>
> of the waters
>
> dilations
>
> of the heart they say
> too much the heart the
> heart of the republic skips
>
> a beat where they touch it

Since the poem opens with the word "words" and goes on to talk about "rain pellets," Oppen may be suggesting that some words — the little, concrete "thing" words — are like drops of rain, tangible and singular, but also that they are "older," preceding those who use them. Oppen tells us they are "older than I," and follows these lines with the phrase "clumsiest // of poets"; he appears to be referring to himself, and in doing so displays a raw honesty about his own writing, an awareness of the mishandling of precious words, a distortion through language, a gap between the naming of the "thing" — an experience, or a sensation — and the inherent ability of what it names (the experience or sensation itself) to touch our lives. Or perhaps Oppen is simply expressing his dislike of over-slick poets: if the "clumsiest of poets" is, in fact, a reference not to Oppen himself but to the poets who "lie" (and the poem may be read in this way), this phrase might be describing those poets in whose hands language becomes wordy and inadequate, whose story, in the words of Macbeth, is "a tale told by an idiot, full of sound and fury, signifying nothing." What *is* clear is that the poem highlights the rain falling on the water; these lines about the rain constitute, both conceptually and also physically in the space they take up, the central part of the poem. The small rain pellets are personified here — they "*live* / on the face // of the waters" (my italics); not only do they "live" but they are also invested with a life-giving power, a power that can swell the heart and stop one's life in its tracks for a moment.

The phrase "they say too much," like other phrases in this poem, may be understood in different ways. If it refers to the poets who "lie," this is a direct criticism of their overuse of language which both veils and trivializes the pure elemental power of nature to move us, to inspire us with awe. These poets' indiscriminate spilling out of language may divert us away from what can truly touch us — not only in the heart, but also in all our organs, in the nerves and bones of our body.

Again, the word "they" in the phrase "they touch it" at the end of the poem is ambiguous. It may refer to the poets, or to the rain's "small pellets." If it refers to the poets, the heart's skipping a beat "where they touch it" may imply simply an irregularity in one's life-rhythms, momentary and fleeting. Certainly, the poets talk of "dilations // of the heart," which has a scientific feel to it as a result of the word "dilations"; what really makes our heart skip a beat is the sudden sense of the dancing of the rain on the face of the water (or on our own face?) — that scene, that sensation.

The lines following "dilations" look rather squashed on the page, all running together, as opposed to the singularity of the word "small" on the page, and the skipped line before the last line of the poem (which may be a physical manifestation of the heart "skipping a beat"). This technique of Oppen's — his individual and careful setting out of the lines — visually reinforces the content, the crowded lines reflecting the rushing onward of poets who "say too much" while the singular prominence of the word "small" reflects the singular and individual impact of each small raindrop on the water. "Res Publica" therefore becomes a poem about gaps: the gap between public and private, between the voicing of an idea and the deep impact of what it stands for and to a certain extent substitutes, between the word and the spaces it leaves behind.

Myth of the Blaze both evolves out of *Seascape: Needle's Eye* and moves in the direction of Oppen's last collection of poems, *Primitive,* articulating more and more a sense of origins, both personal and universal but also poetic. These origins are substantiated in the increasing use of elemental natural forces such as water and light and wind, but also in the inner force personified most clearly in the Tiger's eye. Many of the phrases and ideas present in *Myth of the Blaze* are also woven into *Primitive,* for example, the "crystal center of the rock," the Tiger "burning," the poem gathering itself together from the lines written, and unfolding through images of spirals, opening hands, and the pull of a secret, elemental darkness. As Oppen draws nearer to the end of his life, combating an increasing forgetfulness and loosening grip on his memory (attributed to the onset of Altzheimer's disease), he looks back through his early experiences but also inward to the sources of his own poetic power, and draws on these for the writing of his later poems. Increasingly, the poetry becomes a kind of "writing on the wall" — enigmatic, prophetic in many ways for the generation of his time and those to come after, uncompromising, carved out of the stones of language to blaze into one's consciousness with a compelling force.

EIGHT
Primitive

Oppen's final collection of poems, *Primitive,* has evoked comments by several critics about the meaning of the title, and also about the use of gaps and disjointed syntax in this and other volumes. The poems in this slim volume, featuring a predominance of nouns and splintered phrases punctuated by those same gaps and spaces that appear in previous volumes, deconstruct syntax to the limits of coherence. John Taggart, in a book on contemporary poets, has explored the significance of these spaces within the body of Oppen's poetry, saying that they indicate "a further move toward the substantive, the atomization of facts' totality now laid down like the giant stones of Macchu Picchu, no mortar between them, only a few verbs of being remaining here and there."[1] The giant stones of Macchu Picchu are an apt image to apply to Oppen's poetry; both embody something elemental and primeval, hugely concrete and yet unfathomable. Further on in his book, in a chapter devoted primarily to Oppen's use of gaps and spaces, Taggart makes the following comments:

> They [the gaps] do provide us with temporary pauses, which make a counterpoint of silence against the opacity of words, the poem's words, a counterpoint against the pull of the poem's syntax. The gaps are gifts of silence in which we may go down, may go into the unspeakable foundations.[2]

This comment places Oppen's gaps within a conceptual framework; they appear in the poem not only to provide a punctuation of sorts (although many of them do function as such), but also to create wordless spaces which allow the reader's consciousness to filter down between the words and phrases and reach a place that cannot be defined in language, but which touches something deep within the human mind. Along the same lines, Taggart comments on the title of Oppen's last book:

> Not primitive as unskilled in the use of tools, but the *new* primitive; one who would ... come upon the universe as if for the first time, who would come to language and the writing of poems as if for the first time.[3]

Taggart's understanding of the term "primitive" (as applied to Oppen's last volume of poems) pertains not only to the discovery of an underlying substantiality of the world and our experience of it, but also to a willingness to penetrate language, to probe through and beyond it to that elemental space where poetry begins. These are the themes of *Primitive;* Oppen wishes to explore the fundamental core of human experience and poetic creativity, to suspend conscious reasoning in one's approach to both experience and the language of poetry in order to reveal the origins of experience and creativity, which lie deep in the unconscious, beyond the grasp of logic and linguistic expression.

The first poem in *Primitive* is called "A Political Poem." Oppen seems to be using the term "political" in its most universal sense here, relating to two of the most fundamental fears which society faces — isolation and loneliness — yet lacing them within a framework which grants them a certain power. However, his opening lines begin elsewhere, making a tentative reference to love: "for sometimes over the fields astride / of love?" Oppen uses this image as a possible starting-point from which to delve down into the unfathomable origins of experience and of creativity. The love image is a very concrete one — passion in a field, the physically sexual connotation of "astride"— but at the same time it represents one of the more fundamental and unfathomable human emotions. Love may be expressed in word and gesture, but it is ultimately beyond one's full understanding. It may be felt, but never completely enclosed in verbal definition. From this point the poem continues:

Eight: Primitive

> begin with
> nothing or
> everything   the nerve
> the thread
> reverberates
>
> in the unfinished voyage

The "unfinished voyage" seems to speak of our passage through life, beginning with birth (which traces back to an act of love) and shot through with a certain thread which connects and unites us with our personal origins. Love may also be an unfathomable state from which we can "begin with nothing or everything," whether it be human sexual love for one another or the aesthetic love of the artist for his craft. Much of Oppen's poetry, it can be seen, reflects a love and concern for humanity, evidenced in Oppen's own decision to leave off writing poetry in the 1930s in order to work with the unemployed, and perhaps as a result of (or as the original reason for) this action, Oppen is not indifferent to suffering; this makes itself clearly felt in his poetry. There is the "loneliness // of becalmed ships and the violent men and women of the cities' / doorsteps unexpected" which provides a transitional image, that of "becalmed ships," connecting the "unfinished voyage" (one's passage through life) with a scene from modern urban life, "the violent men and women of the cities' doorsteps." Both the "becalmed ships" and the "violent men and women" are images of isolation and loneliness, appearing as both cause (of modern urban violence) and effect (as in the case of the becalmed ships). From the image of modern urban violence Oppen traces back to the origins of all poetic images, through "this sad and hungry // wolf walks in my footprints fear fear" and then "birds, stones, and the sun-lit // earth turning, that great // loneliness all / or nothing / confronts us." We have come full circle, back to "all or nothing"; from the unfinished voyage, the becalmed ships and the violent men and women of the cities, the poet traces back through images of wolf and bird to the final elemental images of stone and planet turning in space. What unites them all is loneliness: the motionless, isolated ships, far from shore, the sad and lonely men and women in cities, the "sad and hungry wolf" and finally the planet turning in vast and empty space. Oppen associates the loneliness with fear, which he emphasizes by repeating the word "fear" twice at the end of the line "wolf walks in my footprints fear fear." Yet the image of the "sun-lit earth turning" seems to be a positive one, associated with light and returning us to "all or nothing"—that state of genesis which provides the poet with creative images and the connecting thread. It appears that the loneliness and fear derive not only from human isolation, but also from that point of genesis where love begins. Loneliness and fear then become essential elements of the creative mode, the loneliness and fear of the poet plumbing the depths of experience, for this reaching into elemental depths is an individual and solitary activity. What lies beyond surface reality and the poet's consciousness of it is the dark, unknown primitive place where poetic origins are to be found. The "sad and hungry wolf" has aroused fear because he dogs the poet's footsteps—he haunts the poet with a primal image. Yet this and other primal images become the stuff of the poem, and, embracing them all, the light of the "sun-lit earth turning" illuminates the poem as a whole. The "sun-lit earth" is a primary image because it is the source of the poem's light, but also because it is reminiscent of the Creation: "Let there be light." The last lines of the poem reinforce the Genesis motif:

> loneliness all
> or nothing
> confronts us
> the image
> the day
> dawns on the doorstep its sharpness
> dazes and nearly blinds us

Here we have the evening and the morning and, in a sense, the first day of Creation, as the earth turns away from the lonely dark into the light, and the day dawns, awakening us with its clarity. We awaken into the light, and this awakening dazzles and stuns us all: the men and women on the doorstep, the poet, and the reader who sees the poem coming into being.

Oppen uses only two gaps in the poem, and they come in the second and fourth lines: "of love?   Begin with // nothing or //everything   ";

Eight: Primitive

these two gaps separate out the phrase "begin with nothing or everything" from the rest of the poem, giving it visual emphasis. But they also signify the "nothing" and "everything" of the phrase they delineate: they are nothing because they are empty spaces, yet everything because they are the places where the unspoken significances of the poem can be expressed. These unspoken elements are also released through Oppen's disjointed syntax: for example, the word "astride" in the first line actually straddles the opening question, breaking up the phrase "sometimes over the fields of love" into two parts. In fact, the love image seems to span across the whole poem, providing a superstructure within which the loneliness and isolation of the poetic images take on a different shape.

The placing of the word "loneliness" in "the unfinished / voyage loneliness / of becalmed ships" seems also to be significant. The word "loneliness" syntactically belongs with the following line "of becalmed ships," but its placement alongside "voyage" links it also to our passage through life: loneliness accompanies us on the voyage of our experiences in life because we are ultimately individuals, each one experiencing life differently. Thus loneliness, like love, also spans the different dimensions of the poem; it is expressed in the images of alienation in city life and in the struggle of the poet to make the deep images reverberate through the poem. Since the word "loneliness" links both the previous and the following phrases, it also acts as a thread of sorts. As opposed to the linking of phrases provided by the word "loneliness," the phrases "the image" and "the day" are each given a line to themselves, preceded by "all / or nothing / confronts us," so that these are what confront us: the image and the day. The image conveys the elements of fear, loneliness and love, while the day brings its clear, sharp light which illuminates the other images of the poem, and our understanding of both the poem and the world we live in.

The structure of this poem divides into two: the only punctuation is a comma which comes after "and the sun-lit // earth turning," and before "that great loneliness." What comes before the comma is a piling up of image on image, all the concrete stuff of the poem, and what comes after is an articulation of their significance in the light of the dawning day. There is thus a division into two sections: a threading of all the images, and how the light dazzles them into being in the poem.

"Disasters" is another poem which begins in the turmoil of modern life, the disasters referring to war and political upheavals. This poem is an attempt by Oppen to express the need to uncover and thereby recover the unacknowledged elements of our world, those underlying elements which cannot be spoken of in everyday discourse because they are too primitive to find expression in words:

> of wars o western
> wind and storm
>
> of politics I am sick with a poet's
> vanity   legislators
>
> of the unacknowledged
>
> world *it is dreary*
> *to descend*
>
> *and be a stranger*

The phrases "o western wind" and "legislators of the unacknowledged world" refer to the poet Shelley, as Norman Finkelstein notes:

> "Disasters," for example, begins with a series of references to Shelley's poetry and prose, ... the "vanity" of the poet ... is appalled in the same way that Shelley's was when he wrote "Ode to the West Wind" following the agitation for social reform in England in 1819.[4]

Finkelstein believes that Oppen inverts Shelley's claim that "poets are the unacknowledged legislators of the world," changing it so that poets become "the legislators of the unacknowledged world" in order to express Oppen's own belief that "the world itself is no longer acknowledged; poets legislate a value system whose existence is no longer suspected; and the mode of discourse out of which Shelley was able to speak is no more."[5] However, there is another way to interpret "the unacknowledged world" as that primary sphere of existence where the undefined and ultimately indefinable belong, and which cannot be articulated in words. Oppen sees the poet's undertaking as an attempt to find expression and order for those unarticulated elements. It is not an easy task, and often turns the poet into a solitary, lonely figure: "*it is dreary / to descend // and be a stranger* how / shall we descend[.]" The poet must immerse himself in the strangeness of the experience, in a song where the established order no longer exists, but is replaced by an elemental flux; the poet is one of those "who have become strangers in this wind that / rises like a gift / in the disorder." The poet becomes a stranger, set apart and different from the everyday world. Yet the wind is a "gift"; it is the element which uncovers, or discovers the underlying core. Then:

> the song
> changes the wind has blown the sand about
> and we are alone the sea dawns
> in the sunrise verse with its rough
> beach-light crystal extreme

Now the song changes; it is no longer dreary, but becomes a "sunrise verse," rising out of the wind-blown sand. The phrase "sunrise verse" encapsulates an image of the poem rising up out of the elemental flux, but also an image of beginnings, as the sun comes up over the sea at the beginning of the day. "Beach-light crystal" is an amalgamation of several of Oppen's recurring figurations: the sea, the light and the cluster of the crystal. These images embody all that is primary and essential in Oppen's poetry, born out of the basic stuff of life:

> sands dazzling under the near
> and not less brutal feet journey
> in light
>
> and wind
> and fire and water and air *the five*
>
> *bright elements*
> the marvel
>
> of the obvious and the marvel
> of the hidden is there

Here is the journey of the poet, through the shift of sand to the heart of all human and poetic experience, wherein lies "the marvel of the obvious and the marvel of the hidden," the acknowledged and the unacknowledged world. This is where all meaning dances, whether through images such as "wasp wings" or through the "mother-tongues" which may refer to one's native language, but may also refer to a primary generic language which gives rise to poetry:

> in fact a distinction dance
> of the wasp wings dance as
> of the mother tongues

At this point a personal vision intrudes, leading Oppen to muse on his own individual and historical origins, and on the solitariness of his Jewish forefathers who wandered the desert:

> O
>
> *O I see my love I see her go*
>
> *Over the ice alone* I see
>
> myself   Sarah   Sarah I see the tent in the desert my life
> narrows my life
> is another

Oppen sees his life receding back into the origins of his people (again, as in "Semite," the sense of funneling back to a point of origin), but links this to the theme of the poem, the uncovering of the hidden or unacknowledged, by emphasizing the nomadic life of the Jewish tribes who lived in caves and were therefore "hidden":

> my young
> brother he is my lost sister her small
> voice among the people the salt
> and terrible hills whose armies
> have marched and the caves
> of the hidden
> people

Thus the poem expresses the "small voice" with its echoes of the "still small voice" of the burning bush in the Bible, exposing the unacknowledged, bringing to the surface the hidden origins from which everything derives, whether it be the genesis of poetic creativity or the undisclosed heart of human experience, and all evolving, fluting upwards and outwards from the single word "people."

Eight: Primitive

Oppen's manipulation of syntax works in this poem, as in others, to disclose underlying elements. The unusual structure of the syntactical units in "he is clumsy and alone my young brother he is my lost sister" welds together brother and sister, turning male into female in a common evolutionary chain leading down through history to Oppen's own present. The final phrase "and the caves of the hidden people" is fractured into three progressively shorter lines, the last line being the single word "people," which chronicles visually not only the singularity of the ancient Jewish people, but also the tapering down to a point of origin. Throughout the poem there are further examples of seemingly jumbled syntax: "in fact a distinction dance // of the wasp wings dance as / of the mother-tongues" and "sands dazzling under the near / and not less brutal   feet journey / in light"; these jumbled phrases may be seen as the "sand" of the poem, stirred up and blown about by the "wind" of the poetic energies, in order to expose the "sunrise verse" in the lines: "the wind has blown the sand about / and we are alone the sea dawns / in the sunrise verse...." And so the whole poem becomes a stirring-up of the familiar, the acknowledged, in order to reveal the strange, the unacknowledged, the essential and primary dimension.

In "The Poem," Oppen describes the process of writing and how poetry emerges into language. This is a self-reflexive piece of work, in which the last line refers to the poem's own "becoming." The rest of the poem leads up to this moment as Oppen synthesizes the elements that make up the poem, while at the same time fracturing the line-by-line structure of the poem into fragments of signification which often run from one line to the next with mid-line breaks. The poem begins:

> how shall I light
> this room that measures years
> and years not miracles nor were we
> judged but a direction
> of things in us burning burning

"This room" may be understood as the structure within which the poem takes shape, and in which all the poet's past experiences and hard work are enclosed. This is where the "direction of things" takes place: a process likened to a burning wind that is both external to and internal in the poet, driving him like a ship towards his goal, which is the completion of the poem. Oppen once again employs the metaphor of a ship sailing, to convey the unfolding of the poem:

> burning burning for we are
> still nor is the place a wind
> utterly outside ourselves and yet it is
> unknown and all the sails full to the last
>
> rag of the topgallant, royal
> tops'l, the last rays
> at the mast-heads

The juxtaposition of the word "still" with the words "burning" and "wind" is reminiscent, once again, of the "still small voice" in the Biblical burning bush, an elemental scene of fire and wind which may be interpreted as the inspiration for the poem, its poetic beginnings. This elemental wind, at once familiar and strange, then becomes the wind that drives the ship at sea, and that also propels the poem along, redeeming both ordinary lives and that of the poet:

> to save the commonplace save myself Tyger
> Tyger still burning in me burning
> in the night sky burning
> in us the light

Oppen returns here to the image of Blake's Tyger, which he introduced into the poem "Myth of the Blaze." In that poem the Tyger functions to represent the sudden and heart-stopping confrontation with an elemental experience, beyond thought or word but deeply felt; here the burning drive within the poet is compared to the awe-inspiring power of Blake's Tyger (also a poem about creativity and the imagination); it flares outward into the night sky, where it becomes a light which illuminates the room where the poem begins:

> burning
> in us the light
> in the room it was all

Eight: Primitive

>part of the wars
>of things brilliance
>of things

Oppen's hallmark — emphasizing the substantiality, the concreteness of things — is apparent in these lines; "things" war against each other, scintillate, form the solid units out of which poems are constructed: in this poem, the sails, the "royal tops'l," the rags at the mast-head. These objects are tossed about in the "appalling seas" (another elemental image) which throw up the poem:

>in the appalling
>seas language
>lives and wakes us together
>out of sleep the poem
>opens its dazzling whispering hands

In these final lines of the poem everything comes together; language comes alive and wakens us into awareness, as the poem emerges with its "dazzling whispering hands," which connect back to the bright light ("dazzling") and "still small voice" ("whispering") of the burning bush image. The phrase "dazzling whispering hands" is particularly interesting. By giving the poem "hands," Oppen turns the poetic art into something physical and concrete and not just an abstract activity of the mind; one's hands are those parts of the body used in physical crafts such as sculpture and (particularly pertinent to Oppen) carpentry, and so the poem becomes tangible, solid, *concrete*. In addition, the poem's "hands" are both "dazzling" and "whispering," and therefore appeal to one's different senses, both visual and auditory. Oppen therefore takes the "abstract" poem — abstract in the sense that reading and writing poetry are intellectual, cerebral activities, taking place in the sphere of the mind and of language, the sphere of signs that replace the concrete thing they represent — and turns it into something almost physical, to be felt, to be touched and to be sensed at a more fundamental and visceral level than the abstractions of language can ever provide.

Oppen uses only two units of punctuation throughout this whole poem, and they are the commas which separate the concrete "things" of the poem: "full to the last rag of the topgallant, royal tops'l, the least rags." The commas separate the concrete images of sail and mast, giving them an individuality in the poem. Other than these commas, the poem has no punctuation at all, so that it drives itself forward like the ship driven by the wind, phrases running into each other like the high waves on the sea. But the lack of punctuation also allows for a variety of interpretation, as some of the words may shift into different units of significance. For example, in the lines "in the night sky burning / in us the light // in the room" the phrasing may take the form of "in the night sky burning" and "in us the light of the room," or alternatively the word may be divided into "in the night sky," "burning in us," "the light" and "in the room it was all." These different arrangements of the words allow for a multiplicity of interpretations, while at the same time linking the idea of the burning illumination, the "us" of the poem and the "room" where it all takes place; we are situated here in a world below ordinary cognition. This kind of syntactic double-flow or ambiguity is also suggestive of water, characterized by fluidity, waves (rather than particles) of meaning. Or to use the metaphors of fire and light, the poem throws out various sparks of meaning, all of which add scintillation to the poem as a whole, and cause it to "dazzle."

One of Oppen's own private memories provides an originary experience which sets in motion the poem "If It All Went Up in Smoke." The "smoke" of the title is reminiscent of the fog described in one of Oppen's earlier poems, "The Forms of Love," from *This in Which,* where he describes an incident involving himself and Mary, who later became his wife:

> We groped
> Our way downhill
> Downhill in the bright
> Incredible light
>
> Beginning to wonder
> Whether it could be lake
> Or fog
> We saw...

Norman Finkelstein tells us that this poem, together with "If It All Went Up In Smoke" and a similar poem "The Natural" (also in *Primitive*) makes

Eight: Primitive

reference to Oppen's first meeting with Mary, a meeting which obviously left a tremendous impact on Oppen; Finkelstein goes on to comment that the fog of that night remained as an indelible image in Oppen's mind and informed much of his poetry.[6] The "light of the fog" that Finkelstein describes becomes the light and smoke of "If It All Went Up in Smoke":

> *that smoke*
> *would remain*
> the forever
> savage country poem's light borrowed
> light of the landscape and one's footprints praise
> from distance
> in the close
> crowd all
> that is strange...

In these opening lines, the "forever savage country" is juxtaposed in the same line with "poem's light borrowed," so that the savage landscape — savage in the sense of primary and pre-civilized — gives off a light which the poem takes on as its own. This savage country is both physical and external (the scene of George and Mary's first meeting), but is also an inner landscape of the poet's, made up of a deeply evoked memory and underlying emotions of desire and need. Thus the root of the poem is embedded in the evoked landscape, and the poet imprints himself on that landscape with his "footprints," revering it as both an external landscape with its light and fog or smoke, but also as an inner source of poetic power, "in the close crowd." Its strangeness and mystery generate the beginnings of the poem:

> all
> that is strange the sources
> the wells the poem begins
> neither in word
> nor meaning but the small
> selves haunting
> us in the stones and is less
> always than that

George Oppen

Oppen attributes the beginnings of the poem to "the small / selves haunting // us in the stones," to some essential sub-verbal self which exists in an inner primal landscape defined not by words but by stones. This self is an elemental, unformed entity, rather like Lacan's "homelette," an invented word blending "homme" and "omelette" to describe the young infant whose identity has not yet been shaped; here is a haunting sense of what once was and can still be evoked but only partially embodied in language, although it can be represented in images of stone and grass:

> help me I am
> of that people the grass
> blades touch
> and touch in these small
> distances the poem
> begins

Oppen is of "that people" — those (poets) who draw on deeply personal sources, the grass roots, to find their poetry. The poem begins in those moments of time, those inner landscapes of memory, sensed but not altogether explicable in language because they belong in a sub-verbal realm, but which are nevertheless as tangible in their way as the small, fragile blades of grass. Oppen represents this ultimately indefinable but essential experience through concrete images of stone and grass, those small nouns that have their own inviolate identity and presence, images of primary matter creating a physical landscape which evokes an inner personal and poetic landscape.

As in most of his poems, Oppen dislocates syntax into individual fragmented phrases and words, piling them up in this poem like the stones he evokes. The fourth line, for example, is composed of four individual nouns — those most concrete units of language — and an adjective, which together make up the essence of the poem: "savage country poem's light borrowed." Towards the end of the poem the lines read: "the grass // blades touch // and touch," giving the words "blades touch" a line of their own, so that there is a visual reinforcement of the ideas expressed: the two words side by side, together in one space, touching on each other. And the last line is composed of the single word "begins," following lines of three and five words, so that there is a visual reduction of words and the poem ends in a point of genesis, a "beginning." Linking this up with the first line, "the forever," we have a sense of the timelessness of certain moments and memories which fuel poetic beginnings, as is the case in this poem.

Many of the lines in the poem juxtapose words which have no natural syntactic connection, but which create a strange poetic fusion that empowers the poem as a whole. For example, the line "that is strange the sources" joins "strange" and "sources" to produce the mystery of that first encounter between Oppen and Mary, and also the mysterious power of poetic origins. Another example, appearing in the line "of that people the grass," produces a bond between "that people" — perhaps Oppen's Jewish origins, perhaps the community of poets — and that most common, down-to-earth form of simple plant life, the grass. Finally, the second-last line reads "distances the poem," raising the possibility of understanding "distances" not only as a noun but also as a verb, and thus placing the poem and its sources far back in the past and deep beyond the conscious mind, yet evoked in the here and now. There is also a sense, in this poem, of an Eliadean "illud tempus," a going back to origins (here, the origins of Oppen's personal relationship with his wife Mary) that have become somehow sacred, because they contain a spiritual or psychological significance which enhances the present of those re-enacting the original scene, whether physically or through memory.

Several of the poems in *Primitive* employ elemental forces — the sea, the wind — which "fling up" the essence of the poem. "The Tongues" is an example of such a poem. Here, the leading image is of a whirlwind which tosses the poem into being, stirring up a strange poetic language. The first line — "of appearances" — echoes the quote from Heidegger which prefaces *This in Which:* "the arduous path of appearance." This expression defines Oppen's ever-present poetic struggle: to bring to the surface of one's consciousness, through concrete images, those underlying elements of poetry which are inchoate and ultimately indefinable. The poem is a short one:

George Oppen

> of appearance
> speak in the unchosen
> journey immense
> journey there is loss in denying
> that force the moment the years
> even of death lost
> in denying
> that force   the words
> out of that whirlwind his
> and not his strange
> words surround him

Oppen speaks here of poetry as a strange, mystic force arising out of a stirring wind which whirls the poetic elements into intelligible language: it is a poem about expressing the inexplicable and inexpressible. For Oppen, the poet's journey is "unchosen"; the poetic force cannot be withstood or denied, for to deny it is to deny the stuff of experience garnered in the moments and years of time; it is to deny one's mortality: "death lost / in denying / that force." It may look as though these lines mean that death is lost (and therefore life gained) in denying the force of poetry; but if we examine this phrase within the context of the previous lines, we find Oppen saying that there is loss in denying the poetic force which derives from the moments and years and indeed mortality (symbolized by death) of our existence. Thus the poetic force arises out of lived experience, which is mortal; immortality would weaken the impact of experience lived within the confines of temporality and the immediacy which that temporality imposes. Oppen is most definitely a poet "of this world," as is illustrated by the concrete images and social concerns given expression in his poetry. To accept the poetic force means immersion in an elemental state of flux, and in a strange and powerful language which is "his and not his." This phrase "his and not his" may relate to the words or to "that whirlwind"; either way, the poet is taken over by a mystic force which drives the poem out of him, as it fluctuates through strange forms of expression — semiotic undercurrents? dream language? — until it breaks through into the words on the page.

Once again, Oppen's syntax and line forms are disjointed and fractured in this poem. Bursts of language unlinked by connectors follow on each other, as if the phrases themselves had been whirled around by the strange wind and set down in a heap. This seemingly random juxtaposition of words creates different possible fusions; an instance of this can be found in the lines "there is loss in denying / that force the moment the years / even of death lost / in denying that force," where the word "lost" may refer back only to the word "death," but can also encompass "the moments the years" which precede it. Also the line "that force the moments the years," if taken as a separate unit of significance, allows the reader to interpret the word "force" as a verb, thus implying that the poem is squeezed out of the poet's personal experiences as lived through time. In addition, Oppen's intuitive use of the line and line-breaks, which often produce surprise and ambiguity, multiplies possibilities of meaning. It also slows down the reading, fixes our attention on separate, discrete elements, so that lines and phrases become physical objects, things.

The single gap in this poem comes after the words "that force" and before "the words," to emphasize the break between the deep elemental forces which stir up the poem, and the modes of expression through which they are conveyed. But the gap also highlights the loss, the vacant space, implicit in denying the poetic force. Thus it serves two functions: it creates a conceptual pause, and it acts as a visual reinforcement of what is being said in the poem. We are also reminded, again, of Roland Barthes' concept of jouissance, that startling jolt to one's senses which is erotic both physically and mentally, and which is created by a sudden break or gap in the text where sub-verbal forces burst through and flood our conscious thought. Here, in addition to the sense of a break or a vacant space, the gap may function as a poetic space where "that force"—the whirlwind energies of the poem—can break through to sweep into the reader's mind.

In "Populist," Oppen once more touches on the tongues of poetry and of communication in general, this time representing them through the "blind word" and the speech of "magic infants." Richard Peaver has declared that "[b]efore it is speech, poetry is a place prepared for speech."[7] Oppen is constantly exploring this "place" in his poetry, populating it with primitive and primal elements which are sub-verbal and which therefore must find other modes of expression in order to communicate themselves to the reader. The gaps, the apparently jumbled syntax, the aura of presence which he attaches to the small, concrete nouns: all these convey tones, rhythms and undercurrents quite separate from the actual language of the poem. "Populist" makes use of the images of the "blind word" and the "magic infants" to point to a form of communication which goes beyond the simply verbal.

"Populist," although regarded by those critics who have written about it as a political statement of sorts, seems to go beyond politics to champion and empower simple lives and highlight primal landscapes, paring social existence down to an essential state divested of civilization. The poem is a tracing back through cities of steel and busy highways to the underlying essentials of life, those sources of energy that both revitalize existence and also fuel the poetic drive. These energies are pre-verbal and unarticulated in ordinary speech; they find a voice through the "magic infants" and in the "blind words" of poetry. The infants (reminiscent of the biblical phrase from Psalms, "out of the mouths of babes and sucklings hast thou founded strength") represent human life in its most elementary stage of linguistic development, when communication is made not through recognizable language but through a more basic and linguistically undefined set of sounds. "Blind" words are those patterns of communication that cannot be "seen"; they rely on a deeper, sub-verbal form of expression. The opening lines of the poem juxtapose the cities with the elemental things of our world:

> I dreamed myself of their people, I am of their people
> I thought they watched me that I watched them
> that they
>
> watched the sun and the clouds for the cities
> are no longer mine   image   images
>
> of existence   (or song
>
> of myself?)

Here Oppen aligns himself with simple humanity, the common people who turn away from the cities, towards the sun and the clouds, looking to the sky, in a sense like the first primitive peoples who saw in nature

Eight: Primitive

the imprint of a great and elemental power. Perhaps Oppen is thinking here of his own Jewish people, who roamed the desert and lived as simple nomads after the Exodus from Egypt. Oppen's questioning reference to Walt Whitman's "Song of Myself" implies a habit he shares with Whitman, who reads himself into others and others into himself. Whitman's "Song of Myself" from his collection *Leaves of Grass* is consequently and simultaneously a song of everyone. In addition, Oppen seems to share Whitman's outlook that the poet's text is at best only an attempt to capture in words those images in nature that arouse awe and wonder by the power of their elemental presence; the natural world embodies an energy beyond even the speech of the poet. The following lines from Whitman's poem illustrate this power:

> Do you take it I would astonish?
> Does the daylight astonish? or the early redstart twittering through the woods?
> Do I astonish more than they?
> This hour I tell things in confidence,
> I might not tell everybody but I will tell you.

There is, in Whitman's poem as in Oppen's, a direct appeal, a personal communication which strives against the paradox of mass isolation in Oppen's cities; Oppen is particularly sensitive, in the poems of *Primitive,* to the loss of individuality inherent in the sweep and crush of fast-paced modern living, the stamping out of the simple and primitive in humanity. Oppen struggles in his poetry to restore something of the basic energies of life, to put people back in touch with stone and sea and sky, and so strengthen an unspoken bond that has been lost. He sometimes seems dubious about his power to do this through the words of his poems (as is Whitman), articulating his fear about exposing himself and his text:

> tho if I stumble on a rock I speak
> of rock if I am to say   anything   anything
> if I am to tell of myself   splendor
> of the roads   secrecy

> of paths for a word like glass
> sphere encloses
> the word opening
> and opening
> myself and I am sick
> for a moment
> with fear let the magic
> infants speak

Here, as elsewhere in Oppen's poetry, we have an example of a thin, column-like poem, where Oppen isolates a word or short phrase in each line, thus turning words and phrases into objects, concretizing and objectifying language. The poem, then, is composed of building-blocks of words, structured like a monument or monolith, each individual stone a word or short phrase.

The fear that Oppen speaks of in this poem (and that he tries to dispel by invoking the "magic infants") is double-edged; it is the fear of exposing himself in his poetry, but at the same time it speaks of words as imprisoned within themselves, and therefore impotent to convey what he wants to say. Instead, he calls on the "magic infants" and later on, the "blind word" to communicate what essentially escapes language but can bind people together:

> we who have brought steel
> and stone again
> and again
> into the cities in that word blind
> word must speak
> and speak the magic
> infants' speech

The "blind word" is an interesting phrase, since it implies both an attitude to words and also something about the nature of words themselves; it is the unseen word, but also the unformed, groping word — the raw speech underlying "finished" discourse. Oppen's invoking of an unformed, more elemental means of communication finds a parallel in the natural landscape; he goes on to talk of

Eight: Primitive

> ... the sunrise the lapping
> of shallow
> waters tongues
> of the inlets glisten
> like fur in the low tides

Using the word "tongues" to describe the inlets of the sea conjures up a picture of the narrow rivulets of water, but may also imply the way the sea "speaks" to us; the poem continues:

> all that
> childhood envied the sounds
> of the ocean
> over the flatlands poems piers foolhardy
> structures

Here, the poem is constructed as a "foolhardy structure," shored like the piers against the elemental power of the sea. The poet in his poem must grapple with that elemental power, harness it to empower the words of the poem. Children, envying "the sounds of the ocean," seem intrinsically to understand the elemental power of the sunrise, and of the sea, and of the wind in the last section of the poem, which appears to deal with elemental images and how they furnish the poem with an essential foundation upon and through which the poem may speak:

> and the lives the ingenious
> lives the winds
>
> squall from the grazing
> ranches' wandering
> fences young workmen's
>
> loneliness on the structures has touched
> and touched the heavy tools   tools
> in our hands in the clamorous
> country birth-
> light savage
>
> lights of the landscape magic
> page the magic
> infants speak

In this last part of the poem, the loneliness of workers building their fences and hefting their tools turns into the sort of experience they share with the poet; their simple lives and simple crafts are equated with the poet's craft as workmen employ basic materials (wood and stone) and the poet, basic images (sun, sea, cloud, "savage light") to fashion the structure of their lives, or in the case of the poet, the structure of the poem. The "birth-light" (perhaps a play on "birthright"?) and "savage light" embody a generic source of energy, something primal and powerful which fuels both human existence and the creation of the poem. Thus, again reminiscent of Whitman, both the simple people and the poet find expression of their lives and work; both are joined in a common experience that draws on fundamental, "primitive" materials to convey their essential selves.

Most of the spaces in "Populist" appear beside repeated words, which they throw into relief: "No longer mine image images" or "if I am to say anything anything" and towards the end of the poem, "and touched the heavy tools tools." These spaces cause the reader to pause in the reading of the poem and to consider the significance of the repeated words — a kind of readerly "double-take." One possible way to interpret the repetition of words is that they refer to the different levels at work in the poem. There are the images of the city — the concrete images such as the rear-view mirror — and also the elemental images of sea and sun which propel the poem; there are the workmen's tools and the poetic tools; and there is the "anything" to be said, which may lie both in the concrete words and also in the underlying and unspoken wonder evoked by the primal landscape.

Oppen's line-breaks in this poem are, as always, interesting; the two main images of "speaking" — the "blind word" and the speech of the "magic infants" — are systematically fractured into two lines, so that the adjectives "blind" and "magic" conclude the lines in which they appear, thus placing visual emphasis on these words. "Blind" and "magic" embody the non-visual element and the awe-inspiring power around which the poem functions, for Oppen wishes to delve beyond appearances to the primary energies of the natural world which encircle us all.

"Strange Are the Products" also compares the alienation inherent in

Eight: Primitive

city life with the mystical primitiveness of All Hallows' Eve. This poem sets the precise but meaningless design of commercial urban planning and the "anger of the streets" against love and joy experienced in the mystical dark of Hallowe'en. Oppen moves from the two-dimensional circle on the drawing-board to the isolated pinpoints of humanity on city streets:

> of draftsmanship   zero
> that perfect
> circle
> of distances terrible
> path
> thru the airs small very
> small alien
> on the sidewalks

and goes on to talk about the "anger of the streets" which lead only to other streets, streets which are "brutal pitifully brutal" and "swaggering." There is a flat emptiness to these descriptions, but also a great anger at the indifference and cruelty of city life. Contrasted with this is the mystical, glorious dark of All Hallows' Eve, the great unbounded joy and love and communion in the celebration of an almost pagan, primeval experience which the poet feels both in the huge dark around him, but also in the small bones of his skull, deep inside his head at some primary sub-verbal level:

> All
> hallows Eve more
> beautiful most
> beautiful found
> here saturnalia the poem
> of the woman the man our dark
> skull bones' joy in the small
> huge dark the
> glory of joy in the small
> huge dark

This poem is constructed very carefully around the contrasts of flat drawing-board circle and round living bones of the skull (which encloses one's deepest and most primary experiences in the mind), anger in the streets and love in the primitive dark of Hallowe'en, the "small alien on the sidewalk" and the glorious joy in the "small huge dark." Oppen's love for concrete elemental images evidences itself in the "dark skull bones' joy." Like the mystic awe of watching the deer in "Psalm," this mystic experience is also captured in the concrete details of bone and skull, as Oppen chooses the basic and essential human framework—the skeleton—to represent the primary and elemental experience of communion in the dark, out of which "the poem of the man the woman" will grow.

Oppen's odd juxtaposition of phrases, his violation of syntactical rules, takes on a strange pertinence in this account of the almost-sacred dark of All Hallows Eve, a time of liminality, the crossing of thresholds and the breaking of ordinary social norms and boundaries. Linguistic frames of reference are fractured in this poem to give a sense of the burst of mystic joy and glory which radiates through poet and poem; the lines invite continuation from one to the next, so that we experience them as a tumble of words like "most beautiful found here the saturnalia the poem of the woman the man" to give a sense of the outpouring of emotion that Oppen feels. This tumble of words has an erotic feel to it, a Barthes-like sense of jouissance as the words spill themselves on the page and swamp the reader in a flood of sensuality. Thus the oddity of Oppen's poetic language becomes strangely appropriate in this case to the context and content of the poem. At the same time, the physical line-breaks act as arbitrary interruptions, preventing the tumble of words and so inviting stasis as well as fluidity. This contradiction, not quite resolved in the poem, may reflect a split (conscious or unconscious) in Oppen's approach to the material of this particular poem: the need for a flow or tumble of language—to reinforce the content of the poem—working against Oppen's view of individual words as discrete units, the building blocks of language.

"Neighbors," the second-last poem in *Primitive,* deals with two kinds of communication: social and poetic. The poem is constructed around what to say and how to say it, both within the framework of social discourse—the poet and his neighbor—and in the poetic sense—how the poem "speaks." The first section of the poem leads from a scene with the next-door neighbor to an attempt to define the voice of the poem as it unfolds itself in the poet's mind while he is talking to his neighbor:

>   the neighbor the actual neighbor we are even friendly
> in a way and I don't know what I am doing
> here there is more
> to wake to
> than these old boards these many
> boards and the voice of the poem a wandering
> foreigner more strange
> and brilliant
> than the moon's   light the true
> native opening
> the nooks and the corners and the great
> spaces clear
> fields of her hands we
> not poets only
> waking are all in her hands

For Oppen, capturing the poem's essential qualities is as difficult as pinning down moonlight; as opposed to the awkwardness of *what* to say to the neighbor, the poet's difficulty with the poem is *how* to say it: the poem "wanders," casts a shimmering light that is as elusive as moonlight, shining into corners, illuminating spaces. Poet and neighbor are both held in that light — the neighbor physically, the poet metaphorically.

The second section of the poem talks about the difficulties of articulating the truth of the poem (and so of experience itself); not that the truth cannot be glimpsed or fleetingly experienced, but that the pinning it down in words involves a tremendous struggle:

>   shall we
> say more
> than this I can
> say more there it
> is I can
> say more we have hardly begun
> to speak walk the round
> earth for dark
> truths and blazing

George Oppen

truths are the same they
move waver almost
stand in my
mind continually
in our
dreams like the shadows
of water
moving if
in time we see
the words fail this
we know this
we walk in and is all
we know we
will speak

to each
other we
will speak

This closing section begins with an ambiguous question and statement: "shall we say more than this" and is followed by "I can say more." The first pronoun "we" intimates that this is a reference to the social contact between poet and neighbor (whether or not the conversation between them will develop), whereas the second pronoun "I" indicates the poetic context of what the poet can say in the context of the poem. There are deep, surging truths to be told, bound up in primary metaphors of moonlight, water and shadow; like the shimmering of moonlight and the glint and shadow of water, these truths are elusive; words are inadequate to incorporate them. The poet's attempt to capture these "dark" and "blazing" truths (which are ineffable and yet scintillate, shimmering, across our minds) creates a strange and brilliant poem, its language glinting like light on water.

The enigmatic language of "Neighbors"—words and phrases slotted into each other, ideas sliding into other ideas—creates a dream-like poem, in which meaning glances off the phrases glint by glint, sliver by sliver, making it difficult to comprehend from one line to the next. The poem has to be grasped as a shimmering whole, the truth of what is being said embodied in the light and dark of the images. The repetition of the last lines "we / will speak / to each / other we / will speak" brings together the social and the poetic context of the poem: it will all come together, communication will be made, both between the poet and his neighbor and also from poet to reader through the poem. Although one might read the curtailment of the last line — the omission of "to each other" — to suggest a loss of certainty that speech will be communicative, and perhaps to imply that it is no longer clear that they will speak to each other, the last word in this poem is nevertheless "speak." Thus the final emphasis in the poem is on the speaking, the expression of the self, one's voice, whether it be social or poetic.

"Till Other Voices Wake Us," the closing poem in *Primitive,* and Oppen's last published poem, provide a fitting closure to his body of poetry, as it comes full circle: in this poem, Oppen reminisces about the writing of his first collection of poems, *Discrete Series.* As do several of Oppen's other later poems, the opening of this poem makes reference to a flight backwards in time:

> the generations
>
> and the solace
>
> of flight memory
>
> of adolescence with my father

The poem, however, explores not only Oppen's personal past, but also the delving down into a fundamental place of origins, like Yeats' "The Circus Animals' Desertion," where poetry begins. The reference to *Discrete Series* is a way to combine both the temporal past of the poet and the timeless poetic origins:

> and writing
> thru the night
> (a young man,
> Brooklyn, 1929) I named the book
> series empirical
> series all force
> in events the imagined
> lights have entered

George Oppen

>   us it is a music more powerful
>   than music
>   till other voices wake
>   us or we drown

Much of Oppen's poetry derives from past events in his life, each of which has its own energy or light, not always fully understood or articulated, but all of which have tremendously affected his poetry, each providing its own illumination. Oppen sees himself as an accumulation of these pinpoints of light, which have penetrated his consciousness in that deep fundamental place of poetic genesis which generates the music of experience and of language. In this last poem, Oppen is paying tribute to those deep primary sources of personal and poetic experience, represented in his poetry as elemental metaphors of light and water and crystal rock, which generate the poem and its "music more powerful than music."

Oppen's rearrangement of the closing lines of T.S. Eliot's "Prufrock" ("till human voices wake us, and we drown") radically changes the meaning. Oppen's line reads "till other voices wake us or we drown" and it may be that here he is drawing our attention to what he called "the greatest mysteries" of the little words like "and," for in this case the replacement of the word "and" by "or" is what makes Oppen's line completely different in meaning from Eliot's original one. Oppen's phrase juxtaposes the conscious, waking world of the poetic voice and all its tones, inflections, rhythms and pauses, with the powerful unconscious which it articulates, where one drowns oneself in memory and the music of poetry, an immersion into a sub-verbal flow at the heart of all experience. This is where Oppen's "arduous path of appearance" begins — the long struggle to bring the powerful presence of things and events up into the conscious language of the poem, through the dislocated syntax, the gaps, the elemental metaphors and the strange juxtapositions. What Oppen does in his poetry is to describe the poetic process and its realization in the finished poem, coming up from the deep sub-verbal regions into the light of day and the poem itself, so that, in the words of Maritain, which preface Oppen's *The Materials,* "We awake in the same moment to ourselves and to things."

NINE
Recurring Threads

On reading through the range of Oppen's work, one finds not only recurring symbols, themes and influences, but also the recurrence of specific phrases and concrete images. Many of these — for example, "the bright light of shipwreck" (poems number nine and nineteen in *Of Being Numerous,* "Two Romance Poems" from *Myth of the Blaze*), "the narrow end of the funnel" ("Myth of the Blaze" and "Semite"), "the grass blades touch" ("If It All Went Up in Smoke" and "The Natural") and "the grass blades hide" ("The Occurrences") — provide pivotal ideas in the poems; they are like the bones of Oppen's body of work on which he hangs the flesh of the poem, lodged in his poetic consciousness and perhaps in his subconscious. They share an elemental quality, rooting the poems in which they appear like an anchor securing a ship at sea or in the harbor, or like a lightning conductor which grounds electrical energy. In particular, the idea of shipwreck appears to absorb Oppen's attention, making its way into several of the poems in *Of Being Numerous,* but also in "Two Romance Poems." Its appeal may lie in the way it harnesses together the concepts of man's helplessness against the furies of the natural elements and his inability to navigate a clear course through the complexities of modern urban life; but it evidently fascinates Oppen in other ways as well, since he couples it with a "bright light." There is warning here, like the beam of a lighthouse, but also a strange beauty; Oppen's fascination with shipwreck may be embedded in its disintegration, its breaking down of structured entities into the basic material from which they were originally structured. Much of Oppen's poetry does just this, breaking apart the mindless accepted norms of modern society and exposing their inability to guide us truly through the maze of urban civilization, as well as breaking down syntax, formal line-breaks and conventional phrases to reveal their underlying elements and release fundamental poetic energies.

    The constant re-emergence in various poems of other words and phrases, such as "grass blades," "funnel" and "crystal," bear out Oppen's preoccupation with the fundamental, the pinpointing of one's attention on what lies beyond and below the surface, the employment of a poetic microscope of sorts. Roots and blades of grass, the roots of plants, appear in several of the poems from *This in Which,* as well as in "The Occurrences," reinforcing the reader's sense that Oppen's poetic camera, or microscope, has zoomed in on the most minute and most particular of elements in the natural world, each leaf and stalk outlined sharply, each individual component standing out for a moment in the greater landscape of field and hill and garden. It is interesting to note how many poets have focused on grass in their poems: Walt Whitman's *Leaves of Grass,* Dylan Thomas's "The Force That Drives the Green Fuse Through the Flower" and of course Carl Sandburg's well-known war poem, "Grass." Oppen's predilection for the little words, the basic bones of language, is paralleled in his picking out of the little things of nature, so that the reader may see and feel the green of the grass blades and the damp feel of the plant threads in the earth: here is a reduction of the great flux of life, a reminder to us to look more closely and carefully, as we go about in the world of modern culture with our unseeing and unthinking attitude to the wonders around us, and towards our everyday use of language. Paul Auster calls this the "primal act of seeing": "The locus is always the natural world, and the process is one that originates in the perception of objects beyond ourselves, in the primal act of seeing."[1] In drawing our attention to the small details — of the natural landscape and of language — Oppen insists that we stop for a moment, tugging at our sleeve and forcing us to take note, to really see and feel and experience at ground level, where everything originates. This is what Auster means when he speaks of "primal seeing" — not only noticing more carefully and experiencing more viscerally those elements of our surroundings, but seeing them as if for the first time.

Nine: Recurring Threads

In a similar vein, Oppen returns several times, in poems from *This in Which,* and in *Primitive,* to the image of hands, which he couples with the idea of the emerging poem. Phrases such as "the poem / opens its dazzling whispering hands" ("The Poem," from *Primitive*), and "fields of her hands," "all / are in her hands" ("Neighbors," also from *Primitive*) — the latter, apparently, referring to the "voice of the poem" — concretize the poem, make it tangible to one's senses, turning the abstract concept into an almost physical entity to be grasped, something the reader can almost feel the contours of. Oppen would always want his body of readers to sidestep the empty realms of language and the windy plains of abstract thought, to come to grips with the *this* of the poem, to touch the phrases and feel them on their tongue, to see, to hear, to feel. His poetry has a hard visual and auditory edge to it, a concreteness, a paring-down to essentials.

This sense of paring-down is echoed in Oppen's linguistic reductions of words like "though" and "through," which he consistently chooses to write as "tho" and "thru." Whether this is deliberate or not on Oppen's part, it conveys the idea of a minimalizing of language, a spareness in his attitude to words; since he cannot write poetry without using words at all, he must choose language as the medium of his art, but always prefers the small, the short, the most concise. As has been noted throughout this analysis of Oppen's work, there is no excess and no superfluity in his writing: his is a spare, lean style, using primarily nouns and essential verbs, the small words he likes, the simple, concrete image and the almost total lack of complex figures of speech such as metaphor or allegory. Or as Michael Palmer puts it:

> By speaking against literary contrivance, Oppen argues both for the possibility, or necessity, of an immediacy of poetic engagement or intervention, and against the "poetic," that is against the devices of a passive and acculturated representation.[2]

Oppen himself comments on the use of metaphor:

> It is possible to find a metaphor for anything, analogue: but the image is encountered, not found; it is an account of the poet's perception; it is a test of sincerity, a test of conviction, the rare poetic quality of truthfulness.[3]

Crusoe imagery appears in only two poems — "Crusoe / We say was / Rescued," from poem number six in *Of Being Numerous,* and "we discover // Friday's footprint" from "The Speech at Soli" in *Myth of the Blaze* — but the concept of the shipwrecked individual (for example, "shipwreck / of the singular" from poem number seven in *Of Being Numerous*) pervades Oppen's work and is directly linked to the fascination on Oppen's part with the idea of shipwreck in general. As mentioned before, the concept of shipwreck embodies a helplessness in human beings when faced with the elements, but perhaps also in the face of the wars and disasters which overtake the simple man as he goes about his daily life. The figure of Crusoe, within this context, takes on a complexity of possibilities; one possibility is that he is the survivor, the one who goes back to nature and lives the life of a simple, primitive man, existing on the basic necessities which his environment provides, meeting up with and co-existing with Man Friday, who has always been at home in these kinds of surroundings. The story of Crusoe, from this perspective, is the story of a man who leaves modern civilization behind and learns to make a new life for himself, based on the elementary needs of those early human beings who once populated the land. "Friday's footprint" becomes a reminder of that mode of existence, the possibility of living a more basic and less complicated life, the footprint imposing itself as the contours of what once was and perhaps could have been again. David McAleavy discusses Oppen's ironic use of single quotes in the phrase "Crusoe / We say was / Rescued," commenting that this "indicates that an apparently happy self-sufficient man was brought back to a civilization which was practically insane." McAleavy compares the poet who writes against the invasions of society to the Crusoe figure, adding: "Both find light and peace in solitude, which the city or society destroys."[4]

Already in "Myself I Sing" from *The Materials* we have our first glimpse of a Robinson Crusoe figure in the man marooned on a beach who "[f]inds a dune / And on the beach sits near it. Two / He finds himself by two." This lone figure, isolated from civilization, seems to find his surroundings conducive to a certain creativity, as he begins to imagine different possibilities in the landscape around him. This is the supreme advantage of Crusoe: undistracted by the noise and flux of the modern "civilized" world, he can allow his imagination to take over, and so embodying the idea that our imagination — our free-ranging mind — is stifled in the urban landscapes of bustling crowds and noisy traffic, and needs the peace of solitude and isolation. In addition, one wonders if the reference to "two" might imply the possibility of being joined by Man Friday.

An entirely different possibility of interpreting the Crusoe figure is as that of the solitary figure who is detached from the human collective, the outsider, the exile. From this perspective, the solitariness of Crusoe is not, as McAleavy sees it, the peaceful state of a meditative man; it becomes more of an enforced loneliness, an enforced detachment from others like himself, from the tribe which can provide a sense of unity, togetherness and security. When we look at Oppen's personal life, we can see how the figure of the exile was pertinent to his own experiences: Oppen joined the Communist party in 1935, describing his politics in the 1930s as liberal and antifascist, and after the Second World War was interviewed by the FBI in 1949, just before the onset of the McCarthy era. As a result, he, his wife Mary and their daughter Linda were forced to leave the USA to live in Mexico for the next nine years, until anti-Communist feeling had subsided somewhat.[5] This self-imposed exile nevertheless marked Oppen as one of a hunted minority; together with many other prominent figures from the world of art who suffered the same persecution at this time, Oppen's removal from the USA to Mexico cut him off from his homeland and from the people he had grown up with. It made him an outsider of sorts, an individual set apart from the collective, separated, like Crusoe, from the mainstream of the society he had been born into. The references in the aforementioned poems to Crusoe and Man Friday do seem to embody, at least in part, this sense of exile from the community, as evidenced in poems like "The Speech at Soli" from *Myth of the Blaze*. Oppen's perception of his own difference lay not only in his political attitudes but also in his Jewishness; *Myth of the Blaze* was brought out in 1975, the year that Oppen went to Israel at the invitation of the mayor of Jerusalem.[6] As a result of this visit, perhaps, several of the poems in this volume evidence Oppen's considerations of his own Jewishness and how it differentiated him from others. In "The Lighthouses" and "Semite," for example (both from *Myth of the Blaze*), the phrase "neither Roman nor barbarian" appears, as Oppen defines himself not only as someone excluded from these categories, but also as what he is *not*—intimating, perhaps, that his sense of self derives not from what he has in common with any other collective group, but from what divides him from others; he sees himself as an outsider. And in choosing Romans and barbarians as those groups to which he does not belong, Oppen emphasizes the social groupings of a former time, goes back in human history to an era closer to his own Jewish origins. And so the phrase "neither Roman nor barbarian" links him to the figure of Crusoe both as an outsider and also as one who belongs to another time, more primitive and more basic than the frantic modern era of urban sprawls and petty politics. In "Populist," for example, Oppen begins with "I dreamed myself of their people, I am of their people" and three lines later declares, "for the cities / are no longer mine"—linking together in this part of the poem the fact of his belonging to the Jewish people and their origins, and also his sense of exile, or at least difference, from the urban populations he once identified with but seems now to have drawn away from.

The idea of being alienated or excluded from the mainstream of society, whether that of a bygone time or that of contemporary life, is linked to Oppen's distrust of political dogma and blind ideology, against which he protests frequently in his poems, particularly in *Of Being Numerous*. Oppen rightly sees mainstream social and political trends as reinforcing the herd instinct and therefore alienating those who do not adopt or adhere to the current ideas and convictions set out in particular political platforms. Oppen distrusts not only political ideologies, but any mainstream fashion (for example, the "jet set," the "vocabularies of the forties" and the "JetStream" of poem number twenty-three in *Of Being Numerous*), whether political, social or artistic, since these erase individuality and encourage a mindless following. This is dangerous not only because of what it does to those followers who embrace an idea mindlessly, without considering its pertinence to their own individual outlook or values, but also because of what it does to those who do *not* adopt it, and are marginalized or even persecuted for not doing so. As both a supporter of Communist (or at least Socialist) views, and also as

Nine: Recurring Threads

a Jew, Oppen must have understood only too well the dangers of being "different," an outsider, as well as the need for one's individual conviction and a firm adherence to the path one chooses to follow, even if it is one eschewed by society at large. His poem "Historic Pun" (from *Of Being Numerous*) ends with the line "Semite: to find a way for myself," showing his need for a way of life which can be adapted to his own individual outlook and values and not those dictated by the majority.

As has been discussed, Oppen's recurring diatribe against political dogma and oratory derives not only from the marginalizing and exclusion of those individuals who refuse to be swayed by populists, but also from its trivialization of authentic dialogue and communication by employing glib language. The catch-phrases and stock vocabularies of politicians and social trend-makers often empty out language of its potential, making it two-dimensional and trite. Oppen's poetry works hard and constantly to reinvest words with power and significance, and activates those sub-verbal elements which can detonate language in order to open up deeper and richer veins of experience. Oppen wants direct, unmediated communication wherever possible, and not the over-digested, second-hand slogans that so often characterize the discourse patterns of those looking for high impact but which in actual fact blunt one's sense of what is real and true. Even the smooth, polished talk of living-rooms and television is shrugged aside by Oppen, who always prefers the hard, clear image and the raw syntax over the linguistic conventions of his time.

Since one of Oppen's major concerns is to illuminate the possibilities of dealing more directly and more fundamentally with our experiences of the world, his poetry is rich in images of light: dawn and sunlight and sunrise, crystal and flame and fire, radiance, glint, glow and gleam, glittering and shining and dazzling, clarity and brilliance and flash, and of course blaze. The word "blaze," appearing both in the name of the collection *Myth of the Blaze* and in its title poem, is also connected to the Tyger of Blake's poem (mentioned in "Penobscot" and "The Poem"), the Tyger being an important image in Oppen's poetry, although it features in only a few poems. In addition to the "blazing" of the Tyger's eye, which embodies primitive forces and energy (both natural and creative), this image also *reflects* a fierce illumination of raw power. It is the blazing of raw power which can be dangerous when used for twisted purposes, and although Oppen does not use the Tyger's blazing eyes to represent this kind of power in his poems, the misuse of power for political ends certainly did occupy his attention. One is reminded of the corrupt Colonel Walter Kurtz in *Apocalypse Now,* and the blazing horrors of the opening scenes depicting Vietnam War combat. Although Oppen probably did not see this film, the madness of the Vietnam War (so memorably portrayed in the film), must have left a deep impact on this poet whose own war experiences and social concerns for the future of his country and people are written into much of his work. The theme of the film, based on Conrad's *Heart of Darkness,* which deals, like the film, with the influence of corruption and decadence born of a rotting civilization, is relevant also to one of the indisputably great poets of the twentieth century, T.S. Eliot, who used the phrase "Mr. Kurtz — he dead" from *Heart of Darkness* as the preface to his poem "The Hollow Men." Although vastly different from Oppen in background, outlook, personality and poetic style, Eliot appears to be a shadowy but significant figure in the background of much of Oppen's poetry, and his influence can be traced through several specific poems. In an article about Oppen's *Of Being Numerous,* David Ignatow places Oppen among the best of twentieth century poets, mentioning him together with Wallace Stevens, William Carlos Williams, Ezra Pound and T.S. Eliot, and calling him "a man who rests his faith in the mind as a value in itself on which the individual may depend." He continues: "Concurrently, there is an awareness of disaster and chaos, this awareness being an affirmation of the possibility of order."[7] In describing Oppen thus, Ignatow links him thematically to T.S. Eliot, whose poems — in particular *The Waste Land*— focus on the lack of, and need for, belief and order in twentieth century civilization. Nevertheless, Eliot's background was cosmopolitan and his poetic approach defined by a critical detachment quite unlike Oppen's strong personal involvement. Eliot was born into a family in New England who instilled in him orthodoxy and discipline, as well as a love of tradition; his upbringing had all the force of a heritage of academic discipline and orthodox faith behind it, and the tone of his poetry, influenced by this upbringing, is controlled and detached. For Eliot, the great creative mind had to be a thinking mind; emotion had to be disciplined before it could be a creative source in art. A poem, according to Eliot's outlook, could portray suffering, but it should not be written directly out of the poet's pain. Eliot believed that there had to be a division between the poet's personal suffering and the creative mind before a great piece of poetry could be written. Interestingly, in a review of *Seascape: Needle's Eye,* Stanley Plumly says of this collection of poems that it "is memorable for its 'symbolic logic' " and finds that in "A Mortality Play: Preface," "the central location of the image is far more ontological than physical — the emotion, to paraphrase Eliot, having become thought."[8] Although this comment places Oppen alongside Eliot in his approach, it is difficult to find this kind of abstraction in any of Oppen's poems. Oppen's orientation is always towards the physical, the concrete, the image which directly arouses the sensual response.

There is no doubt that the misery, alienation and destruction which characterized the first half of the twentieth century affected both Eliot and Oppen profoundly, yet we do not sense Eliot's own personal response to the human condition within his own poetry. We are made deeply aware of a civilization teetering on the brink of a great chasm — but this awareness is brought home to us through the actions and emotions of the various personae of the poems. In contrast, Oppen's presence is strongly felt in his poetry, battling and struggling with forces which threaten to corrupt or overwhelm humanity, and the speaker in his poems is almost always his own personal voice. This is not to say that Oppen's poetry is in any way confessional, but that he speaks out of his own experience and looks directly into the eyes of the reader as he does so. Yet in spite of these quite radical differences between Oppen and Eliot, the pervasive influence of the latter, whether consciously recognized and admitted by Oppen, or sensed only at a sub-conscious level, is evidenced in several similarities of theme and approach shared by both poets.

Eliot's poetry portrays post-war society as a jumble of fragmented humanity, a "heap of broken images," as Oppen's *Of Being Numerous* often does, although Oppen conveys the sense of fragmentation though his disjointed use of syntax as well as through specific images. Eliot's passage from "What the Thunder Said" in *The Waste Land,* beginning "Who are those hooded hordes," presents a truly apocalyptic vision of civilization in chaos, a civilization which has undergone the traumas of revolution and war: the hordes of the homeless are here, cities razed to the ground, earth cracked and scorched by fire. Oppen's poem number twenty from *Of Being Numerous,* opening with a statement about those who live for the prospect of war, goes on to talk about "armies [a]nd the ragged hordes moving and the passions of that death." It seems that Oppen, too, was haunted by the same spectacles of war: the razed landscapes and the homeless refugees, fragmented humanity. Elsewhere in his poetry we come across words like "madness" and "conspiracy," and "catastrophe," as well as references to crimes both social and political. If Eliot presents the great panoramas of war and history from a universal and mythic point of view, Oppen takes these to our doorsteps in newspapers and into our living-rooms on television.

There are other phrases or fragments of ideas in Oppen's poetry which suggest the influence of (or at least an acquaintance with) Eliot's poems. In "Eros," from *This in Which,* Oppen talks of an "old man" with a "bulging" head which is "eroded." The poem goes on to discuss the influences of history and the effects of wars, just as Eliot's "Gerontion" begins with an impotent old man and touches on the way history affects us. Also in "Gerontion" we find the phrase "Signs are taken for wonders. 'We would see a sign!' " referring to the birth of Christ and the star which guided the Wise Men; Oppen's "Guest Room" from *This in Which* describes the dawn and its light coming up over the San Francisco hills, which the poem tells us are "signs" and "promises," things they "took as signs." These similar-sounding phrases indicate similar issues in both poets' poetry: how history affects us, the place of faith and belief in our everyday lives, our search for significance. But it is the destruction caused by war that most often unites the poetry of Eliot and Oppen; Eliot's concern is how war affects whole societies and cultures, while Oppen looks at the effects of war on the individual (often himself); but both poets come back to this theme again and again in their work. Elsewhere in Eliot's early poetry we get sudden flashes which reflect the kind of devastation that war brings, for example the "fractured atoms" of "Gerontion": the first splitting of the atom was announced in 1919, and Eliot's "fractured atoms" carry — for the reader of today — connotations of nuclear warfare. Nuclear warfare was a very real threat to Oppen: Rachel Blau DuPlessis, in an interview with the poet, describes his "apocalyptic fears of the atomic age when Linda was a 'child.'"[9] We can see that Oppen's poetry is shot through, too, with phrases like "the war's huge air" ("Some San Francisco Poems," number three), "mad kings gone raving mad" ("The Speech at Soli"), "disorder so great the tumult wave upon wave" ("The Book of Job") and "murder comes to our dinners ... of a planet the size of a table-top ("Semite"), this last phrase relating to newspaper headlines on global affairs which come to our dinner table, but also reducing our world to virtual insignificance exactly as nuclear war can so easily do. The tenuous and flimsy nature of modern existence is borne out in Eliot's "Hollow Men," prefaced (in addition to the quotation from *Heart of Darkness*) by the phrase "A penny for the Old Guy"; this is a reference to Guy Fawkes, one of those "hollow men" who was thwarted in his attempt to blow up the British Houses of Parliament, and subsequently executed. It is the straw effigy of this original figure that is ceremoniously set alight on bonfires across Britain every year on the fifth of November. Eliot sees the treachery of war embodied in the figure of Guy Fawkes, and perhaps the annual bonfires remind him of the inferno of the First World War; in "The Hollow Men" he shows us a civilization hollowed out from within, paralyzed and hopeless in the aftermath of war. The poem portrays the land of the Shadow and those who lack human substance; it is peopled with hollow, empty figures living in a kind of limbo, straw men subject to the winds of history and change, who seem (as they go round and round the prickly pear cactus in a parody of the children's game "Ring a Ring of Roses") to embody the hopelessness and desolation of the "hooded hordes" of *The Waste Land*. Likewise, in Oppen's "From a Phrase of Simone Weils's" we come across the line "like a fire of straws," a reference, within the context of the poem, to the empty creeds and dogmas which appear to sustain the adherent with a guiding principle but in the end provide no substantial belief or value. Like the hollow men, these creeds are just straws in the wind. Oppen's distrust of political dogma had to do with his view of language and his intense dislike of flippantly used words, but this distrust probably also derived from the political persecutions of the McCarthy era, and almost certainly also from the war oratory of politicians and from political speeches made during the Vietnam War. If Eliot's despair at the ravages of war and the futility inherent in so much of modern society makes itself felt on a grand panoramic scale, Oppen's own concern is trained in on more specific and particular events, some from his own personal life and others from his immediate society. Yet in both poets' cases the shadow of war and its outcomes falls across the poetry. Eliot is concerned with the loss of faith and belief in early twentieth century civilization; Oppen seems more disturbed by the debilitating effects of misdirected political convictions and the facility with which they appear to convince those who are easily swayed.

In the poetry of both Eliot and Oppen the theme of alienation is one of the leading issues. In almost all of Eliot's early poems — "Prufrock," "Portrait of a Lady," "Preludes," *The Waste Land* and of course "The Hollow Men," we are confronted with images of the anonymity of the city and the vacant figures of those who lead aimless urban lives with no real substance to them. Eliot's "Unreal London" pervades most of the poems written in the second two decades of the twentieth century; the figures in these poems have nothing substantial to communicate, all of them avoiding real communication because there is nothing left for them to say. Oppen's major poems of alienation, with their social gaps, their urban compartmentalizations, their bland incomprehensions, appear, for the most part, in *Of Being Numerous:* number seventeen, for example, with its "ferocious mumbling" and "rootless speech," number thirteen peopled by those whose only mode of communication is argument and who "become unreal," the detachment and isolation of poem number two's "city of the corporations // Glassed / In dreams," the slick but empty talk of the jet set at their parties in poem number twenty-three, like the women "talking of Michelangelo" in "Prufrock." So many of Eliot's figures are bored, skimming the surface of life and trying to be enthusiastic about paltry excitements; a sense of boredom seems to pervade the majority of Eliot's early personae, as they mindlessly go through the motions of rituals long emptied out of any real significance, rituals both fake and somehow sordid. Eliot himself perceived this as one of the primary diseases of modern civilization, and his poetry — both from earlier periods and from the later decades — constantly addresses this issue. Oppen, too, in his early poetry, appears concerned about the issue of boredom; the first poem in his first collection, *Discrete Series,* mentions the "knowledge not of sorrow ... but of boredom ... with which one shares the century," and portrays a figure of someone listlessly looking out of the window as if "to see / what really was going on." Oppen, of course, felt that boredom was the prime enemy; this is why so much of his poetry demands of us that we look below the surface — of things in the world, of ourselves, of words — to rediscover awe and wonder.

Eliot's Waste Land typist seems to embody the modern urban persona who goes through the motions of living without being engaged in any kind of genuine emotional interaction with others. She comes home to prepare for an evening with a young man, but busies herself with dishes and tins of food, and when the brash house agent's clerk arrives ready for his sexual encounter she is "bored and tired"; afterwards she thinks to herself: "Well now that's done: and I'm glad it's over." The figure of Eliot's typist seems to have crept into one of Oppen's poems, number eleven in *Of Being Numerous,* in the guise of Phyllis, whom we see "[c]oming home from her first job / On the bus in the bare civic interior / Among those people, the small doors / Opening on the night at the curb"— except that Oppen's poem provides a redemption of sorts, in that the girl's heart is "suddenly tight with happiness." Oppen's poems, for the most part (although not exclusively) in *Of Being Numerous,* do seem to have this difference, that Oppen is as concerned as Eliot with the vacant and trivial nature of modern urban living, but is ultimately a much more affirmative poet: for all his myriad portrayals of urban populations and their blunted emotional responses, their mental blindness and deafness at times, there is a counterbalance of affirmation in many of his poems. A good example of this can be seen in "Strange Are the Products," where the "small alien // on the sidewalks thru the long / time of deaths // and anger" leading to "brutal" and "swaggering" streets is set against the "glory of joy in the small / huge dark" as the speaker fills up with an almost pagan rush of happiness at the mystic celebrations of All Hallows' Eve. Eliot's poetry of the 1920s rarely featured such possibilities of redemption. Even at the end of *The Waste Land* the question "Shall I at least set my lands in order?" remains essentially unanswered. It is only in his later poetry of the 1930s (during which time Oppen was not writing poetry), in *Ash Wednesday* and *Four Quartets,* that Eliot explores the concept of redemption, conveying it most consistently and pervasively through the "still point." It is worthwhile to consider the idea of Eliot's "still point," since it is both complex and abstract, but also because Oppen also presents his own kind of "still point," albeit very different in nature from that of Eliot.

Eliot's concept of the "still point," developed in *Four Quartets,* is one which refers to time and the timeless; it is where past and future meet in an immeasurable moment. It exists, for Eliot, in the mystic revelation of the saint and the perfection of art, and it links into a transcendental reality which is out of time. The "still point" is presented first in "Burnt Norton," the first of the quartets, as a moment which is both in and out of time; it is a spiritual reality outside the realm of chronological time, yet experienced within it. Eliot is dealing here with a sphere of existence which is mystical, revelatory and spiritual. The glimpse that we may have, if we are privileged, of this other realm at the intersection of time and the timeless, both belittles man's day-to-day living, but also adds significance to what went before, and what comes after, in time. Common man, whose "still point" is the ecstatic but fleeting gleam of a spiritual existence beyond time, finds his everyday existence diminished; yet for the redeemed — the saint, the mystic, perhaps the artist, those with spiritual values — the "still point" is the apprehension of an ever-present spiritual reality existing alongside but beyond the temporal, which illuminates their whole lives; it both conquers and reconciles time. Eliot believes that this "still point" is most accessible to those who seek it through prayer, discipline and surrender, and therefore his is the viewpoint of the ascetic and the seeker after spirituality.

If the nature of Eliot's "still point" is spiritual and transcendental, Oppen's "still point" — if it can be called that, and I think there *is* such a concept in Oppen's poetry — is fundamental rather than transcendental, and not exclusively spiritual. While Eliot's "still point" is primarily the domain of the saint and the mystic, Oppen's "still point" is very much of this world, and accessible to the common man. The "still point" of Eliot's poems diminishes the common man's existence, making it appear paltry and useless, whereas Oppen's "still point" is an uplifting experience which illuminates and adds significance to the often disregarded everyday moments which pass us by unheeded. Such moments, in Oppen's hands, are cracked open to reveal fundamental truths not ordinarily perceived; they immerse one in a deeply significant experience of one's world, *as it is*. One example of a possible "still point" in Oppen's poetry has been discussed in "The Occurrences"; but Oppen has already presented a "still point" in one of his earlier poems, "The Image of the Engine," from *The Materials*. The silent moment of comprehension occurs here when the clanking engine has finally come to a standstill, and in the ensuing silence there appears "a still and quiet angel of knowledge and of comprehension." As already discussed in chapter three, this quiet angel who appears in the silent aftermath reminds us of the "still small voice" in the biblical story of the burning bush; the coupling together of angel and biblical story provides the only example of a "still point" in Oppen's poetry which approximates the spiritual and transcendental nature of Eliot's "still point." Nevertheless, like all of Oppen's "still points," this one also manifests itself out of the physical and concrete — in fact, in this particular poem, from the mechanical workings of a run-down car.

Another example of Oppen's "still point" is to be found in "Psalm" (from *This in Which*), where the sudden and startling encounter with the deer suspends time for a moment as the leaves "[h]ang in the distances / Of sun" and the poet's carefully chosen words are "crying faith." In this encounter, Oppen succeeds in bringing language to bear on the delicate beauty of what is "there" all round us, and to which we are so often blind. There is another revelation in this poem: the discovery of certain words, the "little words" and how they can cause us to stop in our tracks if set up carefully enough in the landscape of the poem. And in "The Forms of Love" (also from *This in Which*), Oppen takes the memory of an experience with his wife on a foggy evening and turns it into a "still point" where different worlds intersect, where fog becomes lake and lake becomes fog, where Oppen and his wife "groped / Our way together / Downhill in the bright / Incredible light." This is obviously a supremely significant moment in the lives of Oppen and his wife Mary, as it appears in several other poems. It is a dazzling experience for them both, one that fused them together in a relationship that was to be always intimate and important throughout their lives. It must have been, like Eliot's "still point," a moment "out of time" for Oppen, but one which enhanced, rather than diminished, his everyday life with Mary.

Oppen's own kind of "still point" is presented again in two of the poems from *Primitive*. In "Disasters," Oppen talks of the elements — "light // and wind / and fire and water and air *the five // bright elements*" — revealing that "the marvel // of the obvious and the marvel / of the hidden is there," and calling it all "a distinction dance // of the wasp wings." In this poem, his "still point" is embodied in the dance, an idea which also appears in Eliot's *Four Quartets*. For Eliot, the different symbolic representations of the "still point" always convey the movement of life revolving around a still center which is at the same time dynamic and vital; this is where "the dance" is. Eliot's choice of the dance as an image of the "still point" is not a random one; dance is the most nearly complete of all art forms. It is both a temporal and a spatial art; it combines movement, music and, most of all, pattern. In Eliot's view, the art of the dance, like the "still point," is paradoxical; it is written and performed in time — that is, it occurs in time — yet exists out of time. In addition, the metaphor of the dance and its pattern directly links the significance of artistic design with the significance of Christian principles; Kristian Smidt believes that "the poet found a pattern when the man found a faith. For one of the main effects of Christianity in Eliot's poetry is the provision of a unifying principle to his vision."[10] In this respect, Eliot's adoption of the dance as a metaphor for the "still point" differs radically from Oppen's representation; although Oppen portrays a perfect orchestration of the five elements, a moment which illuminates "the marvel // of the obvious and the marvel / of the hidden," this dance is neither abstract nor spiritual in a religious sense, as Eliot's is, but a dance of "wasp wings." This is a specifically physical image taken from the natural world. Oppen takes his image from the world of insects, a world both fragile and transient, and uses it as an embodiment of all the elements, transforming it into a moment of awe for the most basic and primary life force. There is

Nine: Recurring Threads

nothing abstract about Oppen's images, although they may be regarded as spiritual in the sense that they both revere and celebrate the real and the tangible in our everyday world. Even when Oppen refers to the emergence of the completed poetic effort *within* the poem, he gives his poems "hands," turning them into something far more concrete than Eliot's beautiful but abstract representations. In "Strange Are the Products," Oppen's "still point" again clothes itself in the physical and concrete, as he describes the startling moment of joy in the "small huge dark" of All Hallows' Eve. Here, the joy is encased in the skull, so that it becomes a sacred, almost ceremonial experience (an "illud tempus"?), yet bound up in the body — a moment out of time, but felt in the physical regions of the mind.

Eliot's "still point," then, embodies a state where one is lifted beyond the boundaries of ordinary human possibilities; its nature is one of striving to reach what may be beyond us, to hope for perfection. On the other hand, Oppen asks us to take notice of what is there around us in our own everyday environment and to learn to revere it; he asks us, too, to confront our own flaws and to find the underlying beauty and wonder inherent in our own human fallibility. The concept of the "still point" which Eliot introduces into his later poetry is, therefore, a predominantly spiritual one, whereas Oppen's moments of revelation are always grounded in the sphere of the physical and concrete, embedded in the tangible elements of the world about us, and touching some fundamental inner place in the human psyche.

Perhaps this essential difference between Eliot and Oppen is highlighted most clearly in those closing lines of the last poem in Oppen's last published collection, *Primitive*. Those same lines, paradoxically, also point to the most clearly evident of Oppen's links to Eliot. The lines from Oppen's poem "Till Other Voices Wake Us" read: "till other voices wake / us, or we drown" and echo the last line of Eliot's poem "The Love Song of J. Alfred Prufrock": "till human voices wake us, and we drown." The closing lines of both "Prufrock" and "Till Other Voices" deal with the strange music of the poetic medium as opposed to the humdrum voices of the everyday world: Eliot's mermaids sing deep "in the chambers of the sea," their music capturing the speaker until "human voices" jolt him back into what is for him the drab real world, while Oppen is immersed in the "music more powerful // than music" of his poetic experiences, in which he may remain submerged unless "other voices" wake him. Jeffrey Peterson interprets Oppen's version of the lines thus: "Oppen revises T.S. Eliot's 'The Love Song of J. Alfred Prufrock' with an ironic turn: replacing an 'and' with an 'or,' and converting the very source of Prufrock's fatality to the 'other voices' of a saving, awakening human community."[11] Eliot's poem ends in a tone of regret and a sense of loss; but Oppen, although not unwilling to immerse himself in the other-worldly depths of the poetic experience, senses the need to come back up into the mundane physical world of everyday human voices because he knows that this is where his poetic voice originates. Oppen's tone may be one of resignation, but it is also one of acceptance, as well as an affirmation of the need for, and the importance of, returning to renew and preserve contact with his fellow men. On the back cover of the *New Collected Poems* there is a quotation from one of Oppen's unpublished poems, "Semantic," which reads: "There is the one word / Which one must / Define for oneself, the word / Us." This is where Eliot and Oppen part ways: Eliot will always be the poet of detachment, whereas Oppen will always be the poet of involvement, human interaction and engagement.

In light of the radical differences in the personality, politics and outlook between these two poets, one may wonder at there being any link at all between them. Yet Oppen was a friend of, and was influenced by, Ezra Pound for many years, although the difference in their political outlook exerted itself on their friendship. Michael Davidson tells us that Pound was very supportive of the Objectivist movement (to which Oppen belonged), and that Oppen helped to publish a book of Pound's in the 1920s.[12] Since Pound also worked tirelessly to gain recognition for T.S. Eliot, and was instrumental in helping Eliot, through his advice and suggestions, to shape the final version of *The Waste Land* (and to whom Eliot was subsequently deeply indebted), it is natural to assume that Oppen was therefore intimately familiar with (and also possibly discussed with Pound) Eliot's poems, his thematic concerns and his writing style. Certainly, of all Oppen's recurring threads, from the use of simple individual words and phrases through the reiteration of more complex and conceptual poetic ideas, the textual relationship with Eliot appears to be the most pervasive. Perhaps this is not surprising; ultimately, both poets are concerned with the idea of communication. Eliot's lost and lonely people such as Prufrock, his city poems overflowing with figures defined by their aimlessness, alienation and indifference, his Waste Land personae whose social interactions — in pubs, rented rooms and winter resorts — are so superficial as to be two-dimensional at most, and whose contact with the past and with their present culture, if it exists, is tenuous: underlying all these is a concern on Eliot's part that what has been lost in the years at the turn of the century, and in particular following the First World War is a sense of unity, a meshing-together of the human collective, a willingness to listen and to sympathize. All of this, of course, is familiar to even the most casual reader of Eliot's poetry. Oppen, too, although through radically different channels and in radically different ways, strives constantly and consistently through all his poetry — from *Discrete Series* to *Primitive* and beyond — to put us back in touch: with each other, with the simple wonders of landscape and habitat, with the pull of our essential and often subconscious selves, with his own poetic creativity. Just as he worked in his personal life towards providing social support for the unemployed of the 1930s, affirming what he saw as a social responsibility for creating a sense of community, so in his poetry he strove towards an awareness in the reader of strong and fundamental bonds between us and our universe, forged through a heightened sensitivity to the deep life-forces which reveal themselves to us in ways beyond what conscious thought and language can represent.

Conclusion

The purpose of this book has been to examine primitive modes as they appear in the poetry of George Oppen, and the ways in which these primitive modes are conveyed to the reader, as the poet attempts to deal with aspects of poetry that are elemental and fluid, and not easily accommodated into language. Since primitive modes have been defined here as primarily pre- or sub-verbal states, we find a dichotomy produced when Oppen attempts to portray primitive, elemental states through language, which is frequently discovered to be inadequate to reproduce them, but must be employed nevertheless as the sole means of communicating these modes of existence. Aspects of language other than words, such as rhythms, spaces, tone and line-breaks, must be brought into play to compensate for this inadequacy. The secondary dichotomy discovered in Oppen's work — his simultaneous fragmentation and synthesis, as he dismantles language into small and often odd phrasings and unusual line-formations in order to achieve a synthesis of poetic ideas — echoes the greater dichotomy produced by this poet's use of language to express the ultimately inexpressible.

The primitive modes with which Oppen engages tend more towards a psychological and social orientation rather than an anthropological one, synchronic rather than diachronic. This is not to say that Oppen shuns completely the use of historical or temporal origins in his poems; we have seen him, particularly after his visit to Israel, introduce in his later poems references to the origins of the Jewish people — to Abraham and Sarah, to the wanderings of the Israelite tribes in the desert, to the guiding pillars of fire and cloud — as we have found him building poems around significant events in his own life which represent for him an "illud tempus," a re-enactment of that event which grants it a sacred and mythic quality. Although mythic consciousness (which projects an added dimension onto some of the primitive modes discussed) may arguably be defined as anthropological, mythic consciousness is universal and transcends temporal boundaries.

The spectrum of poetry written by Oppen is shot through with primary landscapes of light, water and stone, basic human instincts of fear and longing, elemental undercurrents of desire and need, mythic dreams and essential energies which fuel the poetic drive. Many of the later poems manifest the "birth" of the poem itself, rising out of these essential energies. In his work, Oppen features animals, elements of myth and ritual, subconscious and unconscious urges, and the exploration of those substrata of experience underlying the social framework of our lives. We find the hawk, the deer, the wolf and the tiger in the poems, as well as Oppen's awe at the natural world, so beautifully captured in "Psalm." He traces the ancestral myths of his people as well as primitive rites and customs such as All Hallows' Eve. In doing so, Oppen strips away the trappings of civilization to expose primal urges of fear, desire and awe, going down into his poetic self to discover the nature and origins of the poetic drive. Primary images of water, stone and fire are prominent in almost all of Oppen's poems, as we have seen, playing a particularly significant role in the later collections of poetry. Julia Kristeva's claims that the disorganized pre-verbal flux of sounds and rhythms which marks the infant stage remains active beneath the linguistic competence of adults, and that these primary processes of sound and rhythm are released from the unconscious by poetry, are given expression again and again in Oppen's work. Kristeva's approach is constantly validated through the ways in which Oppen strengthens the link between subject-matter (pre- and sub-verbal elemental modes) and vehicle (rhythms, sounds and gaps in the poetry), by bringing into play those rhythms and spaces which express aspects of the sub-verbal modes he portrays.

Many, though not all, of Oppen's primitive modes are conveyed through static primary images such as stones, the crystal heart of a rock, starlight, "the five bright elements," and elemental imagery of ocean and desert. Oppen's depiction of primary states through basic images of stone, water and light, elements which for him are "just there," which embody their own existential nature independent of onlooker or perceiver, may correspond in a sense to Lacan's description of the Real, an ineffable and inaccessible state beyond words and beyond definition.

Oppen has written several poems which feature animals, and in these poems he has done for the status of animals (and our perception of them) what, in as sense, he has done for language: he has restored an essence of animal which human domestication and subsequent exploitation of animals has destroyed. The animals in his poems — the sharp-eyed hawk, the shy and light-footed deer, the lone wind-blown sea birds, the padding wolf, the blazing tiger — all these retain a dignity and power which, according to Jean Baudrillard, has been lost to animals as a result of modern scientific and technological developments. Baudrillard claims that man's domestication and exploitation of animals has led to their "de-animalization," as we experiment on them, send them to zoos (ostensibly to protect them, but in actual fact because we have often endangered their natural habitat), relegate them to a position of inferiority in the hierarchy of living things when we take charge of their well-being, often championing their cause in a condescending manner (Baudrilllard gives the example of Brigitte Bardot and the baby seals), and trivialize them in sentimental funeral services and King Kong–type films. Even a film like *Free Willy* becomes ludicrous when we consider that the "heroic" release of the whale could only come about because we ourselves removed it from its natural environment in the first place. Baudrillard refers to the once-symbolic status that animals had in the past: "animals have always had, until our era, a divine or sanctified nobility that all mythologies recount. Even murder by hunting is still a symbolic relation, as opposed to an experimental dissection."[1] This last statement vindicates the character of the wolf and tiger in Oppen's poems, as animals who are stately even in their primitive and predatory nature. Hunting, for these animals, is an activity in which they engage in order to provide food and to survive on their own terms. Baudrillard goes on to discuss the non-verbal aspect of the animal kingdom in comparison with the hyperspeak of today's electronic world:

Conclusion

> In a universe of increasing speech ... only they remain mute, and for this reason they seem to retreat far from us, behind the horizon of truth.... In a world bent on doing nothing but making one speak, ... their silence weighs more and more heavily on our organization of meaning.[2]

Here, Baudrillard gives credence to the silence of animals by juxtaposing it with the vacuous language of today's media-controlled world, a language and form of discourse we have seen Oppen hold up to ridicule and criticism in many of the poems from *Of Being Numerous*. In his vindication of the muteness of animals, Baudrillard critiques so-called technological advances, as well as giving us reason to pause in our subordination of animals, for they maintain a "horizon of truth" which has been all but obliterated in our human world of virtual communication and cyber-reality. In his animal poems, Oppen reinvests the animals with a primitive honor and dignity that has in many ways been lost to them in our "progressive" culture, which counts animals as inferior to man in the hierarchy of living creatures. The animals in Oppen's poems are independent and vibrant, sometimes cruel but always dignified, our equals in every way and sometimes our superiors. All the animals portrayed share a true voice, a more primitive but more authentic means of communication which does not lie and never demeans, never trivializes. In contrast, this modern era of media-controlled technology has made us humans shallow and trite in our communication, slicking over the truth in favor of clichéd e-messages and catchy advertising slogans, and so we live in a world made bland and desensitized to real feeling and thought.

In some ways, Oppen himself shares characteristics with those same animals he portrays in the poetry. His engagement with the world about him is direct and unflinching, without mediation, while his poems evidence honesty and a simple integrity. There is nothing coy or pretentious about Oppen's poetic style; instead, it sometimes appears raw and unformed. He does away with linguistic superfluities, preferring most of the time not to use figures of speech, since these, too, are a form of poetic mediation. His language is, for the most part, pared down to the most basic essentials: what can be said poetically by other poets in five words,

Oppen will say in three, and say it no less poetically. His view of the world that surrounds him is presented through the most basic elements from which that world is made up: grass and trees, stone and rock, sea and ocean, sunlight and shadow. This must be how animals see their environment: in terms of heat and cold, food and drink, shelter and exposure. Oppen's poetry has a black-and-white quality to it, uncompromising; in this way it embodies something of the nature of animals, whose needs are clear-cut and whose world, too, is defined by simple contrasts: hunter or hunted, hungry or satisfied, protected or exposed, winner or loser of territory. Mark Linenthal identifies this clear-cut, spare style in Oppen's work, believing that it contributes to, and even creates, an intensity in the poems: "The concentration or intensity of the poetry, its weight, comes from an abstemiousness, a plain speaking, a determination to say (and say only) what is so for him."[3] This is part of Oppen's integrity, as a man and as a poet: he will not be compromised by whim or swayed by trend, and he never allows his emotions to overrule the importance of what he has to say. This does not mean that his poetry lacks passion, only that his way of speaking channels that passion into a voice of clarity and single-mindedness.

As has been discussed throughout this study of his work, Oppen is engaged, particularly in *Myth of the Blaze* and *Primitive*, and whether overtly or implicitly, in mapping the creative process in his poetry. There is something elemental about this process; as we read the poem, we often discover the creative origins from which the poem begins, and then, as we read on, we find the poem emerging from the words like Aphrodite rising out of the sea. Oppen thus reveals to us the underlying workings of the poetic mind, as if a brain surgeon had made an incision in the brain and allowed us to see the inner workings of the different lobes, the sources of all our memories, thoughts, and speech and other physical actions. Often, Oppen — like the brain surgeon — employs visual tactics such as gaps, line-breaks and fractures in syntax, to expose the inner workings of the poem, or to crack open the text and allow the underlying sources of energy to ooze up to the surface. Lacan's concept of desire as a disruptive influence triggered by pleasure and poetry, one which subverts orderly syntax, is relevant to the poetry of Oppen, who deliberately

Conclusion

makes use of this disruptive syntax to allow more primary processes — often of deep-seated desires and fears — to surface. Oppen's extensive use of gaps in his poetry punctuates the language of the poems, allowing for conceptual pauses which have their own non-verbal significance.

In summing up his style, it is of crucial importance to review the primary language that Oppen employs in his writing. The kind of language that Oppen employs has been discussed in depth throughout this study, partly because it is a hallmark of his work, but also because it is intrinsically bound up in what Oppen is doing in his poems, as he explores again and again the fundamentals of human experience: the primary drives which motivate our actions, the underlying significance of what our senses perceive, the ways in which we can draw on elemental energies to create a more dynamic and at the same time more stable existence. Oppen frequently presents the world and our engagement with that world through a poetry comprised almost exclusively of nouns and simple static verbs, undecorated by adverbs and adjectives, or uses disjointed phrases with no conjunctions to connect them. For Oppen, the elementary aspects of the language he employs mirror the elemental states he wishes to convey. Thus the primitive modes are expressed in the imagery of the poem, but also in the structural aspects of the language. Roland Barthes claims that significance in a piece of writing derives from the "text at work," and says:

> "Significance"—the glow, the unpredictable flash of the infinities of language—is at all the levels of the work without distinction: in the sounds ... in the monemes ... in the syntagms.... This running-together of the scientific "fields" of language makes "significance" ... closely resemble the dream-work, such as Freud began to describe it.[4]

In equating "significance" with the dream-work, Barthes emphasizes that subtle and illogical interplay which characterizes so much of Oppen's shimmering poetry, where linguistic logic is absent but significance all-pervasive. Oppen makes use of multiple logics — the logic of sound, the logic of rhythm and the logic of the unconscious — to produce texts that flash with a significance unconnected to the logic of discourse.

The poetic motivations behind the depiction of primitive modes in

Oppen's poetry are as diverse as the style and content of the poems themselves. The content of these poems ranges freely among cities, forests, oceans and deserts, in houses, gardens, streets and offices; the poems run the gamut of awe, puzzlement, fear, hunger, cunning and worship; some are short and clipped and even raw, while others are long outpourings; the language used is at times clear and straightforward, at other times enigmatic or reshuffled until all common sense seems beaten out of it. Oppen's interest in the primitive is sometimes stimulated by the desire to explore the world of animals and children, who retain a purity and clarity, and embody a simplicity which has been lost to adult humankind through the contamination of a civilized lifestyle. At other times Oppen explores the origins of the creative process, which go beyond words and conscious reasoning. And there are times when exploring the primitive mode is a way to release what Ted Hughes once called "archaic energies of feeling"[5] which put us back in touch with a universal and personal primitivity — the underside of our conscious, social selves — and which also fuel the poetic drive. Oppen wishes primarily to delve into the creative process, but also to reveal the collective self that binds us all in the midst of the maze of modern living, exposing the primary layers of our existence by stripping bare the surface cast of everyday life to reveal the underlying sources of energy which can revitalize the mundane. At the turn of the millennium, so much in the way of communication has become trite and pretentious and two-dimensional; Marjorie Perloff investigates the issue of media-based communication, examining poetic experiments being made in an age of media discourse. She questions the "viability of the 'natural style' [of writing] in a world where nature is increasingly subject to the hitherto unimaginable operations of the various 'quiet' revolutions of our time, especially that of the information revolution." She goes on to say that "what [T.S.] Eliot called 'the ordinary everyday language which we use and hear' has now entered an arena where 'natural talk,' filtered through the electronic media, packaged and processed, becomes the T.V. 'talk show.'"[6] Common social discourse, or "natural" speech as Perloff describes it, has been trivialized to the point of meaninglessness; our language is loaded with empty catch-phrases, e-card clichés and slick advertising slogans which have emptied communication of any real meaning. Our interaction with each other and with reality has become a two-dimensional affair, a simulation, as Jean Baudrillard succinctly points out.[7] Helen Vendler looks at Barthes' metaphors of truth and meaning in relation to the surface text and its intrinsic significance:

> To ... the notion of meaning as the pit of a fruit, Barthes opposes his metaphor of the onion, which consists of its successive peelings. Or he compares the braidings of various "codes" in a text to the interweavings of polyphonic music, where no single strand is definitively "the" music. In either case, Barthes argues against the separation of essence from surface — always an aesthetic argument.[8]

Baudrillard claims that in this age of electronic media there is no essence, only surface; what Oppen does in his poetry is to return the essence to the surface, so that the visible and aural aspects of the text — those immediately evident elements — spark off the essence, mobilizing underlying significances which radiate to the surface and invest it with depth. In this way, our language is invigorated with meanings and truths which have been flattened out by the triteness of e-mail abbreviations and talk shows, one-dimensional multiple-image video clips, shoddy song lyrics and the plethora of self-conscious and sentimental poetry which floods the Internet as a result of lucrative competitions.

Marjorie Perloff has a wonderful description of today's "Waste Land" of communication:

> [I]nevitably, our Waste Land is no longer Eliot's, no longer the "Fire Sermon," where Tiresias witnesses the fornication of typist and clerk is a debased reenactment of the great adulterous unions of Greek mythology, but a Waste Land where typist and clerk might make a videotape on "How to Create a Glamorous Setting for Romance in an Efficiency Apartment That Has No Washer/Dryer and Only a Small Kitchenette." As for Tiresias, he will no doubt continue to "walk among the lowest of the dead." But not in Hades, only up and down the studio aisles where Geraldo is now prophesying the future.[9]

This is the sort of Waste Land against which George Oppen implicitly struggles in his poetry, as he deconstructs language and reinvents form, brings rhythms and gaps into play, taps into primary energies and elemental currents, and probes the sources of creativity; and in doing so, he restores to us, his readers, an essential dimension of communication and experience which we have often chosen to ignore, or have forgotten.

Appendix: Additional Reading

- McAleavy, David. "A Bibliography of the Works of George Oppen." *Paideuma* 10 (Spring 1981), pp. 155–169.

- DuPlessis, Rachel Blau. "A Bibliography of Interviews of George and Mary Oppen Chronologically Arranged." *Sagetrieb* 6 (Spring 1987), pp. 137–139.

- Oppen, Mary. *Meaning a Life: An Autobiography.* Santa Barbara: Black Sparrow Press, 1978.

- Altieri, Charles. "The Objectivist Tradition." *Chicago Review* 30, (Winter 1979), pp. 5–22.

- Davidson, Michael. "Forms of Refusal: George Oppen's 'Distant Life.'" *Sulfur* 26 (Spring 1990), pp. 127–134.

- Davidson, Michael. "Palimtexts: Postmodern Poetry and the Material Text." In *Postmodern Genres*. Ed. Marjorie Perloff. Norman and London: University of Oklahoma Press, 1988, pp. 75–95.

- Dembo, L.S. "The Existential World of George Oppen." *Iowa Review* 3 (Winter 1972), pp. 64–91.

- DuPlessis, Rachel Blau. "'The familiar / becomes extreme': George Oppen and Silence." *North Dakota Quarterly* 55 (Fall 1987), pp. 18–36.

- Finkelstein, Norman. "What Was Objectivism?" In his *The Utopian Moment in Contemporary American Poetry*. Second edition. London and Toronto: Associated University Presses, 1993, pp. 35–46.

- Hatlen, Burton. "'Feminine Technologies': George Oppen Talks at Denise Lertov." *American Poetry Review* 22 (May/June 1993), pp. 9–14.

Appendix: Additional Reading

- *Ironwood* 5, special issue on Oppen, 3 (1975).
- *Ironwood* 26, special issue on Oppen, 13 (Fall 1985).
- Kenner, Hugh. "Oppen, Zukofsky, and the Poem as Lens." In *Literature at the Barricades: The American Writer in the 1930s*. Ed. Ralph F. Bogardus and Fred Hobson. University: University of Alabama Press, 1982, pp. 162–171.
- *Paideuma*, special issue on Oppen, 10 (Spring 1981).
- Pound, Ezra. "Preface to Discrete Series." Reprinted in *Sagetrieb* 10 (Spring 1981), p. 13.
- Rakowski, Carl. "George Oppen, the Last Days." *Talisman: A Journal of Contemporary Poetry and Poetics* 2 (Spring 1989), pp. 82–89.
- Silliman, Ron. "Third Phase Objectivism." In his *The New Sentence*. New York: Roof Books, 1987, pp. 136–141.
- Taggart, John. "To Go Down To Go Into." *Ironwood* 31/32, 16 (Spring/Fall 1988), pp. 270–285.
- Tomlinson, Charles. "Objectivists: Zukofsky and Oppen." In his *Some Americans: A Personal Record*. Berkeley and Los Angeles: University of California Press, 1981, pp. 45–73.
- Young, Dennis. "The Possibilities of Being: The Poetry of George Oppen." Dissertation, The University of Iowa, 1989.

Notes

Introduction

1. Reproduced in *The Symposium*, January 1933, p. 114. This review provides an overview of the Objectivist movement's aims and style, throwing light on Oppen's use — as an Objectivist poet in the 1930s — of hard clear images in his poetry.

2. From *A Homemade World*. New York: Knopf, 1975, p. 171.

3. In *Contemporary Literature*. 10, 2 (1968), pp. 159–177. See also Dembo's interview with Oppen in *George Oppen: Man and Poet*.

4. From "Poetry and Politics," in *George Oppen: Man and Poet*. Orono, Maine National Poetry Foundation, 1981, pp. 23–50.

5. In *Poetic Thinking: An Approach to Heidegger*. Chicago: University of Chicago Press, 1981, p. 5. Heidegger's notions of time have been adopted into many of Oppen's poems, fitting in well with Objectivist aims in general.

6. In an essay titled "The Place of Being in the Poetry of George Oppen," in *George Oppen: Man and Poet*, pp. 89–112. Chilton's essay makes a comparison between Oppen's poetry and that of his contemporary and co-Objectivist, William Carlos Williams, relating, among other things, to the influence of Heidegger on Oppen.

7. Ibid., p. 100.

8. From the article "The True Art of Simplicity," reproduced in *Ironwood* 5 (1975), pp. 31–34. Wakoski is, herself, a poet employing a simple, sometimes austere style.

9. Quoted from an essay titled "What Do We Believe to Live With?" in *Ironwood* 5, pp. 62–67. Rachel Blau DuPlessis was a close correspondent and friend of Oppen's; two of her other essays on Oppen are included in the collection of essays *George Oppen: Man and Poet*.

Chapter One

1. In *Myths, Rites Symbols*. Ed. Wendell C. Beane and William C. Doty. New York: Harper Colophon Books, 1976, p. 3. Eliade, a French researcher of mythic origins in human culture, also sets out, in his book *The Myth of the Eternal Return*, the notion of the "still point" in T.S. Eliot's poetry. The idea of the "still point" is presented and discussed in chapter nine of this book.

2. Ibid., p. 51.

3. Ibid., p. 37.

4. Ibid., p. 88.

5. In *Symbolism, the Sacred and the Arts*, ed. Diane Apostolos-Cappadona. New York: Crossroad Publishing Company, 1985, p. 3.

Notes: Chapter Two

6. Ibid., p. 5.
7. Ibid., p. 86.
8. From his essay "George Oppen, *Discrete Series*, 1929–1934." In *George Oppen: Man and Poet*, p. 272. Sharp investigates the ways in which Objectivism grew out of Imagisme, as well as the ways in which Oppen evolved his images from within the tradition of Objectivist writing.
9. In *Crowell's Handbook of Contemporary American Poetry*. New York: Thomas Y. Crowell Co., 1973, pp. 39–40. In his description of how the Deep Image works, Malkoff makes reference to several poets who make use of the Deep Image, including Robert Bly, W.S. Merwin and Galway Kinnell.
10. From *Romantic Image*. London: Routledge and Kegan Paul, 1957, p. 44. Frank Kermode is known primarily as a Yeats critic, but his Romantic Image, as explored in Yeats' poetry, has elements in common with the Deep Image.
11. *Crowell's Handbook of Contemporary American Poetry*, p. 41.
12. In "Swimming up into Poetry" from *The Atlantic*, Dec. 2003. Merwin is given attention in this chapter not only because Deep Images are pertinent to his work, but also because Merwin, like Oppen, often writes a poetry whose total meaning derives as much from the sub-verbal as from the verbal.
13. In *Enlarging the Temple*. Lewisburg, PA: Beckwell University Press, 1979, p. 6.
14. From *The Spirit in Man, Art and Literature*. Princeton: Princeton University Press, 1971, p. 90. Jung's theories of the collective unconscious are particularly relevant to the exploration of sub-verbal states, since some of those symbols embedded in the collective unconscious are mythic and pre-verbal, belonging to a primordial time in man's consciousness when linguistic competence had not yet been developed.
15. Ibid., p. 90
16. These three comments of Freud's appear in Abel's book *Freud on Instincts and Morality*. Albany, New York: State University of New York Press, 1989, p. xvi.
17. *The Psychology and Biology of Emotion*. New York: Harper Collins, 1994, p. 15. Plutchik's book explores different emotional states and how we enunciate them in language. He claims, among other things, that words are an unstable medium for the articulation of emotion, since emotions belong to the senses and not to cognitive processes.
18. Printed in *World Poetry*. Ed. Clifton Fadiman, Katherine Washburn and John Major. New York and London: W.W. Norton and Company, 1998, p. 999. This collection of poetry features the work of poets from many different cultures and languages, and spanning a period of 4000 years. Poems from other cultures and languages have been translated into English for the collection.

Chapter Two

1. In *Literary Theory*. Second edition. Minneapolis: University of Minneapolis Press, 1996, pp. 52–53. Eagleton's book is an invaluable survey of the leading literary theories of the twentieth century from Russian Formulism onwards, and includes an afterword which looks at current postmodern theories like cultural theory. The work of Derrida, Lacan, Kristeva and Barthes is succinctly summed up in a chapter on psychoanalysis.
2. From Eliot's well-known *Selected Essays*. London: Faber and Faber, 1933, p. 22. In this essay, Eliot is discussing the work of Ben Johnson.
3. In "Revolution in Poetic Language," in *A Kristeva Reader*. Ed. Toril Moi. Columbia: Columbia University Press, 1986, pp. 93–94. Kristeva's exploration of what she calls the "semiotic" is integral, as she sees it, to the understanding of how sub-verbal elements manifest themselves in po-

etry. She examines, among others, the work of James Joyce and the French poet Stephen Mallarme.

4. Ibid., p. 96.
5. Ibid., p. 113.
6. Ibid., p. 113.
7. From *The Pleasure of the Text*. Trans. Richard Miller. New York: Hill and Wang, 1975, p. 14. Barthes, a French poststructuralist, examines the underlying energies of the text and the almost sexual nature of their effect on the reader.
8. Ibid., pp. 20–21.
9. From the aforementioned book, *Literary Theory*, p. 116.
10. In Derrida's seminal work *Of Grammatology*. Corrected Edition. Baltimore and London: The John Hopkins University Press, 1998, p. 14. Derrida's deconstructionist approach, which "unravels" the text, provides a leading twentieth century theory of how language destabilizes (also poetic) meaning.
11. From *The Situation of Poetry*. New Jersey: Princeton Press, 1976. Pinsky is both critic and poet, having investigated the part memory and myth play in American lives. He was named Poet Laureate in 1997.
12. From her book *Radical Artifice*. Chicago: The University of Chicago Press, 1991, p. 43. Perloff's book explores the view that words are often misleading and impotent to reveal the essential poetic voice. Perloff has also analyzed Oppen's poetry, including specific poems, in this and other works.
13. Ibid., p. 46.
14. In *Trying to Explain*. Ann Arbor: University of Michigan Press, 1979, pp. 200–201. Donald Davie, in addition to being a literary critic, is also a well-known poet and author.

Chapter Three

1. From his essay "Not Altogether Lone in a Lone Universe," in *George Oppen: Man and Poet*, pp. 335–336. In addition to being the author of this essay, Burton Hatlen is the editor of *George Oppen: Man and Poet*. His previously quoted essay "Poetry and Politics," also in the book, is, in fact, a conversation with Oppen and his wife Mary. In addition, Hatlen has put together, with Julie Courant, an annotated bibliography, appearing at the end of *Man and Poet*, of reviews and discussions of Oppen's work

2. From "Oppen on His Poems: A Discussion," in *George Oppen: Man and Poet*, pp. 197–213. This is actually an interview with Oppen in which the poet answers questions about specific poems such as "The Image of the Engine," "Party on Shipboard" and "Technologies."

3. Also taken from "Not Altogether Lone in a Lone Universe," p. 338.

4. From "The Place of Being in the Poetry of George Oppen." *George Oppen: Man and Poet*, p. 91. See the notes for the introduction to this book for further comments on the essay.

5. "Not Altogether Lone in a Lone Universe," p. 340.

6. Ibid., p. 342

7. From "Building a Phenomenological World," in *George Oppen: Man and Poet*, pp. 243–256. Shapiro makes an interesting comparison in this essay between Cubist techniques in art and the techniques Oppen employs in his poetry. References are made, for example, to ambiguous relationships and an apparent lack of logic which Shapiro discerns as common to Cubist art and Oppen's poems.

Chapter Four

1. From the first page of "The Dialectic of *This in Which*," in *George Oppen: Man and Poet*, pp. 359–374. Finkelstein's essay traces political issues in several specific poems from *This in Which*, to claim that

Oppen offers a way of dealing indirectly with these issues through his poetry.

2. Ibid., p. 372.

3. From "Out There Is the World," in *George Oppen: Man and Poet*, pp. 169–180. In this essay, which examines the poetry of Oppen and Charles Tomlinson, Edward Hirsch looks at these two poets' emphasis on the visual aspect, and the relationship between observer and observed as set out in their poems.

4. In "The Dialectics of *This in Which*," p. 365.

5. In "Boy's Room: A Note on Clarity and Detachment," in *George Oppen: Man and Poet*, pp. 239–242. This is a short article, dealing with Oppen's personal yet objective commitment to his own moral vision.

6. In *Contemporary Literature* 10, 2 (Spring 1969), pp. 159–177. This interview is reproduced in *The Contemporary Writer: Interviews with Sixteen Poets and Novelists*. Ed. L.S. Dembo and Cyrena N. Pondrom. Madison, Wisconsin: University of Wisconsin Press, 1972, pp. 172–190.

Chapter Five

1. On the second page of "Clarity and Process: George Oppen's *Of Being Numerous*," in *George Oppen: Man and Poet*, pp. 381–404. David McAleavy's long article deals with the perception of a dynamic world and the difficulty of giving it shape without limiting it to any specific set of determining principles. The article is based on chapter five of his dissertation on Oppen. McAleavy has also put together a bibliography of discussions on Oppen's work, also included in *George Oppen: Man and Poet*.

2. From "'Of Being Numerous' by George Oppen," in *George Oppen: Man and Poet*, pp. 375–380. Weinfield discusses here the paradox of the One and the Many, the shifting world unfolding and the desire for cohesiveness. He views "Of Being Numerous" as a modernist version of the epic poem.

3. In "The Political Responsibilities of the Poet," in *George Oppen, Man and Poet*, pp. 149–167. Mottram's essay, based in part on comments made by Oppen to L.S. Dembo, explores the relationship between the poet's position of honesty within the social framework of the political dogma of the time.

4. See page 339 of the aforementioned essay by McAleavy.

5. In "The Place of Being in the Poetry of George Oppen," p. 100. See note 6 in the introduction.

6. In *Being and Time*. New York and Evanston: Harper and Row, 1962, p. 457. Heidegger's view of being-in-time is integral to the understanding of Oppen's approach to objects, which he believes have their own existentiality both within, but also independently of, the spectrum of time.

7. From "Out There Is the World," in *George Oppen: Man and Poet*, pp. 169–180 (p. 174). See note 3 in chapter four.

Chapter Six

1. In "Shorthand," *Poetry* 26 (June 1975), p. 172. Perlberg's review of *Seascape: Needle's Eye* casts doubts on Oppen's ability to convey poetic significance through the medium of language.

2. In "Language Made Fluid: The Grammetrics of Oppen's Recent Poetry." *Contemporary Literature* 25 (Fall 1984), pp. 305–322. Berry notes Oppen's use of fragments and his lack of punctuation, as well as his unusual line-breaks, in this article.

3. From the sixth chapter of McAleavy's dissertation on Oppen, "If to Know Is Noble: The Poetry of George Oppen." Reprinted on p. 484 of *George Oppen: Man and Poet*. McAleavy's dissertation, accord-

ing to Burten Hatlen, is an essential resource for the student of Oppen's work.

4. Excerpt from *The Mayan Letters*, reprinted in *Selected Writings*. Ed. Robert Creeley. New York: New Directions, 1966, pp. 81–82. Olson was a fellow-poet of Oppen's: *The Mayan Letters* was written to Robert Creeley, and ranges over mythology, anthropology and language. His manifesto, *Projective Verse* was quoted in William Carlos Williams' *Autobiography*. Olson's manifesto deals with aspects of poetry that are non-cognitive and non-verbal.

5. From "Reticence and Rhetorics," in *Man and Poet*, pp. 231–237. Bernstein's essay analyzes the balance between Oppen's use of rhetoric and his emotionally spare style, to produce the "clarity" and "honesty" Oppen continually refers to in interviews about his work.

6. In "Conviction's Net of Branches," in *Man and Poet*, pp. 417–428 (p. 426). Heller's essay discusses Oppen's struggle to render the human condition through the visual (both in terms of images and also in terms of what one sees on the page).

7. From "Poetry: Pure and Complex." *The New Leader*, February 18, 1963, pp. 26–27. Levertov knew Oppen personally, and although they did not always see eye to eye, there seems to have been mutual respect for each other's work. Levertov, like Oppen, was politically active, giving interviews in which she talked about her political views.

8. From the previously mentioned article, "Conviction's Net of Branches," p. 419.

those personal events, memories and viewpoints which made their way into his poems.

2. In the preface to the *New Collected Poems*, p. x. Weinberger allows the reader to peep into Oppen's life and see the man and his personality, as well as placing him firmly within the spectrum of influential poets, particularly of the '60s and '70s.

3. In "The Archetypal Gesture: Myth and History in the Poetry of George Oppen," in *George Oppen: Man and Poet*, pp. 113–122. Lake's essay links Oppen with the great mythopoeic poets like Pound, Eliot and Joyce as far as the scope of Oppen's work is concerned. He sees Oppen as a poet whose poetic approach to history searches out a deeper mythic pattern. He also makes reference to Eliade's *The Myth of the Eternal Return*, in connection to the ancient Jewish people and their god Yaweh.

4. From "Objectivist Poetics and Political Vision: A Study of Oppen and Pound," in *George Oppen: Man and Poet*, pp. 123–148 (pp. 142–143). In this article, DuPlessis traces the connections between Pound and Oppen from a socio-political point of view and also from the point of view of poetic style.

5. From "Syntax and Tradition: George Oppen's *Primitive*," in *George Oppen: Man and Poet*, pp. 429–443 (pp. 439–440). Finkelstein sees *Primitive* as a collection of poems which explores man's consciousness of the world, an exploration which began, in Finkelstein's view, with *Discrete Series*. There are several analyses of individual poems in this essay.

Chapter Seven

1. From the introduction to the *New Collected Poems*. Manchester: Carcanet Press, 2003, p. xx. Davidson's enlightening introduction to the *New Collected Poems* provides an interesting historical and social survey of Oppen's life, as well as discussing

Chapter Eight

1. In *Songs of Degrees: Essays on Contemprary Poets and Poetics*. Tuscaloosa and London: The University of Alabama Press, 1994, p. 9. In addition to this book, Taggart has also written about other Objectivist poets, including Louis Zukofsky.

2. Ibid., p. 233.
3. In "The New Primitive." *Chicago Review* 30:3 (Winter 1979), pp. 148–151.
4. From "Syntax and Tradition," in *George Oppen: Man and Poet*, p. 437. See note v following chapter seven. In addition to exploring subjective and poetic consciousness, Finkelstein looks at how Oppen's language, particularly his syntax, reflects that consciousness.
5. Ibid., p. 437.
6. Ibid., p. 442.
7. In "A Poetry and Wordlessness." *The Hudson Review* 19, 2 (Summer 1976), pp. 317–320. Peaver disagrees with other critics who see Oppen's work as a poetry of the visual; Peaver's view is that Oppen is not an empirical poet.

Chapter Nine

1. In "Private I, Public Eye" *Bookletter*. 3, 11 (January 31, 1977), pp. 12–13. Paul Auster's review of *Collected Poems* praises Oppen's manipulation of syntax in the poems, as well as expressing an admiration for the philosophy behind Oppen's craft.
2. "On Objectivism." *Sulfur* 26, 10 (Spring 1990), pp. 117–126. Palmer admires Oppen's refusal to adopt accepted poetic norms and values and his naked engagement with the poetic idea.
3. From "The Mind's Own Place." *Kulchur* 3 (Summer 1963), pp. 2–8. A key passage in this article, where Oppen sums up his poetic viewpoint.
4. In "Clarity and Process: George Oppen's *Of Being Numerous*," in *George Oppen: Man and Poet*, pp. 381–404. See note 1 following chapter five. Here, McAleavy discusses the Crusoe figure in Oppen's poem in conjunction with *Moby Dick*, both texts dealing with the man forced to be self-sufficient.
5. See Joseph Kronick's "George Oppen's Life and Career" in *American National Biography*. New York: Oxford University Press, 1990.
6. See Michael Davidson's introduction to the *New Collected Poems*, p. xxvii. Davidson adds here that Oppen stayed with a group of Israeli poets, and that this encounter — and his stay in Jerusalem — left a strong effect on Oppen, foregrounding the issue of his Jewishness. This evidenced itself in the poems written during that time.
7. From "Poet of the City." *The New Leader*, July 8, 1968, pp. 20–21. This article is also mentioned in the Burton Hatlen bibliography at the end of *George Oppen: Man and Poet*.
8. In *Ohio Review* 14, 2 (Winter 1973), p. 104.
9. In *Sagetrieb* 6 (Spring 1987), pp. 137–139.
10. From *Poetry and Belief in the Work of T. S. Eliot*. Revised edition. London: Routledge and Kegan Paul, 1961, p. 191.
11. In the *Dictionary of Literary Biography*, volume 165: *American Poets Since World War II*, fourth series. Ed. Joseph Conte. State University of New York: Buffalo, 1996, pp. 188–206. Peterson's contribution to this collection gives both an in-depth review of Oppen's life and work and also a list of works by, and about, Oppen.
12. See Davidson's introduction to the *New Collected Poems*, p. xvii.

Conclusion

1. In "The Animals: Territory and Metamorphosis," in *Simulacra and Simulation*. Trans. Sheila Faria Glaser. Ann Arbor: University of Michigan Press, 1994, p. 134. Baudrillard's comments on animals bear out his views that contemporary reality is so thinned out as to be two-dimensional, glossy but lacking depth.
2. Ibid., p. 137.
3. In "An Appreciation." *Paideuma* 10, 1 (Spring 1981), pp. 37–38. This particular

publication of *Paideuma* was dedicated to articles and essays on Oppen.

4. From "The Text and the Work," in *Untying the Text*. Ed. Robert Young. Boston and London: Routledge and Kegan Paul, 1981, p. 40. As a leading post-structuralist, Barthes takes a skeptical approach to the ability of language to define what we wish to say, as he constantly probes and diffuses the linguistic aspects of the text.

5. Quoted in *Myth in the Poetry of Ted Hughes*. Ed. Stuart Hirschberg. New Jersey: Barnes and Noble Books, 1981, p. 205. Hughes, like Oppen, was interested in those primary drives which propel speech; he also, like Oppen, portrayed primitive modes in his poetry, particularly in his collection *Crow*.

6. In *Radical Artifice*. For bibliographical details, see note 12 following chapter two.

7. See *Simulations*. Trans. Paul Foss, Paul Patten and Philip Beitchman. New York: Semiotext(e), 1983. In this book, Baudrillard poses the issue of two-dimensional interaction; he believes we are now living a reality so superficial that it has lost the power of metaphor to give it depth.

8. From the essay "The Medley Is the Message: On Roland Barthes" in *The Music of What Happens*. Cambridge, Massachusetts: Harvard University Press, 1988, p. 66. Vendler's book deals — as the title suggests — with the underlying "music" of a text, that sub-verbal aspect without which the surface text is nothing more than a "skin."

9. In *Radical Artifice*, p. 199.

Bibliography

Primary Sources: The Works of George Oppen

The Materials. New York: New Directions, 1962.
This in Which. New York: New Directions, 1965.
Discrete Series. Cleveland: Asphodel Bookshop, 1966.
Of Being Numerous. New York: New Directions, 1968.
Collected Poems. New York: New Directions, 1976.
Primitive. Santa Barbara: Black Sparrow Press, 1978.
New Collected Poems. New York: New Directions, 2002.

Secondary Sources

Abel, Donald. *Freud on Instinct and Morality.* Albany, New York: State University of New York Press, 1989.
Altieri, Charles. *Enlarging the Temple.* Lewisburg, PA: Beckwell University Press, 1979.
Auster, Paul. "Private I, Public Eye." *Bookletter* 3, 11 (January 31, 1977).
Barthes, Roland. *The Pleasure of the Text.* Trans. Richard Miller. New York: Hill and Wang, 1975.
_____. "The Text and the Work." In *Untying the Text.* Ed. Robert Young. Boston and London: Routledge and Kegan Paul, 1981.
Baudrillard, Jean. "The Animals: Territory and Metamorphosis." In *Simulacra and Simulation.* Trans. Sheila Faria Glaser. Ann Arbor: University of Michigan Press, 1994.
_____. In *Simulations.* Trans. Paul Foss. Eds. Paul Patten and Philip Beitchman. New York: Semiotext(e), 1983.
Bernstein, Michael. "Reticence and Rhetorics." In *George Oppen: Man and Poet*, edited by Burton Hatlen. Orono, Maine: National Poetry Foundation, 1981.

Bibliography

Berry, Eleanor. "Language Made Fluid: The Grammetrics of Oppen's Recent Poetry." *Contemporary Literature,* 25 (Fall 1984).
Chilton, Randolph. "The Place of Being in the Poetry of George Oppen." In *George Oppen: Man and Poet*, edited by Burton Hatlen. Orono, Maine: National Poetry Foundation, 1981.
Davidson, Michael. Introduction to *New Collected Poems.* Manchester: Carcanet Press, 2003.
Davidson, Peter. "Swimming up into Poetry." *The Atlantic,* Dec. 2003.
Davie, Donald. *Trying to Explain.* Ann Arbor: University of Michigan Press, 1979.
Dembo, L.S. Interview in *Contemporary Literature* 10, 2 (Spring 1969).
_____. "Oppen on His Poems: A Discussion." In *George Oppen: Man and Poet*, edited by Burton Hatlen. Orono, Maine: National Poetry Foundation, 1981.
Derrida, Jacques. *Of Grammatology.* Corrected edition. Baltimore and London: The John Hopkins University Press, 1998.
DuPlessis, Rachel Blau. "Objectivist Poetics and Political Vision: A Study of Oppen and Pound." In *George Oppen: Man and Poet*, edited by Burton Hatlen. Orono, Maine: National Poetry Foundation, 1981.
_____. Comment in *Sagetrieb* 6 (Spring 1987).
_____. "What Do We Believe to Live With?" *Ironwood* 5 (1975).
Eagleton, Terry. *Literary Theory.* Second edition. Minneapolis: University of Minneapolis Press, 1996.
Eliade, Mircea. *Myths, Rites, Symbols.* Ed. Wendell C. Beane and William C. Doty. New York: Harper Colophon Books, 1976.
_____. *Symbolism, the Sacred and the Arts.* Eds. Diane Apostolos-Cappadona. New York: Crossroad Publishing Company, 1985.
Eliot, T.S. *Selected Essays.* London: Faber and Faber, 1933.
Fadiman, Clifton, Katherine Washburn and John Major, eds. *World Poetry.* New York and London: W.W. Norton and Company, 1998.
Finkelstein, Norman. "The Dialectic of *This in Which.*" In *George Oppen: Man and Poet*, edited by Burton Hatlen. Orono, Maine: National Poetry Foundation, 1981.
_____. "Syntax and Tradition: George Oppen's *Primitive.*" In *George Oppen: Man and Poet*, edited by Burton Hatlen. Orono, Maine: National Poetry Foundation, 1981.
Halliburton, David. *Poetic Thinking: An Approach to Heidegger.* Chicago: University of Chicago Press, 1981.
Hatlen, Burton, ed. *George Oppen: Man and Poet.* Orono, Maine: National Poetry Foundation, 1981.
_____. "Not Altogether Lone in a Lone Universe." In *George Oppen: Man and Poet*, edited by Burton Hatlen. Orono, Maine: National Poetry Foundation, 1981.
_____. "Poetry and Politics." In *George Oppen: Man and Poet*, edited by Burton Hatlen. Orono, Maine: National Poetry Foundation, 1981.
Heidegger, Martin. *Being and Time.* New York and Evanston: Harper and Row, 1962.

Bibliography

Heller, Michael. "Conviction's Net of Branches." In *George Oppen: Man and Poet*, edited by Burton Hatlen. Orono, Maine: National Poetry Foundation, 1981.
Hirsch, Edward. "Out There Is the World." In *George Oppen: Man and Poet*, edited by Burton Hatlen. Orono, Maine: National Poetry Foundation, 1981.
Hirschberg, Stuart. *Myth in the Poetry of Ted Hughes*. New Jersey: Barnes and Noble Books, 1981.
Ignatow, David. "Poet of the City." *The New Leader*, July 8, 1968.
Jung, Carl. *The Spirit in Man, Art and Literature*. Princeton: Princeton University Press, 1971.
Kenner, Hugh. *A Homemade World*. New York: Knopf, 1975.
Kermode, Frank. *Romantic Image*. London: Routledge and Kegan Paul, 1957.
Kristeva, Julia. "Revolution in Poetic Language." In *A Kristeva Reader*. Ed. Toril Moi. Columbia: Columbia University Press, 1986.
Kronick Joseph. "George Oppen's Life and Career." *American National Biography*. New York: Oxford University Press, 1990.
Lake, Paul. "The Archetypal Gesture: Myth and History in the Poetry of George Oppen." In *George Oppen: Man and Poet*, edited by Burton Hatlen. Orono, Maine: National Poetry Foundation, 1981.
Levertov, Denise. "Poetry: Pure and Complex." *The New Leader*, February 18, 1963.
Linenthal, Mark. "An Appreciation." *Paideuma* 10, 1 (Spring 1981).
Malkoff, Karl. *Crowell's Handbook of Contemporary American Poetry*. New York: Thomas Y. Crowell Company, 1973.
McAleavy, David. "Clarity and Process: George Oppen's *Of Being Numerous*." In *George Oppen: Man and Poet*, edited by Burton Hatlen. Orono, Maine: National Poetry Foundation, 1981.
———. "If to Know Is Noble: The Poetry of George Oppen." Ph.D dissertation, Cornell University. Ann Arbor Microfilms, Inc., 1975.
Merwin, W.S. *The Lice*. New York: Atheneum, 1967.
Mottram, Eric. "The Political Responsibilities of the Poet." In *George Oppen: Man and Poet*, edited by Burton Hatlen. Orono, Maine: National Poetry Foundation, 1981.
Olson, Charles. *The Mayan Letters*. Excerpt reprinted in *Selected Writings*. Ed. Robert Creeley. New York: New Directions, 1966.
Oppen, George. "The Mind's Own Place." *Kulchur* 3 (Summer 1963).
Palmer, Michael. "On Objectivism." *Sulfur* 26, 10 (Spring 1990).
Peaver, Richard. "A Poetry and Wordlessness." *The Hudson Review* 19, 2 (Summer 1976).
Perlberg, Mark. "Shorthand." *Poetry* 26 (June 1975).
Perloff, Marjorie. *Radical Artifice*. Chicago: The University of Chicago Press, 1991.
Peterson, Jeffrey. *Dictionary of Literary Biography*. Volume 165: *American Poets Since World War II*. Fourth series. Ed. Joseph Conte. Buffalo: State University of New York, 1996.
Pinsky, Robert. *The Situation of Poetry*. New Jersey: Princeton University Press, 1976.
Plumly, Stanley. Review of *Seascape: Needle's Eye*. In *Ohio Review* 14, 2 (Winter 1973).

Bibliography

Plutchik, Robert. *The Psychology and Biology of Emotion*. New York: Harper Collins, 1994.

Shapiro, Abby. "Building a Phenomenological World." In *George Oppen: Man and Poet*, edited by Burton Hatlen. Orono, Maine: National Poetry Foundation, 1981.

Sharp, Tom. "George Oppen, *Discrete Series*, 1929–1934." In *George Oppen: Man and Poet*, edited by Burton Hatlen. Orono, Maine: National Poetry Foundation, 1981.

Seidman, Hugh. "Boy's Room: A Note on Clarity and Detachment." In *George Oppen: Man and Poet*, edited by Burton Hatlen. Orono, Maine: National Poetry Foundation, 1981.

Smidt, Kristian. *Poetry and Belief in the Works of T.S. Eliot*. Revised edition. London: Routledge and Kegan Paul, 1961.

Taggart, John. "The New Primitive." *Chicago Review* 30, 3 (Winter 1979).

_____. *Songs of Degrees: Essays on Contemporary Poets and Poetics*. Tuscaloosa and London: University of Alabama Press, 1994.

Vendler, Helen. "The Medley Is the Message: On Roland Barthes." In *The Music of What Happens*. Cambridge, Massachusetts: Harvard University Press, 1988.

Wakoski, Diane. "The True Art of Simplicity." *Ironwood* 5 (1975).

Weinberger, Eliot. Preface to *New Collected Poems*.

Weinfield, Henry. "'Of Being Numerous' by George Oppen." In *George Oppen: Man and Poet*, edited by Burton Hatlen. Orono, Maine: National Poetry Foundation, 1981.

Williams, William Carlos. Review of the Objectivist Movement in *The Symposium*, January 1933.

Index

Abel, Donald 16
All My Sons 81
Altieri, Charles 14
"Animula" 118–20
"Anniversary Poem" 125–7
"Antique" 44–47
Apocalypse Now 186
Ash Wednesday 192
The Atlantic 14

Barthes, Roland 26, 27–8, 35, 71, 167, 203, 205
Baudrillard, Jean 200, 201, 205
Berry, Eleanor 114
"Birthplace: New Rochelle" 39–40
Blake 133, 160, 185
Bly, Robert 13, 15, 18
"The Book of Job" 189
"The Building of the Skyscraper" 723–4
"But So as by Fire" 127–9

Chilton, Randolph 6, 7, 37, 96
"The Circus Animals' Desertion" 177
Collected Poems 33, 115
Communism 4, 115, 183, 184
"Confession" 141–2
Conrad 186
Contemporary Literature 6
Coolidge, Clark 30
Crusoe 43, 182

Davidson, Michael 132, 196
Davidson, Peter 14

Davie, Donald 31
Deep Image 13, 18, 19, 69, 72, 117
Deep Imagists 12
Dembo, L.S. 4, 6, 35
Derrida, Jacques 2, 20, 26, 27, 28, 29
"Disasters" 156–9, 194
Discrete Series 3, 4, 12, 32, 114, 177, 191, 197
DuPlessis, Rachel Blau 2, 7, 138, 189

Eagleton, Terry 20, 21, 27, 28
"Eclogue" 33–4
Eliade, Mircea 9, 11, 13, 92, 128, 165
Eliot, T.S. 21, 33, 54, 71, 84, 178, 186, 187, 188, 190, 191, 192, 193
"Eros" 188
"Exodus" 129–30

Finkelstein, Norman 56, 57, 71, 156, 162, 163
"The Force That Drives the Green Fuse Through the Flower" 180
"The Forms of Love" 59–61, 162, 193
"The Founder" 67–9
Four Quartets 54, 70, 192, 194
Frazer, James 105
Free Willy 200
Freud, Sigmund 11, 16, 21, 22
"From a Phrase of Simone Weil's and Some Words of Hegel's" 115, 189

Genesis 154
George Oppen: Man and Poet 2, 76

Index

"Gerontion" 188
The Golden Bough 105
"Grass" 180
"Guest Room" 188
Guy Fawkes 189

Hadrian 118
Halliburton, David 6
Hatlen, Burton 2, 5, 6, 32, 37, 44
Heart of Darkness 186, 189
Heidegger, Martin 5, 6, 28, 29, 39, 56, 69, 101, 165
Heinlein, Robert 56
Helen of Troy 136
Heller, Michael 120, 124
Hirsch, Edward 61, 113
"Historic Pun" 185
Holden, Jonathan 12
"The Hollow Men" 186, 189, 190
Hughes, Ted 204
Husserl 20

"If It All Went Up in Smoke" 162–5, 179
Ignatow, David 186
"Image of the Engine" 34–5, 193
Ironwood 2

"Jouissance" 26, 28, 35, 71, 167
Joyce, James 23
Jung, Carl 9, 30, 84

Kenner, Hugh 3
Kermode, Frank 13
Kristeva, Julia 2, 11, 21–5, 28, 44, 50, 117, 199

Lacan, Jacques 2, 22, 24–6, 44, 48, 82
Lake, Paul 136
"A Language of New York" 61–5, 81, 89, 108
Leaves of Grass 41, 169, 180
Levertov, Denise 121
"Leviathan" 52–4
Levine, Philip 30
The Lice 14
"The Lighthouses" 138–40, 183

Linenthal, Mark 201
"Looking for Mushrooms at Sunrise" 15
Lu Chi 105

Malkoff, Karl 12
Mallarme, Stephen 23
Maritain 178
The Materials 4, 6, 32, 33, 50, 52, 56, 89, 178, 182, 193
McAleavy, David 79, 80, 115, 182, 183
McCarthy, Joseph 183, 190
Meaning a Life 2
Merwin, W.S. 14, 15, 52
Mexico 4, 183
Miller, Arthur 81
Moby Dick 100
"A Morality Play: Preface" 124–5, 187
"Myself I Sing" 41–3, 96, 182
"Myth of the Blaze" 132, 179, 182, 183, 184, 185, 202

"A Narrative" 74–5
"The Natural" 162, 179
The Need for Roots 116
"Neighbors" 174–7, 181
New Collected Poems 196
Nominalist Poets 29

Objectivism 3
Objectivist (poetry) 12
An "Objectivists" Anthology 3
"The Occurrences" 69–71, 179, 180, 193
Oedipus 135
Of Being Numerous 1, 3, 52, 79, 81, 84, 104, 111, 113, 114, 115, 179, 182, 184, 185, 186, 187, 188, 190, 191, 202; *#3* 82–3; *#7* 83–5; *#11* 85–7; *#12* 87–9; *#13* 89–91; *#14* 91–2; *#17* 92–5; *#22* 95; *#23* 96–8; *#25* 98–9; *#26* 99–102; *#27* 102–3; *#35* 103
Olson, Charles 116
Oppen, Mary 2, 5, 163, 164
"Ozymandias" 110

Paeiduma 2
Palmer, Michael 181
"Party on Shipboard" 7
Peaver, Richard 167

Index

"Pedestrian" 50–2
"Penobscot" 65–7, 185
Perlberg, Mark 114
Perloff, Marjorie 30, 31, 204, 205
Pinsky, Robert 21
Plumly, Stanley 187
Plutchik, Robert 17, 18
"The Poem" 159–62, 181, 195
"A Political Poem" 152–6
"Population" 36–8
"Populist" 167–72, 184
"Portrait" 18
"Portrait of a Lady" 190
Pound, Ezra 116, 186, 196
"Power, the Enchanted World" 111–2
Primitive 1, 4, 5, 7, 132, 150, 151, 152, 181, 194, 195, 197, 202
"Prufrock" 33, 60, 84, 93, 178, 190, 195, 196, 197
"Psalm," 16, 57–9, 128, 193, 199

The Real 24, 25, 44, 48, 82
"The Red Wheelbarrow" 93
"Res Publica: 'The Poets Lie'" 148–50
Reznikoff, Charles 3
"Route": *#1* 105; *#4* 107–9; *#13* 109–10

Sandburg, Carl 180
Saussure, Ferdinand de 20
Seascape: Needle's Eye 114, 115, 118, 150, 187
Seidman, Hugh 72
The Selected Letters of George Oppen 2
"Semantic" 196
"Semite" 132, 137–8, 158, 179, 184, 189
Shapiro, Abby 53
Shelley, Percy Bysshe 110, 156
"Some San Franciscan Poems" 124, 189
Song of Myself 41
"Song, the Winds of Downhill" 121–4

"The Source" 47–9
"The Speech at Soli" 182, 189
Spring and All 98
Stevens, Wallace 186
"Still point" 10, 54, 71, 192, 193, 194, 195
"Strange Are the Products" 172–4, 195

Taggart, John 151, 152
This in Which 5, 56, 57, 67, 77, 162, 165, 180, 181, 188, 193
Thomas, Dylan 180
"Till Other Voices Wake Us" 177, 195
"To Elsie" 98
"To the Poets: To Make Much of Life" 143–5
"The Tongues" 165–7
"Two Romance Poems" 145–8, 179

Ulysses 136

Vendker, Helen 205
Vietnam War 186, 190

Wakoski, Diane 7
The Waste Land 186, 187, 190, 191, 192, 196, 205
Weinberger, Eliot 133
Weinfield, Henry 80
Wen Fu 105
"West" 120–1
Whitman, Walt 41, 169, 171, 180
Williams, William Carlos 3, 93, 98, 186
Wittgenstein 20
"Workman" 43–4

Yeats, William Butler 177

Zukofsky, Louis 3

www.ingramcontent.com/pod-product-compliance
Lightning Source LLC
Chambersburg PA
CBHW032052300426
44116CB00007B/697